GUNS N' ROSES

THE BAND THAT TIME FORGOT

PAUL STENNING

THE BAND THAT TIME FORGOT
The Complete And Unauthorised Biography Of Guns N' Roses
Revised Edition

by Paul Stenning

A CHROME DREAMS PUBLICATION

First Edition 2004
This Edition 2005

Published by Chrome Dreams
PO BOX 230, New Malden , Surrey
KT3 6YY, UK

WWW.CHROMEDREAMS.CO.UK

ISBN 1 84240 314 1

Editorial Director Rob Johnstone
Editor Rob Johnstone
Cover design Sylwia Grzeszczuk
Interior design Marek Krzysztof Niedziewicz

Photos courtesy of
Starfile
Mick Hutson
Paul Stenning
LFI
Record covers courtesy of Geffen Records
Lyrics courtesy of Warner Chapel Publishing

A catalogue record for this book is available from the British Library.

Printed and bound in Great Britain by William Clowes Ltd, Beccles, Suffolk

The Complete Unauthorised Biography

GUNS N' ROSES

THE BAND THAT TIME FORGOT

REVISED EDITION

PAUL STENNING

ACKNOWLEDGEMENTS

It can be difficult writing an unauthorised book. People either make a supreme effort to help and give the right side of the story – or they can be aggressive and unwilling to assist. It was no surprise to me that in writing a history of G N' R I encountered a few unwanted reactions to the project. I would have been happy to include up to date interviews with the current band, and also the ex members. Some were willing to co–operate, others sneered at the idea of the book. I am grateful to those, such as Steven Adler who sought to help out. However I decided that without everyone's side of the story – the story might not be fair.

The book thus became a platform with which to provide the readers with an objective viewpoint hopefully seen from all sides.

I tried and failed to speak personally to Axl Rose. It's my belief he does not even know about this book or my interest in contacting him. If you're reading Axl, then please do and I hope this book sets the record straight.

I extend my gratitude to the following people for their help and assistance:

Vicky Hamilton, Ruben Macblue, Rick Roll, Maribeth C. Beekman & Resort Babysitters Inc, Johnny Kreis, Shari Black Velvet, Mark Kostabi… Extra Special Thanks To Joel Mciver (the man for all seasons).

Thank you to my family and my wife to be, for love, support and guidance.

CONTENTS

In 1987 most new bands made little impact with their first record. Before the advent of the Internet it was harder for a new band's music to be heard, but the advantage back then was if you were special in any way, you were quickly spotted. Guns N' Roses were special in many ways. To look at them you could not predict they would sound as competent as they actually were. Yet reading closely between the lines it's easy to ascertain how all the right elements were in place for this band to take over the world, even if they did not realise it themselves.

The two album covers for the *Appetite For Destruction* debut (one featuring the infamous robotic molestation scene, the other the censored band members' cross logo) each had enough allure to draw even the most anti–metal or rock person into its charms. The back cover displayed five of the most ragtag urchins ever committed to musical photographic history. They were so motley that in hindsight they seem as if they were deliberately picked out as a glam metal boy band. But this was the 80s and rock boy bands were a twinkle in the eye of commercialism. Guns N 'Fuckin' Roses were the real deal and the buying public knew it.

Rarely do highly publicised bands fully justify the hype that surrounds them, but Guns N' Roses courted their own publicity without even trying. They fashioned mayhem and self–fulfilling destruction as a matter of course. The songs on *Appetite For Destruction* were controversial enough but they were not purposely so. These were savage Los Angeles converts who lived in a world of intoxication, loose women and rock n' roll. They perpetuated their own myth by simply being *of* that myth; indeed, the myth was reality.

In being completely unpredictable and volatile they bought into public perception enough uncertainty no one even knew which Guns N' Roses would show up for an interview or a gig. That they showed up at all was often reason enough to be satisfied. Thus, the quality of the music contained on their debut album did the business of not disappointing those who bought the album due to the hype. Once legions of other potential fans heard how good the actual music was, the album stratospherically soared in sales terms; a feat that continues to this day.

After such a high profile entry into musical stardom it was hard to see the band matching their initial impact. Yet since 1987 their reputation has retained its appeal, despite years between each album and changes in personnel, not to mention musical style. From the unprecedented release of two comeback albums in the form of the *Use Your Illusion* double set, which focused on emotions as well as pure rock n' roll, to the equally unparalleled punk covers album which predated the pop punk phenomenon, it's been a world of insanity for the band and everyone around them.

The world is different now, but Guns N' Roses stay the same. They remain unpredictable and of incredible importance to their patient legions of fans and they are still capable of the same heartfelt, relevant music they were in the beginning. Members come and go but at the core remains W. Axl Rose and as long as Axl remains alive and creating music – whether we hear it or not – Guns N' Roses will remain a living legend.

The Band That Time Forgot covers the period of the bands inception to their anticipated *Chinese Democracy* album. Inside also is a view into to the psyche of Axl Rose and a large part of the book concentrates on what exactly he has done for the last decade, creating a highly personal and probing profile previously unwritten or explored. Finally this edition focuses on Slash, Duff McKagan and Matt Sorum's latest band, Velvet Revolver.

The Guns N' Roses logo is etched into the soul of every single fan who fell upon the band whether it be via *Appetite For Destruction* or any subsequent album. The band remains in spirit, as defiant as ever and like their fans allegiance, G N' R refuse to go away.

If you have any comments regarding this book, please contact me via e–mail at czechzebra@yahoo.com

Paul Stenning January 2005

CHAPTER 1 APPETITE FOR DESTRUCTION

"They'll be great, if they live long enough" Music Connection describing Guns N' Roses in 1985

The date is June 2000 and the venue The Cat Club in West Hollywood. A mere 250 unsuspecting audience members witness Axl Rose jamming with ex Guns N' Roses guitarist Gilby Clarke and the club's house band The Starfuckers. It is Axl's first live appearance since 1993. All the rumours whether the volatile and virtually reclusive singer had shorn his locks or put on weight were instantly scotched as he looked fit and slender with what seemed to be braided coloured hair, still as long as ever. The makeshift band performed renditions of the Rolling Stones' 'Wild Horses' and 'Dead Flowers' to a startled crowd.

Later that month Axl also granted Rolling Stone magazine a rare interview in which he reveals that the *Appetite For Destruction* album had been re–recorded with the new Guns N' Roses line up to 'spruce up' the old sound, and also to rehearse for upcoming live performances. He discussed the supposedly imminent *Chinese Democracy* album, which at the time had already cost an estimated \$6,000,000. Today that figure is quoted at \$8,500,000.

It seemed Axl and the remaining Guns N' Roses hierarchy were finally getting somewhere after so long away from the spotlight. The singer was happy to talk and in December of the same year the bands first concert in seven years was confirmed as the Rock In Rio III festival in Brazil. The date of January 14th was set to be the time when the full new Guns' line up would be revealed. Fans were already aware that one of the new guitarists was the aptly named Buckethead who played with a bucket of Kentucky Fried chicken draped over his head, with only slots for eyes. As ridiculous as it sounded and in drastic comparison with Slash and Izzy Stradlin's more rock n' roll tenure, it was indeed completely true.

Completing the often revolving line up was Buckethead's partner ex Nine Inch Nails guitarist Robin Finck, additional guitarist Paul Tobias, former Primus drummer Brian Mantia and bassist Tommy Stinson (ex Replacements). There were also two keyboard players,

Chris Pittman and beside Axl, the only remaining member from the 'Use Your Illusion' period Dizzy Reed.

This line up played two New Year shows at the House Of Blues in Las Vegas, where the band played to 1800 fans with tickets costing $180 each.

Since then Guns N' Roses has played festivals here and there, they have even completed tours of one kind or another, all of short duration. There is only one thing missing, the mooted *Chinese Democracy* opus. The album has been in the pipeline for over a decade and aside from one song on the *End Of Days* soundtrack, there has been no new Guns N' Roses studio material. Is the band really a coherent unit? Will the album ever emerge? Only one man knows and he still has the G N' R fans hanging in uncertainty.

"You wanted the Best! Well they didn't fucking make it so here's what you get! From Hollywood, Guns...And...Roses!"
Live Era '87–'93 Introduction

Guns N' Roses was the first band other than perhaps Motley Crue who truly epitomised the rock n' roll idiom that so many pretenders sang about and proclaimed to be 'living' in the glam rock period of the 80s. Other bands had brainless lyrics, ridiculous images and seldom lasted more than a couple of albums. Looking back at the bands of the time, it is perhaps with relief to comment around 80% of them split and currently reside well and truly in the 'where are they now?' folder.

The biggest bands of the time such as Guns N' Roses, Motley Crue and Poison are still together in one form or another, which is testament to not only their longevity but also something akin to a miracle. The audience is still there for the style of music; it is simply more underground than it once was. Yet unlike their peers Guns N' Roses did not fit the usual mould of glam rockers, the nearest definition of any real magnitude was certainly rock n' roll. And though many glam bands of the time would dearly love to have been true rock n' rollers the truth is something would always be missing. They might have had the attitude but the songs would be below par and the image was nearly always a commodity. Where were they without the make up and the oodles of chicks draped over their shoulders as they slugged back the Jack and Coke?

Usually with the music itself taken in context, the peers of Guns N' Roses were anything but contenders. In 2001 reflecting on the Guns' legacy Slash commented "I saw a special on VH1 the other night for a brief second. It was hair bands of the 80s on VH1. And I just laughed. But we were so not a part of that scene. We were a breakout band for the 80s because we were the only band like us around. I think that is what made us so popular. We hit a certain nerve that nobody else was really doing. When the 80s came and went, we were so out of the loop as far as trends go. It never really mattered to me or any of the other guys what anybody else was doing. We just listened to the music. We never cared about being in a popularity contest with anyone. We just did what we did good. It's not about being in a contest."

It was their lack of ego ironically enough, which led the band to hit the heights the other bands of their ilk were trying so hard to attain. The aforementioned Motley Crue were doubtless more about decadence and sampled more than their fair share of rock n' roll but the music was something quite removed from the Guns' rhetoric. Crue did not have an Axl, or even a Slash. Their ensemble was more about the four guys playing together as a unit and they produced their best work when all working in tandem. Guns' on the other hand could produce magic from the fingertips of just one member. As evidenced from Motley Crue's poorly received album minus Vince Neil, their chemistry relied on the four original members gelling. For Guns N' Roses to produce great songs they could easily rely on Izzy or Duff to sing and on the occasions when band members began to split or be fired until only Axl was left, the chemistry still remained.

Quite simply Guns N' Roses were and still are an enigma and they single–handedly changed the face of rock music in their most active period of 1987–1992. Where they came from and how they got to be who they are is as crucial to the current state of play as the monthly reports of what colour or length Axl's hair is and it is at the beginning we must therefore start.

RECKLESS LIFE

In *Kerrang!* in 2000 Slash said "The word got out that there was this band and we had this huge audience in LA comprised of all the different fads that were going on – old school rock n' roll people, punks, Beverly Hills High School teeny boppers, model chicks, drug dealers, it was great. When the 90's rolled around, Axl got really, really into the whole trip and became a more exaggerated version of someone I already knew. Nothing that Axl does now surprises me. It's just a bigger, more exaggerated version. That's where he was headed. But the rest of us didn't give a fuck, because we liked doing what we were doing. As long as we could do that, we were fine."

Axl, the only original remaining member of Guns N' Roses had long been the embodiment of a close friend as well as a mystery to his band mates. Slash once talked of how Axl could be the nastiest, vitriolic character, then turn around and be "the nicest guy in the world". It was also an opinion that virtually everyone who came into contact with Axl Rose seemed to share. The guy was a psychotic, paranoid control freak who built a living legend out of the Guns N' Roses name he would eventually exclusively own. His early days were fraught with confrontations and abuse, which he would be unable to deal with constructively. Revelations as to why this happened and what exactly occurred would eventually appear to Axl. From provoking police to assaulting his girlfriends Axl pushed away those who tried to enter his world and would eventually turn into the second coming of his persona as a child – albeit in front of the entire rock n' roll world. Before then however it is necessary to inspect each step of his journey to discover how he came to be where he is now.

Depending on the reports you read, Axl was originally either called William Bailey or William Bruce Bailey. It has even been stated his full name is William Bill Bailey, though logic suggests naming your child with a full and then a shortened version of the same name renders this unlikely. So, though no proof has ever been given it seems Axl had initially been named William Bruce Bailey. He was born in Indiana on February 6th 1962 in the small community of Lafayette.

The accepted idea is that West Lafayette is white–collar middle class, home to Purdue academics and professionals. However it's more of a blue–collar town with a population of about 65,000. The Wabash River from West Lafayette and Purdue University separates the eastern part of the city. The river is something of a demarcation zone and divides the lower middle class residents of east Lafayette that tend to work at AE Staley 's corn syrup plants, or at Eli Lilly Pharmaceuticals.

Monica Gregory is an old friend of Axl's who has always resided in the Lafayette area.

She runs Lafayette's Rock Vault, which is something of a novelty for the area being the only clothing store that caters for rock fans. Gregory and her ex husband Dana were friends with 'Axl' before he even changed his name.

She has said of Axl's early days: "He got hassled a lot, for a variety of reasons. I don't want to go into it other than to say that it is legitimate. It happened to him in Chicago once – he was with my ex husband at the time – and for very little reason, these guys started hassling them: 'who do you think you are? Bon Jovi?' It was like: 'No, leave me alone'. The guys with the ties and short hair were yelling obscenities at Axl and Dana 'cause they got long hair. All the cops came in and basically beat the crap out of Axl...Just because".

"I remember being sexually abused by my Step–father and watching something horrible happen to my mother when she came to get me. I got a lot of violent, abusive thoughts towards women out of watching my mom with this man" Axl Rose

Axl's real father was William Rose who had been a well–known local rabble–rouser and when young Bill was only an infant William Rose bailed out on him. Axl's real father is now believed to be dead.

Axl's original name was indeed William Rose yet as his mother had remarried one L. Stephen Bailey, Axl's name was automatically changed. This was something, which caused complete and utter consternation when Axl found out (some time in his teens) of his past, and his real name. He then on insisted everyone calling him W. Rose. The transition was anything but smooth however. Some days he would prefer to be known as plain old Bill, some days he would be Axl, and on other occasions it seems Axl and those around him didn't know who he was. The errant red head would change moods so regularly it became hard for even those close to him to be able to predict or know what to do around him. For a long time he wanted to dispel the fact that he had ever lived in the Midwest – preferring to be known as either an unknown entity or an urchin from the streets, a status which more closely suited his outlook.

After an upbringing, which included singing in a Pentecostal church choir, by the time Axl was into his late teens he began trying out in several local bands, one of which was a band known as Axl. This became his nickname and eventually he carried it with him wherever he went. That band then changed its name to Hollywood Rose but the Axl stuck with the bands front man.

As a young child both Axl and his siblings were regularly beaten. "If a kid's being beaten, and someone offers help, and the kid goes off, a lot of the time the punishment is just compounded. Instead of helping him and trying to break through to him, it's like, "No, you're going to work on your problems right now! Do you understand me?" That doesn't work. "Shut up, sit down" commands are outdated if you're trying to help someone heal. I was brainwashed in a Pentecostal church. I'm not against churches or religion, but I do believe, like I said in 'Garden of Eden,' that most organized religions make a mockery of humanity". So Axl said in *RIP* magazine in 1992 when reflecting on his upbringing.

Defining his further hatred of rules and church domination he commented, "My particular church was filled with self righteous hypocrites who were child abusers and child molesters. These were people who'd been damaged in their own childhoods and in their lives. These were people who were finding God but still living with their damage and inflicting it upon their children. I had to go to church anywhere from three to eight times a week. I even taught Bible school while I was being beaten and my sister was being molested. We'd have televisions one week, and then my step dad would throw them out because they were satanic. I wasn't allowed to listen to music." In fact, Axl was allowed to listen to music, just as long as it was gospel. His Father frequently reacted brutally if Axl disobeyed him. "Women were evil. Everything was evil. I had a really distorted view of sexuality and women," Axl explained. "I remember the first time I got smacked for looking at a woman. I didn't know what I was looking at, and I don't remember how old I was, but it was a cigarette advertisement with two girls coming out of the water in bikinis. I was just staring at the TV – not thinking, just watching – and my dad smacked me in the mouth, and I went flying across the floor."

This was no isolated incident. The children were forbidden to watch anything remotely sexual on television. Anything from heavy petting to a simple kissing scene was strictly prohibited. This led to arguments between the rest of the family who were so oppressed by the leader of the household they allowed themselves to be torn apart by him. Axl believed that it was his Mother's refusal to help out from her own fear of his father that led him to such extreme emotional problems in later life. Once Axl was famous he considered returning to his mother to save her from continuing abuse, but realised he should not be her saviour as she had not rescued him.

OUT TA GET ME

One of Axl's girlfriends during his turbulent youth was Gina Siler. At the age of 20 Axl had already visited L.A. twice by hitch hiking and it was no surprise when the equally erratic Siler joined him in moving there herself permanently. It was late 1982 and up until 1985 the pair were engaged nine times, though a wedding never took place. Gina and Axl left Lafayette (for good) in her car on December 19, 1982 and moved into a dingy dump, reminiscent of a Charles Bukowski novel, at 1921 Whitley Avenue in Hollywood.

Gina's recollections of Axl at the time were something of a revelation given the image of many is of the Hollywood Rose members living off the streets and sleeping anywhere they could. It seemed however that Axl always had the safety and sanctuary of a car at the very least. Gina recalled: "He knew he wanted to be in a band. He was made to be a musician. I went to West LA Community College, and had some cheesy part time job somewhere. We lived there for five months, and then I moved out. He stayed there, and then Izzy moved in for a while. In fact, while we were living there he got into the band Hollywood Rose. There were times when he would take my car to practice. I would help him do his make up. No, he didn't live on the streets entirely. I helped him out quite a bit. I don't

think he likes to think about that, though. There were times, granted, when he lived on the streets after I'd kick him out because I got
tired of trying to support the both of us, and I got tired of fighting.
I would describe the two of us as putting a nuclear warhead in your
living room and hitting it with a hammer and just waiting. That was
what the two of us together were like."

In Axl's brush with public infamy in the latter part of the 80s he
would refuse to acknowledge he even knew Siler but it is very likely he did as she has described in intimate detail his character in the
early days not to mention his dress sense and behaviour.

In an interview she stated, "When I met him I was having my sev-
enteenth birthday party. He had on a long trench coat, dark glasses;
collar pulled up, and said he was trying to stay away from the police. I asked: 'What happened?' He said: 'nothing. They just always
bother me. They always harass me, no matter where I am.' But he
would do some pretty wild things. They would go out and drink and
do some stupid things, like smash windows along Main Street."

During the years 1983 through 1985, Axl networked in L.A. and
would often say he was going to dye his hair black or blond. Several
times he also spoke of his desire to cut his hair, return to school or
become a 'suit'. Axl and Gina had barely enough money to eat, let
alone do drugs or drink anything other than very cheap wine. Axl
kept himself fit with regular workouts.

With regard to one time Axl was returning from L.A, Gina said:
"He was walking down the street, and it was probably two o'clock
in the morning. From the back, he looks very effeminate, with his
long hair – not common for that area – and very thin legs, and he
had a long coat on. These police were making comments, making
gestures, because they thought he was a woman. Until he turned
around, and they were very embarrassed to find out it was a male.
So they started hassling him, because they were homophobic as hell.
They questioned him, and then found out it was Bill Bailey, who'd
obviously been in trouble before, and threw him in jail."

This is classic Axl Rose behaviour and it sits well with his later
comments regarding homophobia and his reasons for calling other
people 'faggots' or misunderstanding those who were homosexual.

It also explains his decision to stop wearing make up and to dress slightly more conventionally around the time Guns N' Roses' first album came out.

Gina further said of Axl, "He'd be in fights a lot. And I don't think he's even conscious of what he does, or how angry he gets. Somebody told me that he's on lithium, to try and control, because he's a manic–depressive. I always thought that there was something chemical that happened to him when he was angry. That image of him sitting in that electric chair in that video 'Welcome To The Jungle', looking crazed, says it all. That's what he looks like when he's pissed off. And when you see that coming at you from across a room, coming near you, it's frightening as hell. And I'm not very big, and that made it even worse. I won't go much into that." It was perhaps no surprise she would not further elaborate on Axl's temper or past with her.

In the summer of 1982 Axl returned from L.A. with Gina and they spent the summer indulging in hallucinogenics. The two experienced a life of regular teenage couples – much like something out of a juvenile delinquent movie. Axl would write pages of poetry but then he also enjoyed more leisurely pursuits such as skateboarding and playing Frisbee. At Purdue University the two of them would join students in their rooms, dropping acid and painting on the walls. The police tended to focus on these impromptu gatherings.

Axl had several negative opinions of religion developed from the fact that the bible was virtually forced down his throat. Axl and his siblings were taught to fear God and as if through some extension of the holy deity. They also learned by experience to fear their father. And of course Axl would learn to fear his father more than God itself.

Axl has said, "With the help of regression therapy I uncovered that my real dad, not my step dad, sexually abused me. The most powerful anger was this two year old child's anger because it was hurt. Nothing could really scare me, because I'd already seen hell. I'd been killed at two and lived through it, and I was miserable because I'd lived through it. I was miserable for 28 years. My step dad came into my life when I was three or four, and I didn't even know my real father existed until I was 17. I was separated from myself at an early age, and my stepfather made sure I never put myself back together, with his confusing mixed messages of love and brutality. He'd love me one minute, then beat me the next. I've had to learn how to shed both of these men's personalities. I'll take two steps forward, then one step back, but I'm into it. A lot of things are new to me now, but I won't let my fears stop me from progressing."

With the benefit of hindsight and after Guns N' Roses' initial success Axl was able to hire a therapist and put his thoughts into words and articulate them for the listening public. Gina claimed she paid for the rose tattoo he now sports for his birthday, the tattoo that reads 'W. Axl Rose' and sealed his character and identity in blood. Another Lafayette acquaintance bought Axl his first PA system for Christmas years earlier on one condition, that he would bring it back when he became a star. Axl, a man of his word did so.

Being a man of honour was something Axl developed of his own accord, in his family when he was a child the truth and parents did not go together. His parents always told him something very "tragic, dark and ugly" had happened. No explanation was ever given to Axl but if ever he mentioned his real father the subject would be changed or he would be reprimanded.

It was only when he was seventeen that Axl was told he had a different biological father. Axl had come across insurance papers, and later his mother's diploma, bearing the surname Rose. Axl would later say "I was born William Rose. I am W. Rose because William was an asshole". Axl was upset when he discovered he was only two years old when his mother had remarried. Through regression Axl learnt he was the only male influence she needed. When Axl's sister Sharon came along, his stepfather proceeded to molest her on a regular basis. This lasted for twenty years. There were beatings, which would consistently be metered out to both Axl and his sister who years later would confide in each other of their experiences and become closer as a result. Axl would only later learn of the extent to which his stepfather had abused Sharon. For a long time he felt victimised and alone in his misery.

In revelations, which would come later to him, Axl discovered he was prevented from growing beyond his inner child due to the abuse he suffered. The so–called immaturity of Axl Rose the man was rooted in the child who had been prevented from proceeding beyond his tender age. The psychosis of his two year old entity barely showed himself to those around him in anything other than spite and venom. In all truth Axl just wanted to be loved in a way that had been taken from him the day his abuse started at the hands of his stepfather. Yet many around him, unsure of how to handle his mood swings and violent temper, knew little of the infant immersed in a secular world of trapped feelings of inadequacy and a vicious circle of control and oppression.

Axl would rationalise his discovering through regression by saying "I couldn't protect the two year old child. And the world didn't protect him. And women didn't protect him and basically thought he should be put out of existence. A lot of people out there think so now. It's a real strange thing to deal with on a consistent basis. I'm around a three year old baby now and then, and sometimes after a few days it's just too overwhelming for me. My head is spinning because of the changes it's putting me through."

"But it's been such a long time since I knew right from wrong…"
'One In A Million'

Axl's initials, which coincidentally spelled WAR probably did not come from a set decision given that, it was the media who picked up on it some years later. Indeed his later revelations about his past gave a much more adequate definition to his life and its meaning than the more simplistic but tainted violent streaks that mindlessly peppered his youth and even his later years.

The 'war' seemed then, as now to be a very fitting sub header for a man who was the proverbial juvenile delinquent. He was jailed over twenty times but according to him was guilty on only five occasions. He has said "the other times I was busted cos the cops hated me. And I didn't trust the public defenders for shit."

His distaste for the way he was treated led to Axl defending himself at the court hearings but this only led to longer spells in jail and correctional institutions. Indeed Axl was once in jail for three whole months, after he couldn't afford to pay a fine on one occasion. Tippecanoe County Court records indicate that Axl spent "a total of ten days in county jail as an adult over a period from July 1980 through September 1982, on charges of battery, contributing to the delinquency of a minor, public intoxication, criminal trespass, and mischief". He was arrested no less than four times as a juvenile.

"Me and my friends were always in trouble" Axl described some time later. "We got in trouble for fun. It finally reached a point where I realized I was going to end up in jail, 'cause I kept fucking with the system. This guy and I got into a fight. We became friends afterwards, and he dropped charges against me, but the state kept on pressing charges. Those charges didn't work, so they tried other ones. I spent three months in jail and finally got out. But once you've pissed off a detective, it's a vengeance rap back there. They tried everything. They busted me illegally in my own back yard for drinking. They tried to get me as a habitual criminal, which can mean a life in prison. My lawyer got the case thrown out of court. I left and came to California. They told me not to leave, but I left anyway. My lawyer took care of it. I didn't go back for a long time. Now when I go back to see my family, I avoid the police there. I try to avoid all police in general".

Though he would unlikely have seen his time as a youth as a pleasurable stepping stone it was clearly an inspiration whether directly or otherwise, for his later actions and gave him a perilous and ruthless selfish streak. As he commented himself some time later "I couldn't make school work for me. I was having to read books, sing songs, draw pictures of things that didn't stimulate or excite me. It just didn't do anything for me. So I dropped out and started drawing and painting at home and spending a lot of my time in the library. Basically I started putting myself through Axl's school of subjects that I wanted to learn about."

If Axl feels nowadays the world is against him it is likely to be rooted from time periods where the world virtually was. His inability to cope with fame, adulation and a messianic tenure stems from feeling lost and alone as a youngster. His memories of the initial music scene were typically robust; "When I was living in Indiana, I was labelled a punk, a punk rocker. When I moved to L.A., the punks called me a hippy and didn't want anything to do with me. The Hollywood rock scene was a war zone back then. I tried out for a punk band and didn't make it because they said I sounded like Robert Plant. I was bummed because I thought I had a gig and really liked the music".

"I remember when I was in junior high and they talked about finding a goal – 'Yeah, I'm gonna do this, I'm gonna do that' – all just trying to impress the teacher to get a grade. If they get a good grade, they get an allowance. I was like, "No. I wanna be in a band and I wanna do great things. So I got an F for thinking grandiose thoughts"
Axl Rose

A desire to sing in bands gave Axl an outlet and through childhood friend Izzy Stradlin (real name Jeff Isabelle) the two forged an alliance which served to see them both almost simultaneously head for the bright lights of Hollywood. As Izzy has since stated, he hated Indiana and couldn't wait to get out of there. In the majority of his early interviews he would always ask the interviewer to write down that "Indiana sucks." Life was still hard in the Los Angeles scene but away from the quietly motivated country life there was at least something happening most of the time.

Izzy moved after graduating college, the only member of the original line up to do so, and met up with Tracii Guns and Christopher Weber who were both attending Fairfax High School. At night times they would meet up with Izzy at the infamous Rainbow Bar and Grill. It was here that Axl stumbled across Izzy, and his two new acquaintances.

Izzy had been born in 1962 like Axl but unlike his histrionic counterpart he was far more reserved and less likely to get into confrontations, preferring to slip in and out of rooms unnoticed. He was also as integral a part of the early Guns' set up as his more excitable counterpart. Axl once said, "None of us were the popular kids in school – we were all outcasts who got together and pooled our talents" and this was undeniably true. As a team Axl and Izzy were due to become an unstoppable force in a variety of different ways.

The pair spent nights cruising the boulevards that featured plentiful sights of denim, leather and spandex. The wide eyed looks of the small town country boys were documented at the beginning of the *'Welcome To The Jungle'* video where Axl steps off the bus chewing straw and looking positively excited and in awe of the city around him.

Yet before this of course nobody knew who Axl Rose and Izzy Stradlin were and the early days were a succession of struggles. Well meaning girlfriends were used for floor space and the occasional monetary handover.

There has been little spoken in great depth of the early days though Axl has stated that he virtually stood around the Troubadour club watching and learning for two years. Aside from the fated Rose and then Hollywood Rose, the very first years of Hollywood living produced little in the way of product.

There was however a burgeoning scene in Los Angeles which included Axl and Izzy, (who originally had been a drummer) songwriter David Lank (now in the LA band Mank rage); Dana Gregory (a struggling artist in Lafayette); Mike Staggs (in Dumpster, now in Los Angeles his band once opened for G N' R in San Francisco); David Pyle (a local musician); and Shannon Hoon (Axl's cousin and singer for Blind Melon who he recorded three albums with in the 90s before succumbing to a cocaine overdose).

"When we started we wanted to be the coolest, sexiest, meanest, nastiest, loudest, funnest band. There was a group consciousness of rape, pillage, search, and destroy." Axl Rose

Yet things really began moving when Axl joined up with Tracii Guns in the band L.A. Guns. Axl persuaded the professional guitarist to form a new outfit and took the vestiges of the Rose name along with Tracii's surname. This was an improvement on the originally mooted 'Heads Of Amazon' and 'AIDS' names Axl had considered.

He roped Izzy back into the fold, fresh from a stint in Hollywood locals London before discovering drummer Rob Gardener working the L.A. club circuit. Axl and friend David Lank had originally designed a huge banner bearing the name of Axl, which Axl had wanted to keep as a moniker. There was inspiration as far as things they wanted to achieve; yet for a long time, even Izzy and Axl didn't click as a partnership. More frightened of one of them upstaging the other – the world did not seem to be big enough for the both of them to co–exist under the Axl name. Eventually, after the name change and several months they finally gelled.

To complete the line up the band needed a bass player and they placed an advert in local music paper *Music Connection*, which young Michael 'Duff' McKagan answered. He, like Axl and Izzy had fled his hometown in search of rock n' roll fantasy. Born in Seattle on 5th February 1965 he developed his 'punk name' of Duff whilst playing in several new wave and punk bands in his native city. The punk scene was always more likely to be Duff's calling and in true punk style he fumbled around on several different instruments including guitar and drums. But his brother Bruce had taught him his first chords on a bass. Eventually Duff stuck with this instrument after deciding that he was less likely to make an impression in the guitar capital of rock n' roll at the time. Duff's bass player brother was not alone in his musical proficiency, most of Duff's eight siblings could play at least one instrument and his Father had sung in a barber shop quartet.

Like a well crafted and perfectly fictitious story, the meeting of the eventual Guns N' Roses line up came from another act that Duff had originally been playing with after his arrival in Los Angeles. The aptly named Road Crew featured drummer Steven Adler and the guitarist who would be Axl's very own Keith Richards, soft–spoken Saul Hudson, better known as Slash. McKagan had played drums or bass for a throng of Seattle bands like the Fastbacks, Fartz, Silly Killers, Vain and 10 Minute Warning, but left the Northwest for south California and the band known as Guns N' Roses in 1985.

"In Seattle back in my formative years as a musician, I played drums, bass and guitar. I couldn't figure out what I wanted to play. I got a record by Prince and was like, 'Wow, this guy played everything.' All my older brothers and sisters liked James Gang, Sly And The Family Stone, Hendrix, Vanilla Fudge... Maybe it was mainstream stuff, but they were hippies. I liked the soulful and ripping stuff and Zeppelin, too. I saw Grandmaster Flash and Melle Mel when they came to Seattle, but mainly I was into Prince," Duff recalled somewhat surprisingly.

With Road Crew barely functioning as a coherent unit; its members mostly more interested in the sex and drugs aspect of the rock n' roll lifestyle, it was Duff who sensed his life in L.A. would be very reminiscent of his time in his hometown if he didn't find a more viable outlet for his talents. As such he began to scour adverts seeking bass players and it was here he stumbled upon Axl and co.

After a succession of incidents that led Axl to suspect Tracii Guns and Rob Gardener were not the right men for the job, Duff knew exactly who to suggest. A small tour had been planned by Duff and at the last minute he had to find two replacements for Guns and Gardener after they decided they basically couldn't be bothered doing it. So it was Slash who received a call from his ex band mate asking if he and Steven could join the threesome for what was to become the 'Hell Tour'.

Initially Slash's only idea was to steal Axl for Road Crew but it was fate that the alliance formed from the problematic tour would create the first stable line up of Guns N' Roses. There are conflicting stories about how the eventual line up of Guns' actually came together. Future makeshift manager Vicky Hamilton claims that it was she who brought the two sides together whereas, according to Slash it was simply a case of watching Axl in L.A. Guns and realising he would go great with Road Crew. The one down side for Slash in joining Guns N' Roses was the existing guitarist Stradlin. There were no personal conflicts but Slash did not want to play in a band with another guitarist. However Slash eventually swallowed his pride and joined the group.

Vicky Hamilton's recollection of first getting together with the band is as follows: "I met Axl and Izzy when they were Hollywood Rose, I was a booking agent at a place called Silverlining Entertainment. Axl called me and said could he come by and play me some songs. I said yes and he and Izzy came down with a ghetto blaster and played me a tape of 3 songs. I loved it, and started booking them right away. I booked them a couple of shows before I even saw them live. I was interested to manage them from the beginning. They were great musicians and performers and as people I found them intriguing. I was also booking a band called Black Sheep in which Slash was the guitarist. So when Chris Weber was out of the band I suggested that Slash go check the band out and it was a perfect fit. Before this I had worked with Motley Crue and Stryper as a management consultant. I had also managed Poison. My background was in concert club promoting and record retail."

Slash was born in Stoke on Trent, England on July 23rd 1965. Though he was a precocious youngster his infamously shy personality meant he was nowhere near the scale his intelligence demanded and rather than study academically he began to play truant at thirteen, by which time interest from the female sex had begun to sway the frizzy haired aspiring guitarist. It was inevitable that young Slash would flirt with if not fully consume the world of rock n' roll. His parents were esteemed frequenters of the business. His mother, a Black American lady, designed the clothes David Bowie wore for his role in *The Man Who Fell To Earth* movie in 1975 and was well known as a costume designer per se. His white English Father Tony was a graphic designer who designed the album cover for Joni Mitchell's *Court And Spark* LP. His parents had split when Slash was just eleven and he moved with his Father to Laurel Canyon in California.

Slash is the only Guns N' Roses member to have been born into a rock n' roll family. He has said he was "fortunate to have been exposed to so much overindulgent, egotistical, just basically ridiculous rock n roll environment. I watched all these things go down. I watched people go down. I watched a lot of heavy shit go down and I learned from it."

An interesting analysis of Slash's handwriting was produced in *Metal Hammer* magazine at the end of the 90s and the findings state that the guitarist "tends to take issues at face value, attempting simplicity in thought, with no 'alternative agenda' in communication with others". Describing his personal characteristics the interpretation suggested Slash was "highly idealistic and artistic."

"Much of the motivation from which the writer operates is concerned with the satisfaction of completing a job successfully and to a high standard. The material rewards appear to be of a lesser importance, and it is suggested that the writer has an opinion of money, which suggests it is strictly a necessary evil. The writer is likely to be generous with money, particularly towards those less fortunate. The writer appears to have a relatively low 'goal orientated' outlook in terms of money, and considers working at something which is enjoyed to be of considerable benefit." No one who knew Slash either by ways of the media or personally would doubt these findings, and from his base level personality it clearly hints at how there would be future problems.

"Axl is just another version of the Ayatollah" Slash

Steven Adler met Slash after a supposed skateboard crash at which they began talking and found a musical theme in common. The pair both attended Bancroft Junior High School. Adler would sit with Slash and bang obtrusively on a guitar plugged into a small amplifier, which Steven would turn as loud as it would go. At first there was little variation in the type of musical instrument Slash wanted to play, by his own admission his first guitar was a plank of wood with a few strings on it, and he chose the guitar because it had the most strings. A friend of Tony Hudson christened the mop haired six stringer 'Slash' and a potential star was born.

Adler, like most sun tanned Hollywood residents (he was born in Cleveland, Ohio on January 22nd 1965) grew up desperately wanting to be a guitarist. The proverbial surf dude, all blond tangled hair and bright blue eyes, decided after a few years watching Slash's ability soar that the guitar was perhaps not his vocation. Instead he at first tried singing before realising his voice was not strong enough. It was then he began playing on any pots and pans he could get his hands on around the house, much to his mother's annoyance. Adler began to save up for his first proper drum kit.

After the years plying their trade as Road Crew and Hollywood Rose respectively it had become a fated meeting between the two sets of high school buddies and the affable outsider, Duff McKagan. As if by a sense of twisted logic, the fact that their first tour together was so dreadfully inept and unsuccessful actually brought the guys together and sealed lasting friendships not to mention band chemistry. Anyone who has managed to hear those early shoddy attempts at a 'band' might scoff now yet it was this musical infancy and plateau, which took them to the heights they eventually scaled.

Like other bands in Los Angeles, the newly christened Guns N' Roses were victims of the 'pay to play' syndrome. After posters and flyers that could once be placed upon telegraph poles and trees were outlawed by the Los Angeles authorities, bands had to literally promise to pay for the cost of their own tickets, so if they didn't sell them they would have to pay themselves – either way, the incentive to find customers to fill L.A.'s most notorious haunt, The Troubadour couldn't have been greater. Friday and Saturday nights were therefore spent walking back and forth along Sunset Strip selling tickets for between $5 and $10 to prospective fans.

This mentality of having to sell usually 500 tickets made the bands work hard to promote themselves and inspired a frenzied atmosphere at the shows. Guns N' Roses began as a band who would only get to play on Monday and Tuesday nights, when the club was basically plying talent with little chance of a loss, but their performances were so staggering they were soon moved to Wednesdays and Thursdays. They quickly became eligible to play on a Friday or Saturday, at which point they became the Troubadour house band.

Garnering a solid reputation not least based on Axl's burgeoning stage presence and appeal, especially with the ladies in attendance – it was with suggestive intent that various record companies and local press people began to watch Guns' in action.

It was evident that here was a band truly living out their on stage personas – Slash was not merely a caricature of a Jack and Coke drinking guitar player, who wore a top hat for effect, tousled hair in his eyes as if he was about to pass out – this was actually him!

"Up until we got signed, I lived on the streets for five years. I never lived in one place for more than two month, always crashing at people's houses. My parents would say, 'Come back home and go to college and we'll pay for it' but I would reply, 'No, I have to do this now'" Axl Rose

The crowds saw the authenticity of the bands performance and their assembled cast – though worthy of a manufactured glam 'boy band' Guns' were nevertheless strewn together completely inadvertently, living and playing by their own rules. Their dedication also led them to play outside of the generic environments for a live band. Short of money to pay for rehearsal space not to mention studio time the band had to play in friends living rooms whether it be for parties or simply to practice. There were many parties where Guns' would play whether it meant rocking the backyard or the living room.

There were also many Saturday evenings spent at a mansion in Laurel Canyon where the band played for both friends and strangers. In Vicky Hamilton's words, speaking with retrospection in 2003, "In the mid 80's in Hollywood the scene was very much alive. People were hanging out on the Sunset Strip just passing out flyers and promoting their bands. It kind of evolved from the Punk scene of the early 80's. All the people of that Big Hair scene knew each other and supported each other's bands. Then they would go to the Rainbow Bar and Grill and hang out. G N' R were simply the best band of that era and had real talent as songwriters, players and performers. It's not surprising that G N' R were the band that everyone loved."

The band was living in the self–named 'Hell house', which was essentially a garage that doubled as a rehearsal and living space. Not unlike the scene one surveys on the *Appetite For Destruction* back cover. By the bands own admission living at the house was something akin to a living hell, and Izzy (who christened their surroundings with the loving tag) could often be found sleeping behind the couch for days at a time.

Axl once famously described living on $3.75 a day, "which was enough to buy gravy and biscuits at Denny's Deli for a buck and a quarter and a bottle of Nighttrain for a buck and a quarter or some Thunderbird. That was it. You survived."

At the parties girls' purses were raided for some much needed sustenance money.

Yet despite the rock n' roll living circumstances the band was anxious to escape the confines of Los Angeles. The band decided to fulfil the tour dates L.A. Guns and Road Crew would not play. The tour would take them North to places such as San Francisco and Seattle. It was on their way to Seattle for their first gig of the tour that their van broke down which meant they had to hitch hike to their destination. Once there – due to the lack of promotion there was barely an audience. The band still played, only to be paid nothing afterwards. This set a precedent for the remainder of the tour, at each venue the story was the same – no crowd to speak of and no money to pay their expenses, though occasionally they received beer or food as payment. Slash said he couldn't believe they even made it back to L.A.

Nonetheless the group that returned had established a bond and a friendship and from then on it was an unwritten motto that Guns N' Roses would stick together. It was a precursor to an incredible next few years.

"It's new to us this business and we meet these people and they say 'Do this, do that'. And we go 'Fuck it, fuck you!' because it's just not us. We do whatever we want to..." Axl Rose

By the end of 1985 Guns N' Roses was one of *the* hottest bands in the L.A. scene. Their dedication and intense live shows had brought something few bands could ever hope to achieve, especially in the saturated L.A. scene of the time – word of mouth hype. The feeling was that Guns N' Roses might not always play the most flawless or technically astute gig but there would always be a sense of excitement in the air that was perpetuated by the ragtag collection assembled before the audiences' eyes.

And so, once the public excitement had boiled over it was the job of the music press to get involved, which then led to several record companies showing an interest. Local magazine *Music Connection* was one of two or three who began to take notice of Guns N' Roses once the band was playing regular Thursday nights at the Troubadour. The others, such as *Scratch* and *L.A. Rocks* took the band outside of the insular glam and metal scene, across town to potential fans who were not remotely interested in the current metal picture, and were still latching on to a post punk musical revival.

These so called punks would not be seen dead cruising the Sunset strip, so it took the magazines to show them that Guns N' Roses was the first band out of the secular L.A. groupings with any original or street vibe. It is a credit to the band that they could cross such strict boundaries even in the early days without even trying. For even before they were expected to perform certain roles Guns N' Roses adhered to them because it was inherent to who they were. There was no pretence or pouting for the audience, it was real, concentrated and powerful.

And the essential element that pricked the ears of the business minded concert attendees was the set of terrific songs the band had collected. Interspersed with covers of familiar future Guns' tunes such as Rose Tattoo's 'Nice Boys (Don't Play Rock N' Roll)' and Aerosmith's 'Mama Kin' were their own compositions which though

in their early stages still sounded impressive and ran more deeply
in subject matter and execution than the other local bands ideas of
'songs' which usually centred around the sizes of their dicks, and
how many girls they'd conquered the weekend before.

Guns' brand of psycho maniac rock n' roll was evident early on in
the likes of 'Reckless Life', 'Shadow Of Your Love', 'Nightrain',
'Move to The City', and 'Welcome To The Jungle'.

As if predicting the tidal wave of success, which was to engulf
the band, *Music Connection* took the unprecedented step of putting
them on its front cover, which was the first time in the magazines
25 year history that an unsigned band had made its front page. By
the time the publication hit the stands however Guns N' Roses were
signed to Geffen records.

*"The EP's a piece of shit compared to the album... that's the most
contrived piece of shit we've done yet. It ain't a live record–if you
think it is you're crazy. What we did was go into a room, record ourselves and put 50,000 screaming people on top"* Axl Rose

After every label in the Hollywood area worth its salt had taken
the band out for expensive meals and bar tabs it was eventually the
Geffen team of Tom Zutaut and Teresa Ensensat who won the band
over with an insistence that they would be able to do things their
own way and on March 25th 1986 the band inked a deal.

Finding a manger proved to be more difficult however. In the past
year Guns' had been loosely 'managed' by Vicky Hamilton, chief
cheerleader and adopted mother who let the band stay with her and
generally helped them out. At the time she was a booker and promoter working with predominantly Guns', Faster Pussycat and Poison.

However it was never a concrete business arrangement and with
various unexpected developments occurring in the Guns' camp it
was becoming impossible to keep Hamilton as a paid hanger on.
"When the band first started, the image that Geffen had of us was
drunken, fucked up rabble rousers and they would do anything to
make that image keep going," Duff McKagan remarked over a decade after the band had been signed by the label. It was something

McKagan felt particularly strongly about, given his condition at the time. Whether all of his own making or a fact exaggerated by his record label, the sad fact was Duff was drinking two half gallons of vodka a day and snorting an eighth of an ounce of cocaine.

Axl's ex girlfriend Gina had returned to Los Angeles from Phoenix to visit Axl at the end of 1985. She remembered a huge apartment with people sleeping scattered all over the place. Gina recalled that at the time Axl and a friend picked her up at the airport. It was not quite the weekend Gina had envisaged, with Axl and friend doing copious amounts of heroin. Her reaction was enough to cause Axl to be defensive and the weekend was spent with the couple constantly fighting. Later Gina would say: "I shouldn't even say this, but when I went to see Axl before *Appetite For Destruction* came out, and all he said to me was, 'I can't wait until this album's done, because I want to lock myself in a room for six weeks and do heroin'".

No wonder Guns N' Roses seemed a frightening prospect for potential new employees. At first it was Aerosmith's manager Tim Collins who was persuaded to come and meet the band with a view to managing them but after the band went crazy by running up a $450 drinks tab in Collins' name after he had retired for the evening the sensible and austere 'Smith manager decided against working with the band. He would later find his decision fully vindicated and there was immediately bad blood festering between him and Alan Niven.

It was Niven who finally secured the band on behalf of Stravinsky Brothers Management. It was his initial belief that the band would not be the biggest on his roster and would sell 200,000 copies of their scheduled album if they were lucky. He shrugged off suggestions of any actual 'hits' the band had in its repertoire.

However Niven did not reckon on the power of the bands song writing nor the desire for the listening public to seek something stronger and more meaningful than the current crop of 'hair' bands were offering. There were repetitive tales of parties plus stories of strippers and vicarious loose women. Such dumb lyrics were ubiquitous among the rock fraternity, especially those bands who believed in their own immortality and contained a strange sense of arrogance despite looking like transvestites at a jumble sale. Whereas groups such as Twisted Sister took the humorous approach to being made up to look like unappealing women, doused in make up and bad spandex, there were thousands of others who were deadly serious.

Bands who had only started up to get 'chicks' and see their name in lights. In the post Nirvana years of modern rock music it seems ridiculous when those new to the scene look back on the way people dressed in the rock scene in the 80s. Where thrash bands now seem equally laughable in their tight black jeans and high top basketball boots they were viewed as the more 'manly' contingent of an otherwise laughably camp set of bands who did not quite see the irony in their dress sense. The 'where are they now?' file of a now thankfully more sensible musical period contains such flops as Jetboy, Ratt, and Danger Danger, many of whom have since reformed to cater to the small underground circuit in America that still seeks such outrageous glam rock.

Guns N' Roses it seems were way ahead of their time. Their songs contained tales of women and excess but they were an altogether darker mixture of resentment, bitterness, anger and non–conformity. To analyse the lyrics of *Appetite For Destruction* against any of the equivalent records of the time gives no surprise as to why the band became huge off the back of the record.

Each of the twelve tracks from the debut album were classics in their own right – from the simplistic refrain in 'Paradise City', "Take me down to the Paradise City where the grass is green and the girls are pretty" to the song written of Axl's child sweetheart, Erin Everly ('Sweet Child O Mine') with lines that you could read between however deeply you pleased. "Her hair reminds me of a warm safe place where as a child I'd hide, and pray for the thunder and the rain to quietly pass me by…" was a line fans would eventually learn was more deeply rooted than at first seemed. The torment suffered by Axl as a child gave new meanings to the otherwise simplistic song.

Axl said, "I had written this poem, reached a dead end with it and put it on the shelf. Then Slash and Izzy got working together on songs and I came in, Izzy hit a rhythm, and all of a sudden this poem popped into my head. It just all came together. A lot of rock bands are too fucking wimpy to have any sentiment or any emotion in any of their stuff unless they're in pain. It's the first positive love song I've ever written, but I never had anyone to write anything that positive about, I guess."

Of 'Paradise City' Axl would say, "The verses are more about being in the Jungle. The chorus is like being back in the Midwest or somewhere. It reminds me of when I was a little kid and just looked up at the blue sky and went 'Wow, what is all this? Its so big out there.' Everything was more innocent. There are parts of the song that have more of a down home feel and when I started putting down the over–layers of my vocals (I put five tracks on there), it seemed that it came out like some Irish or Scottish heritage."

"I want this to be the biggest selling debut album from a rock act ever!" Axl Rose

There was also the ambiguous 'Rocket Queen' that Axl would say was him singing as if the song were about him but actually referred to a girl he knew who had very little of her life left after abusing herself through mental torture and substance abuse. He said it was a "fucked thing" that since he was in L.A. he had lost "five or six friends" he used to hang out with every day. Elsewhere topics covered were much the same as other 'glam' acts of the time but all told with a shadowy resonance that lurked behind every sordid note.

Axl also said "I wrote this song for this girl who was gonna have a band and she was gonna call it Rocket Queen. She kinda kept me alive for a while. The last part of the song is my message to this person, or anybody else who can get something out of it. It's like there's hope and a friendship note at the end of the song. For that song there is also something I tried to work out with various people – a recorded sex act. It was somewhat spontaneous but premeditated; something I wanted to put on the record... It was a sexual song and it was a wild night in the studio."

There was the dedication to the cheap wine the members would slug like water, 'Nightrain' which featured the tell tale line "I'm on the nightrain so I can leave this slum", loosely translated meaning the wine helped them forget the hell house they were quite literally singing of. 'Mr Brownstone' was a candid and witty tribute to the heroin that all the members had dabbled in, most of all Axl, Slash and Izzy to varying degrees. Either way there was a sinister tone to lines such as "I used to do a little but a little wouldn't do, so the little got more and more. I just keep tryin' to get a little better, a little better than before," which suggested trying to kick the habit, or kick the boredom of life *with* the habit was par for the course even before the band could afford copious amounts of junk.

One of the most obvious titles was 'Welcome To The Jungle' which served a double meaning as a tale of a country boy arriving in the big bad city for the first time, and an equal initiation into the Guns' world, which *Appetite For Destruction* so accurately described. It was a welcoming to their jungle and anyone who listened to it had to "learn to live like an animal in the jungle" where the band played. Axl said of the meaning in the song, "I wrote the words in Seattle. Its a big city, but at the same time, its still a small city compared to L.A. and the things you're gonna learn... I just wrote how L.A. looked to me. If someone comes to town and they want to find something, they can find whatever they want."

There was also the straightforward Axl refrain of 'Out Ta Get Me' which focused on his misdemeanours as a disturbed youth (which he still mostly was) and the notion that the police were quite literally out to get him. It was characteristic of Axl's spirit which exists all the years on from 'Appetite...' when he spat the words "They break down doors and they rape my rights but they won't touch me... I lose my head I close my eyes they won't touch me. Cause I got something I been building up inside, I'm already gone". Axl himself did believe he was "gone" but there was also a snarling 'fuck you anyways' attitude all so evident in every gnarled vocal line.

Axl's description of the song was "Like every time you turn around, someone is trying to screw you over financially, or the cops are banging on your door and you didn't do anything. It's just being railroaded into something and trying to get out from underneath it. You know, parents, teachers, preachers... everybody. The last verse Slash and I put together as a joke 'cause we were talking about how we get in fights sometimes, and how some people get pissed off that you're drunk. But they're the ones that bought the bottle of whiskey to get your drunk on. Some people say I got a chip on my shoulder."

The tantalising epic 'My Michelle' featured one of the bands best loved riffs and a howling chorus. The lyrics were centred around just another of the women (Michelle Young) Axl had frequented. "I know this girl named Michelle and she became a really good friend of the band's and I was going out with her for a while" he said. "It's a true story. Slash and some other members of the band said that's kinda too heavy to say about poor, sweet Michelle; she'll freak out. I'd written the nice sweet song about her, and then I looked at it and thought, 'that really doesn't touch any basis of reality', so I put down an honest thing. It describes her life. This girl leads such a crazy life with doing drugs, or whatever she's doing at the time, you don't know if she's gonna be there the next day. Every time I see Michelle I'm really relieved and glad. I showed her the lyrics after about three weeks of debating, and she was so happy that someone didn't paint just a pretty picture. She loves it. It was a real song about her."

The real beauty of the record laid in its musical simplicity, yet its competence and inspired arrogance. Where else in the history of modern rock n' roll had a band epitomised such a large collective of worldwide vagrants and castaways as Guns N' Roses had managed with a single swipe of their tattooed hands? Nowhere was the answer and no other band had a retort to rival the eloquent beauty of 'Sweet Child O Mine' or the vicious vengeance of 'You're Crazy'. 'Anything Goes' was gutter rock, which was pure in its filthy echoes. 'It's So Easy' was tinged with a punk feel and was just one of the tracks where Axl's repertoire of different voices gleamed. There were some who believed it was another singer entirely who sang on the tracks where Axl took advantage of his repertoire with an utterly unique voice. Slash said on *The Friday Rock Show* "Axl has five or six different voices he can just break in to whenever he likes depending on his mood".

The demands of the song were never beyond Axl's reach and thus *Appetite For Destruction* is peppered with diversity. Enough to please the casual listener of radio rock, with the eventual singles from the album, but enough flair and hunger for depravity to fulfil rockers the world over. For the uninitiated to the world of rock (of whom many were enlisted thanks to Guns N' Roses) this was a world, which they had never seen before. A dirty cacophony of downward reprobates walking it like they talked it and igniting the listeners' passion as well as their emotions and spirit. It was a record that would comfort the listener as if it were written just for them – a record that was over all too quickly, where the traveller could walk through a dream world of other realities, ones the band had lived for them. All of a sudden Axl Rose was a hero, an idol, and 9 out of 10 rock n' rollers wanted to be just like him.

He was the Jim Morrison of a new generation, unbelievably handsome, lithe and perfectly formed with flowing red hair that suggested the volatility which was so clearly part of his make up. Where others fronting bands of a similar ilk tried too hard to attract the ladies and flaunt their charms with exaggerated swagger and too much effort, it was second nature to Axl to not only be a consummate front man but to invite his unisex audience to either want to be him or fuck him. That he was initially oblivious to this power (much like the originally shy Jim Morrison who would perform with his back to the audience) was a further element of attractiveness. A rock star that did not quite know he was a rock star yet, and regardless worked his job like a ten–year veteran, throwing tantrums that bequeathed his status.

"Everything about Axl as a performer and singer comes from his personality, so the shit that makes him crazy or the shit that he finds hard to deal with is, at the same time, what makes his talent" Slash

This was epitomised in the bands first live shows in England, which precipitated the release of the album. The English press had a field day anticipating the arrival of the self styled 'Most dangerous band in the world', unflinchingly raising concern at the potential for England's subdued and serene countryside and suburban homes to be blighted by a band who outgunned the Beastie Boys in terms of bravado and potential 'fuck with your kids' mentality.

Parents were suitably distressed and tales of a rhythm guitarist who was referred to as anything from Slosh to Slug (so called in both cases due to his extreme alcohol addiction) who had supposedly been on a drinking binge for two years and faced each morning with hands that "shook like windmills" in his own words. Some papers even managed to get his name right but even when Slash was name checked correctly the stories of the band were equally outlandish.

Quite what publication had provided the source material for Axl's comments remains a mystery but a squalid daily paper quoted Axl as previously saying that he liked to kill small dogs, especially those such as poodles. "Everything about them means I must kill them" he supposedly spouted, confusing rock n' roll animal lovers everywhere and given Guns N' Roses the unwarranted distinction of being unwanted in England before they even arrived.

The first of three shows at the seminal Marquee venue in London saw the band hailed with a barrage of beer cups and spit, much to Axl's chagrin. Was this what the band had just written a supremely strong record to expect? Had their own assumptions and those around them been too wayward, or was this just a typical reaction of the British crowd who so often are un–favoured by American bands? It did not sit well with Axl who called one audience member a "pussy" when he threw a glass into Steven's drum kit upon the opening night at the venue. He threatened to leave the stage if people didn't stop throwing things and gradually the passion for offending the band subsided but quite expectedly reviews of the shows missed the bands otherwise sterling performances in favour of pointing out their weaknesses and warranted reaction of the crowds.

"It's great to be in fuckin England finally", Axl gushed on the first night before the band had begun but other than a free trip to merry old England the band felt they had accomplished little with their initial visit to British shores and were unenthusiastic about returning to a country with crazy press and moronic audiences. The thankful truth was that at least the band was in support of a remarkably strong record though unbelievably *Appetite For Destruction* faced mixed reviews upon its inception to the world. It was released on 31 July 1987 worldwide.

Some rock institutions like the ironically English *Kerrang!* greeted it like a fabulous new friend, the review in issue 151 gasped "Rock n' roll is being wrestled from the hands of the bland, the jaded, the tired, the worn, and thrust back into the hands of the real raunch rebels". Other publications were not so gushing. *Rolling Stone* for instance initially distanced itself from the grandiose and pompous take on heavy metal and would be one of the magazines most delayed in following the rush for Guns' attention.

As an American establishment it could however behave how it wanted and its power strangled the life from *Appetite For Destruction* one minute, only to fall over itself to embrace it the next. Thus it seemed at first that only the hardened rebels of the metal and hard rock persuasion could possibly grow to like an album so voracious and snotty it even had a rape scene on its front cover. The controversial painting on the sleeve built the record into further extremes, as if it were needed.

Perhaps a knowing tactic from the Geffen honchos to elicit greater swathes of publicity, but more likely a painting which the band themselves just 'dug'; the choice of cover art was a strange one. Drawn by fantasy artist Robert Williams the scene was one with a nefarious robotic creature leering over a half naked woman with her underwear pulled down unkindly low. It was open to interpretation what had happened to the woman with a bare breast on show and a look of unerring horror on her face.

The stores across the US were appalled and many refused to carry the offending sleeve. Likewise, the prim and proper chain stores in England such as W H Smiths also turned away the album. It was not enough for the record to include more f–words than the average PMRC advocate would despair of; this record was positively offensive in its audacity and luridness. The cover art was quickly censored and provided Guns N' Roses with a duel reason to be content. Not only did the furore surrounding the cover draw even more glances toward the album, whether approving or aghast the result-ant publicity did sales no harm, but it also gave the band an instant-ly definable image – one that was inked onto the arm of Axl Rose already.

Bill White Jr. drew the cross tattoo design initially but for the al-bum art it was rehashed by Andy Engell. It would surely have been equally well carved by the bands almost resident tattooist Robert Benedetti, who was immortalised in the notes for 'Appetite…' and his sunset strip parlour name checked. Business was far swifter a few months later.

Credit must also go to Michael Hodgson whose credit for art direc-tion and design was not undeserved. With the cover art so famously derided and lauded the actual guns with roses logo was also quaint-ly placed on the inner sleeve of the record and CD. This gave fans a choice of tattoos to replicate their idols! The art for the album was so unique to the bands peers that it would have set them apart in it-self. This was before the record even blared out to its unknowing lis-tener. Produced by Mike Clink the easy going legend (who had pre-viously worked with Ozzy Osbourne and Survivor), *Appetite For Destruction* belied its initial indifference by becoming one of the biggest selling albums of all time.

"The whole album is about someone we've known and hung out with or something we've done" Axl Rose

Axl said of the album some time later "What people don't under-stand is there was a perfectionist attitude to *Appetite For Destruction*. There was a definite plan to that. We could have made it all smooth and polished. We went and did test tracks with different people and they came out smooth and polished. We did some stuff with Spencer Proffer and Geffen records said it was too fuckin' radio. That's why we went with Mike Clink". Eventually the band captured the sound they were looking for, which they felt underlined their respective tal-ents and Mike Clink was rightly credited for highlighting the bands chaotic strains through volumes of distorted rage, yet equally being capable of indicating their more mellow side with acoustic sections and the 'keep singing 'til you get it right' system with Axl.

The singer would further say: "we went for a raw sound because it just didn't gel having it too tight and concise. We knew what we were doing, and we knew this: we know the way we are onstage, and the only way to capture that energy on the record, is by making it somewhat live, doing the bass, the drums and the rhythm guitar at the same time."

Amazingly the band and production team had managed to capture the bands' onstage intensity. Even the portraits of the band members on the albums back cover were perfectly representative of their individual contributions. There was the reflective Axl, front person extraordinaire carefully holding a bottle of beer in one hand, his other hand caressing his hip, bandana astride his tilted head which suggested he was deep in thought even while the photo was being taken. At odds with the other members it is Axl who stands alone behind the others. Is it merely to draw attention to him deliberately from the photographers' point of view, or was it the natural hierarchy already portraying itself?

There were the cameo roles for the other members; Izzy is quietly reflective looking pensive as he grasps an acoustic guitar. Duff, another member to be clutching alcohol sits looking resolutely wasted, hair slung back in wanton disarray while Slash takes the conclusion of a rebel rousing band of alcoholics to suitable depths, staring blankly through a haze of unkempt hair, top hat and bottle between his legs – happy enough with all he needs and all he had at the time. Steven sits, carefully holding bongos looking every bit the young mischievous pretty boy of the band – all girly blond hair and baby features. The music simply underlined the respective personalities of the band members, being as brash and carefree as it was heartfelt and serious.

Axl gave the analysis of making the record in typically cryptic fashion. He explained in 1992, "That's why recording is my favourite thing, because it's like painting a picture. You start out with a shadow, or an idea, and you come up with something and it's a shadow of that. You might like it better. It's still not exactly what you pictured in your head. But you go into the studio and add all these things and you come up with something you didn't even expect." And therein lay the secret, it wasn't a deliberate or conscious attempt to create music to the backdrop of their lives and their hopes and dreams, it was something, which happened accidentally, a beautiful amalgamation of talents coming together at the right time in exactly the right manner.

"We were headed to a Roxy show and got pulled over by four cops. They picked a bag off the street; said we threw it out the window and there were drugs in it. There were no drugs in it. And they were just trying to hassle us, saying our advance money in our pockets was drug money. They searched everything, pushed us around, and we were late for the show" Axl Rose

The band was quick to start playing live gigs and they began touring in support of The Cult in America in August. The six week tour was a perfect match – two diverse bands with distinct front men (The Cult featured Ian Astbury as singer, who Axl claimed spent more time in Guns' dressing room than his own) who were both able to invite audience members to eat out of their hands. Guns' notoriety was still being cultivated in the States and on a bill with the seemingly clean and trouble free Cult it was left to Axl to steal the show as usual.

In Atlanta there was another parallel with the antics of Jim Morrison when police stormed the stage to arrest Axl following an earlier incident where he had attacked a security guard just before the band went on. Guns' had just warmed up and were into their second song of the set when the melee happened. It could not have been planned better. Despite the remaining members being left in a state of limbo and a hurried improvisational scenario where Slash and Steven played a fifteen minute and ten minute solo respectively (not to mention the rather awkward debuting of a roadie on vocals!) The reputation the band had begun to formulate was strengthened on the back of Axl's backstage police questioning and resultant warning.

There was then the potential of a bill that looked mouth watering on paper, Guns N' Roses were touted to tour England with America's favourite rock n roll band, Aerosmith. However at the last minute Aerosmith pulled out (perhaps a fear borne of their manager Tim Collins' expectations outlined earlier) and Guns' were faced with either touring alone or finding a hasty replacement. The band chosen to support Guns' was Faster Pussycat who had garnered favourable reactions to their more straightforward glam rock self titled debut. Even this more likely go ahead pairing could not continue unabated. Adler broke his hand in a street fight and it needed Cinderella's Fred Coury to step in and take over the drum hot seat.

The bands played at prestigious venues such as the Hammersmith Odeon in the capital and the Manchester Apollo, instantly proving their new found fame in performing at the larger theatres. It was in Manchester however that ticket sales were not quite as glorious as Geffen perhaps anticipated, despite having just released 'Welcome To The Jungle' as a single.

The Apollo theatre had its upper balcony cordoned off due to lower ticket sales than the 2,000 capacity venue could hold and it was therefore a more subdued show that ran at only just over the hour. In Nottingham, the reaction was more fanatical and Axl responded in kind. The band played with such gusto they had the hundreds of Rock City regulars stamping their feet in rebellious bravado, lasting the full two hours of the bands live show, including the encores which threatened to boil the crowd into shadows of steam. The resultant exodus of fans onto the quiet Nottingham streets outside saw a frenzied gathering of still stoked fans, who almost pushed the Guns' tour bus on its head as it tried to weave its way out of the confines of a dreary English winter evening.

"We're not afraid to go excess with substances, sexually and everything else. We know we're always going to be at odds with people on something. A lot of people are afraid to be that way; we're not. And the reason is that bands who have made it big have been that way. And Guns N' Roses plan on making it real big" Axl Rose

Before the show had even taken place Axl had set the precedent, and perhaps explained the bands furious performance when he ripped his hotel room phone out of the wall and promptly dispatched it towards the head of the meek female receptionist at the bottom of the stairs, who had been attempting to discover the source of the noise in Axl's room.

Despite the English press reacting as impassibly as before, by speaking in derisive tones of a band on the verge of collapse with words like 'volatile' and 'temperamental' being used liberally to define Axl's personality, it seemed England wasn't big enough for Guns N' Roses.

Although by the time of their final show in the country, at the Hammersmith Odeon, immortalised by metal legends such as home grown favourites Iron Maiden, the band almost sold out the venue and took it upon themselves to play their longest set of the tour, clearly enjoying the rapturous reception they received. They underlined their desire to do their own thing by playing for shorter periods when the crowd did not suit them or were not vociferous enough, as in Manchester (often a place American bands are loathed to play) – to revelling in their status if the attendant throng embraced them more readily, as in London.

The band was soon to receive the kind of crowds it thrived on, more regularly. As one potential support act had been torn away from them; another fell into their sights. As a replacement for the newly rejuvenated Whitesnake, Guns' had the unprecedented honour of being chosen as the band to join Motley Crue on a tour of the States.

The fast rising popularity of the band was difficult for its members to deal with but for a period of some years afterwards they seemed to ride the wave unerringly and simply go with the flow, without realising the effect it was having on them. Duff reminiscing in 2003 commented, "Back when the band started, we all came from humble backgrounds. We got our first cheques for forty grand and it was like, whoa!" he says. "We'd been living on a hundred bucks a week. None of us had seen anything close to that before. Then the next cheque came, and then the really big cheques came, and they just kept coming."

In gross understatement he also observed that no one in the band could really merge the payments with the work they had done. He laughingly remembered, "We didn't know what anything was, what anything was for. It was only later that I started tying it all together. I started wanting to know: 'Okay, the interest rates have gone up today'".

Unbeknownst to the other members at the time, Axl had already progressed beyond a mere street rogue who did not know what his money was for or exactly what to do with it. He quickly developed a business sense that would soon land him with the dubious honour of leader of the band. For all intents and purposes they were a motley collection of ragamuffins when they joined Motley Crue around America.

Unknowingly making promoters thousands of dollars and living out a dream which had seemed too wild to comprehend truly even a year ago, the band was now part of something it could not fully control. The merger of two such narcotic hungry groups of vagabonds was bound to create interest and frenzied anticipation. Such a tour could not take place nowadays without a great deal more capital than it took in 1987.

"I just liked coke. I liked the way it felt. And fuck, I didn't know if I did it four or five days in a row I'd get fucking hooked on it! And that's a different subject altogether. That drug takes you over mentally and physically, so much that to come back is hard. I had not so much a drinking problem as to just want to drink and get rowdy. I really don't feel that I have the intense addiction people believe"
Slash

In retrospection it is easier to see how bands like Guns N' Roses and Motley Crue broke out of the otherwise small tightly knit 'glam' scene. Not only did their reputations precede and define them but also they both equally outshone other hard rock acts by virtue of their distinctive styles, equally breaking the mould of the time.

Both bands were real and the crowds knew it. Speaking to *Terrorizer* in 2003 Nikki Sixx recalled Crue's and Guns' legacy by explaining, "to me the other bands like Poison and Faster Pussycat missed the fuckin' point altogether so I didn't really pay attention. The point they missed was that we didn't care if we lived or died. And they were really celebrating yeah man rock n roll! Girls! Talk dirty to me! And I was like, fuck you man…shout at the fuckin' devil. I didn't get it. I didn't like it. I have no social skills and I definitely wasn't going to be hanging out at a party with the likes of them. We had our own world and I cherished that."

It was an insular world, which Guns N' Roses had already begun to encompass themselves. Where Crue had rebelled against the otherwise tame looking and sounding bands of the time with tongue in cheek satanic imagery and make up, Guns N' Roses took a more street savvy approach, much like another band of distinctive upstarts, Metallica. Sixx explained more in the pages of *Terrorizer* as to what set his and Axl's band apart. He said, "We were the real deal. It was doom, gloom, destruction, girls, 24 hours a day, the fastest cars, the loudest guitars, it was all the shit that makes Spinal Tap wonderful. And it was scary to people on the outside, and frustrating because we wouldn't do what we were told. To be honest I don't see that in those other bands. I see them as being a fabricated version. Some of them, like Cinderella, did write some good songs but it just wasn't real, that's all."

Real was something both Motley Crue and Guns N' Roses most definitely were and the crowds knew the real thing when they saw it. As early as 1981 Crue's singer Vince Neil had been as much a tearaway as any member of G N' R. Police questioned him after he had beaten up a drag queen in a night club (because he was sold baby powder instead of cocaine). The dreaded crack was responsible ten years later for Neil's porn star girlfriend Savannah being hospitalised after convulsions, brought on by four days of sustained cocaine use along with her boyfriend.

It was not just Vince Neil who had a penchant for excess, as anyone who has read the Motley Crue story in *The Dirt* will know. From tales of the whole band entering rehab in the first month of 1987, to the revelation that their manager Doc McGhee was given a five year suspended sentence for smuggling 40,000 lbs of marijuana into the United States in 1982 – Crue's passion for excess was relentless. Nikki Sixx was the most famous of their drug addicts given that he was to officially 'die' for two minutes after ingesting a heroin overdose.

Axl's take on drugs was something of a mystery for his fans and the media. Though it seemed highly probable he indulged as much as his band mates, he was always seemingly volatile at any time of day and was the only band member not to perpetually have a drink in his hand. Axl told *RIP* magazine, "I have a different physical constitution and different mindset about drugs than anybody I've known in Hollywood, because I don't abstain from doing drugs, but I won't allow myself to have a fuckin' habit. I won't allow it. I'll have done blow for three days and my mind will go "Fuck no". I'll have the physical feeling of knowing my body needs it, and I'll just refuse to do coke that day. I'm not going to do it, because if I was going to do it, I know I won't be able to hit my goals with what I want to do with this band. I can't let myself get into coke as much as I'm into the band. The same thing with heroin. I did it for three weeks straight and had one of the greatest times in my life, because I was with a girl I wanted to be with in this beautiful apartment, and we just sat there listening to Led Zeppelin, doing drugs and fucking."

This would bear out Axl's ex girlfriend Gina's comments about his past heroin use. But Axl insinuated in the same magazine interview that he was always on hand to take care of issues that needed him to be clear minded.

He added: "It was great, 'cause at that time I had nothing to do but sit on my ass and make a few phone calls a day. I stopped on, like, Saturday, because I had serious business to attend to on Monday. I felt like shit, sweated, shook, but on Monday I was able to function. I can't hide in drugs. A lot of people can, but whenever I do any drugs – pills, booze, smack, whatever – to enjoy it, my life has to be perfect – no fuck ups, nothing going wrong. Otherwise, when I'm high, I'll analyse the shit out of everything that's happening in my life and why things are going wrong. That's not enjoyable. And if I have shows to do, I won't touch drugs because it fucks up my throat. My advice is don't get a habit, don't use anybody else's needle and don't let drugs become a prerequisite to having a good time. Do

things in moderation, and just be careful." Being careful was something it seemed only Axl was capable of in Guns N' Roses.

Though Slash would claim his indulgences were equally under
control it seemed he could always be guaranteed to get involved
with those who weren't so careful. Slash had a very close friend
who used to bail him out in the physical and emotional sense of
the word. When Slash was housed in L.A. between tours and was
virtually comatose from a chemical binge; she would often receive
a phone call from an unknown caring person who had found her
number on a note in Slash's pocket.

One New Years Eve at 7pm, Slash called the friend saying he was
ensconced in a hotel with Motley Crue's Nikki Sixx. Tellingly Slash
is none too articulate and in broken diatribe of himself and, whoever, the friend deciphers the following story.

Nikki had announced at one stage he was going to another room to
find his guitar for an impromptu jam of some sort when, a full hour
later Slash realises Nikki hasn't actually come back. Opening the
door on his way to find the lanky bassist, Slash trips over the numb,
blue body of Nikki Sixx. Like a scene from a bad rock n' roll movie, Sixx has overdosed.

In a mist of quick thinking poise Slash confided his fear to the
friend, of being found in a hotel with a dead rock star, and whatever potential blame attachments that might conjure up. So it is with
mindful and intense velocity that the quick thinking friend races
down to pull Slash from the scene, not forgetting to dial Sixx an am-
bulance.

In order to fully sanction Slash with a believable alibi, the friend
magic's a Guns N' Roses party to which copious people are rapidly invited. In a hurried bout of mastermind thinking she turns all the
clocks in the house back two hours – after which it is safe to greet all
the guests with an acknowledgment that they had indeed got to her
house pretty fast. So Slash, enjoying a typical G N' R style party re-
laxes in the knowledge he cannot be tainted with any responsibility
in Sixx's potential fatality. Thankfully, Nikki Sixx made it through.
There were other incidents involving not only overdoses but also
general debauchery, as you might expect. The fact that Sixx's heart

had actually stopped for a full two minutes, was immortalised in the Crue song, 'Kickstart My Heart' which appeared later on their *Dr Feelgood* album.

All the members of Guns N' Roses, Motley Crue and their entourages had survived a tour which, had it occurred at the height of both bands fame and relative excesses might well have had a different ending. It is now only with hindsight that Motley Crue and Guns N' Roses playing together seems ludicrously impossible but the one enduring triumph of the union was Guns' growing popularity. The fact that Axl was arrested (at the L.A. Cathouse, for leaping into the crowd and fighting with a security guard who was harassing one of the band's friends) only served to highlight his notoriety.

In time Guns N' Roses would easily surpass their touring partners in ways beyond mere record and ticket sales.

"Those guys have to do about two million dollars' worth of dope be-fore they're ready for recovery" Aerosmith Manager Tim Collins af-ter Aerosmith had toured with G N' R

1988 was one of Guns N' Roses' most tumultuous years, and for many reasons, a lot of them negative, was also one of their most memorable. After just twelve months in the public eye, the band's popularity had grown to astronomical proportions, which balanced their unavoidable fame with much rock n' roll style activity, much of which seemed to be ignored amidst the other events of the year.

Both media and the public anticipated every Guns N' Roses move with frenzied hawk eyes – waiting intently for something to go wrong. The band however quickly picked up on the superficiality of fame and the disregard for their personal well being. The band was to bring out a mini album and make the unprecedented move of two new releases in the space of as many years.

Before a new EP was even contemplated however, the band be-gan the year on an ironic note. On January 5th they opened for Great White at the Santa Monica Civic Centre in Santa Monica, CA. Although this particular show passed without incident (other than Guns' blowing the then institutional Great White off the stage), sev-eral months later G N' R would be famous for performing a set at Donington at the Monsters Of Rock Festival in England.

Their fame rose due to the deaths of two audience members. Fifteen years on Great White would play an equally historic show where their own guitarist Ty Longley died along with 99 fans and work-ers at the Station, a rock club in Rhode Island (between New York and Boston). Longley was part of a human logjam that followed the band's set – where supposedly forbidden pyrotechnics were used and promptly ignited the club roof causing an inferno throughout the venue. Hundreds headed for the main entrance, which consisted of just one exit. Where the other four members of Great White es-caped through a backstage exit, Longley went for the main entrance and was unable to escape. The incident reached the international news. It was the last thing the band wanted to be remembered for.

The remainder of the first part of 1988 for Guns N' Roses was spent continually promoting *Appetite For Destruction* and focus was most definitely on keeping the band in constant view. It seemed a worldwide trait that the band was in heavy rotation everywhere you looked or happened to hear. Whether it was in a car driving by or on a shop P.A. system, Guns N' Roses had well and truly grabbed the 80s by the scruff of the neck and achieved something no other band had quite managed on the same scale. Where bands that were certainly considered more straightforward heavy metal (still a dirty set of words to mainstream America and the rest of the developed world) such as Iron Maiden and Judas Priest had certainly conquered America as well as their own home country – they were still minority celebrity bands compared to Guns N' Roses. Never before in the world of rock and metal had a band received credibility from both the underground rock fraternity as well as the corporate mainstream – whose preference for radio friendly ballads, popularised by the so called 'soft' metal acts of the time such as Bon Jovi and Poison would constantly override musical ability or integrity.

Axl spoke later with hindsight, when their EP had been released – about the potential of their anticipated full length follow up album. "A lot of groups are trying to outsell *Appetite For Destruction*. For a debut, it was the highest selling album in the history of rock and roll. Definitely in America, but I'm not sure that's true worldwide. I read where Bon Jovi was saying nobody's out done their biggie, *Slippery When Wet*. He knew it was their biggie, and he didn't know if *New Jersey* would be as big. Of course, you're going to want to outdo it. What I want to do is just grow as an artist and feel proud of these new songs."

Regardless of the bands own perceptions on following their already legendary debut, a certifiable believable act such as G N' R was a breath of fresh air. A band who had made it minus the rules. They did not adhere to the conventional ways of doing things – from performing to interviews, their words were often misguided attempts to set the record straight but often would land them in ambiguous light

– and leave them open to intense scrutiny from all quarters. Had the band known what they would learn over the course of the next five years back in 1988 it is questionable whether there would have been such a phenomenon around Guns N' Roses.

Despite their protestations and reactions to the media misquoting or misunderstanding their words – it was this rancour of popularity, which lent the public's affection to them. This fondness stood despite such actions as cancelling shows, which were due to begin in March of 1988 in support of David Lee Roth. Roth was still a top draw in America and enjoying something of a resurgence not withstanding his acrimonious departure from Van Halen.

However, vacuous excuses concerning either commitments elsewhere or Axl's throat problems were bandied around and the band didn't play a single show with the star jumping entertainer. They did however join Alice Cooper onstage at the Long Beach Arena, playing 'Under My Wheels' with him and whooping the unexpectant crowd to delight – the big guns were in attendance, Axl, Slash and Izzy. At the end of March the band gave a hint at their new material's supposed direction by performing on the Fox Late Show. They played an acoustic version of 'You're Crazy' and also a song which was used as a future b–side 'Used To Love Her' – a blatant G N' R swipe at ironic humour regarding an ex girlfriend who would be better buried in the back yard than in the house to constantly curse at her partner.

Slash pointed out that everyone who heard the song usually found it funny except those who never laughed at jokes. Axl himself described the song in the liner notes for the album as to be taken as nothing more than a joke.

Speaking of 'You're Crazy' after the release of the *G N' R Lies* EP that it appeared on, Axl was scathing, "I think 'Crazy' sucks. The band's great but I think I sound like shit. It's a very special, magical song. Every time we record 'Crazy' something happens. When it's really on, the band goes into a trancelike state. You leave everything else behind. I don't think I quite hit what I was looking for. I don't think there's a major problem with it, I just don't think we quite hit it, I think everything else kicks ass!" Despite this cursing from the front man himself, the fans although surprised the band played 'un-plugged' seemed to like the alternate version and as if to predict the future of televised live shows the band played at The Ritz in New York City and had the entire concert aired on MTV.

Playing acoustically for however short a time was a precursor to more familiar unplugged sessions MTV would regularly run in the future. Slash had a different idea about the new version of 'You're Crazy' than his front man. He said of the song, "it's a lot bluesier which is the way me and Axl and Izzy originally wrote it. I think I prefer the slower version it's got something. I don't know but every time we play it in that slower style something weird happens, some-thing magical. We've never done it the same way twice."

The band managed to dispel rumours of any problems with Axl's voice – though later the same year the band would pull out from supporting Iron Maiden due to the continual throat difficulties Axl was facing. Two months after pulling out of various commitments due to Axl's voice troubles the band were paired with Aerosmith for a tour of the states which has assumed legendary status as a ground breaking tour. Their manager Tim Collins said of the pairing "John Kalodner said we needed a great opening act for the summer shows and suggested Guns N' Roses. I said 'we can't do this. We're sober, they're heroin users and drug addicts.' But he insisted we find a way to handle this so we came up with a plan."

That plan involved Guns N' Roses limiting their use of drugs or al-cohol to the confines of their own dressing room which seemed fair to all involved. Besides, it wasn't the first time Aerosmith had is-sued such regulations. Both White Lion and Dokken who had re-cently opened for the Boston group had been given the exact same instructions. Guns N' Roses were felt to be a whole different type of band however and the revelation that Aerosmith's men in control had been clearing all bars containing alcohol before they arrived might have scared the Gunners had they known the exact nature of the bands paranoia and rehabilitation.

However this was an opportunity too good to pass up. It might also have been assumed by fans of both Guns N' Roses and Aerosmith that both could handle such a tour without the use of narcotics. This time, after the proposed shows that were cancelled by Aerosmith the year before, all hoped the tour would go ahead and be a success.

The idea of Aerosmith usurping their supposed successors to the kings of rock n' roll throne was more common than any civility between the two bands but surprisingly given the G N' R penchant for continuing excess aside the recently sober 'toxic twins' of Aerosmith, the bands maintained a healthy respect for each other and while Guns' didn't exactly usurp their heroes at the top of the pile just yet, they certainly embellished their reputation with some perfectly choreographed rock n' roll shows, one of which saw the band play to 65,000 fans in New York's Giants Stadium on a bill that also included Deep Purple. A week after that memorable show the bands sold out three shows at Great Woods, a recently built amphitheatre in Mansfield, Massachusetts that was close to Aerosmith's hometown of Boston. As an opening band the scene was set for G N' R if not to steal the show then certainly to keep it running in the time honoured tradition Aerosmith had grown accustomed to.

After a series of remarkable shows of their own it was no risk for an American rock n' roll institution to throw caution to the wind and take a band on the road who were every bit the young upstarts they had once been themselves. At the Mansfield shows Guns' took to the stage with Axl wearing his 'Eat The Worm' t–shirt in jovial mood, introducing Slash as "the king of beers" and Steven Adler as "the biggest pothead I know" to rapturous audience response.

The joviality was absent on the 4th August show however. A parking lot attendant in Philadelphia told Axl's brother, Stewart, to "fuck off". Axl promptly responded with a punch in the face of said attendant and was jailed for the privilege. The band only just made the show after manager Doug Goldstein managed to bail Axl out in time.

Guns N' Roses had long been protagonists in the Aerosmith story given their championing of the recently reinvented act – their respect had been there for one of the key bands in their own story. From the very beginning they would cover 'Mama Kin' off the first Aerosmith album and it was a fact that 'Smith guitarist Joe Perry had certainly noted.

He picked out their take on the Aerosmith legacy when he commented to *Tower Pulse* "They were the first band that really picked up on the way our music actually sounded. Just certain things about the way they constructed passages and riffs. Like they listened to Aerosmith and didn't pick up on what we looked like but what we were trying to do musically. They told us that. They made no bones about it and I'm really glad. They're just going from what we did with the Stones and Zeppelin and The Yardbirds. It's no secret. Nobody invented this shit."

It was flattering in itself that Perry was flattered over Guns' take on Aerosmith's rock style but he omitted the fact that G N' R had rewritten the rule book on the 'shit' that nobody invented. Taking equal influence from their respective idols gave them a solid base on which to work but the craft with which they constructed their own songs was all their own.

The truth, in all irony Aerosmith was now competing with bands such as G N' R and not just in terms of sales. They had themselves updated their sound in order to successfully make a comeback into the rock arena and keep up with acts like Bon Jovi and Poison. Their *Dude Looks Like A Lady* single from *Permanent Vacation* was a perfect blend of Motley Crue (and was supposedly written about Crue front man Vince Neil) and Guns N' Roses and it was therefore even more commendable such rival bands managed to tour together. Furthermore tour harmoniously.

As Slash would say in *Kerrang!* "Aw, man, it was great... Some funny shit went down on that Aerosmith tour. We were so similar, and yet we made such a contrast. They're all 'straight' now; clean. And their whole operation runs like clockwork; they stay in one place for four or five gigs, then when the tour moves a little further up the road they move to another place and make that their base for the next five gigs, or whatever. The whole thing is kept well under control... Which is exactly the opposite; of course, from the way we usually get things done. We travel the whole time, and very little of what we do is done, uh, straight..."

The professionalism with which Aerosmith now ran their band was borne from decades of not only playing together but touring in tan-

dem and it sat in contrast as Slash observed to the frenzy of the Guns
N' Roses road show. Though the bands managed to co exist there
was a stipulation that certain things could not be done around the
now completely sober Aerosmith. Manager Tim Collins stated to
BAM "we made a deal with them. We told them we wouldn't pay for
any of their drugs or alcohol – we didn't want to enable their activities. But if they chose to use drugs they could do that in their dressing room. At the beginning it worked so well that the bands had no
contact but it gradually loosened up when the gunners were respectful and everyone got along great."

Slash observed that the band could still be themselves around their
now reformed idols. He said, "They were exposed to us the whole
time, and we got to hang out together a lot. Which was really cool,
because those guys have all been heroes of mine since I was a kid
and first started listening to rock n' roll." And as for drinking away
from their presence, it was not a problem though Slash did concede
that he used a cup to drink his Jack Daniels from. Indeed the band
were no preachers given their new found sobriety and it seemed the
members of Guns' were more concerned with how Aerosmith would
react to their activities than Aerosmith themselves were.

Slash was in reflective mood when he remembered one incident
that happened while the bands were playing together. He remarked
"There was one time when Steven Tyler came into the room I used
to use for tuning my guitar. I'd stepped out of the room for a minute
and when I got back there was Tyler standing there looking through
my tapes and stuff. I had one empty, one half empty, and one full
bottle of Jack lying around in there. Anyway, I walked in and we
started talking. And he says, 'Did you drink all that today?' And I
was, like, yeah, I did. And he just gave me this look. He started to
say something, but then he changed his mind. He's been through
some scenes of his own, I guess."

This was some understatement and it was incredible how the bands
co existed, even to the point where Steven Tyler imparted valua-
ble and well versed advice to Steven Adler when the drummer had
become very disillusioned at one point on the tour. As Tyler told
Musician magazine, "I don't push my shit on anybody. I don't say

you're an asshole for using drugs. There's a time and a place for it. You don't go backstage and brag about your time. You just try to pass it on. Tell them how hard it is, how beautiful it is. I tell them there's a whole world of music out there and they're living in a cave with a boulder at the door and the boulder is drugs. You kick the boulder out the way you can go in and out invite your friends in."

This was a more philosophical comment from Tyler who also said of his opening act in more simplistic terms (somewhat fuelling the Aerosmith ego): "What got me is they were us. The bass player *is* Tom Hamilton, Slash *is* Joe Perry, Izzy *is* Brad and the drummer is that close to Joey Kramer. Axl is the same as me, a visionary ego-maniac. Sometimes I walked into their dressing room and it was like looking in a mirror. I talked to them a little about drugs. Aerosmith was upset that the press was giving us a lot of shit about supposed-ly not letting them drink and smoke and do drugs. That offended us because we never presumed to tell anyone that. Before the first show I got Izzy – who I once did drugs with – and Slash and maybe Duff to come to my dressing room. I told them where I came from with drugs and booze and just told them 'look if you've got any blow please keep it to yourself. Do it in your dressing room. If you do it in mine I'm going to have to leave my own dressing room.' But they were ok they told us we were their idols. We had shirts printed up with the names of the rehabs we had gone through instead of tour dates and we gave them to the guys in Guns'. That was our state-ment."

Slash maintained a vibe offstage and off tour that underlined both his and Guns' respect for Aerosmith but also their desire to overtake them as kings of rock. He was quoted as saying on one hand that he felt like a kid again when he had watched old footage of Aerosmith playing in 1975 and in essence he remembered then why he wanted to be a musician, yet he also suggested Guns N' Roses were the best placed band to take that mantle, now some 13 years on.

He believed, "We filled a void which someone had left a long time ago, Aerosmith used to do, I think, what we do. But even Aerosmith isn't the same thing any more. Even though they're still around, be-cause they're older and experienced been through the mill and this and that, they're on another plateau now where they're not going to fill that gap that they left. So along come these guys, us right? And we're just going for it." Slash would have done well to learn from his elders mistakes and realise their own rock n' roll lifestyle would be lucky to last as long as Aerosmith's did. For the moment Guns' were clearly respectful of Aerosmith but also felt they had the ability to become like their idols and perhaps even surpass them.

When the bands joined each other on tour and on stage they made sure they played 'Mama Kin' and when they got to L.A. the feeling of support between the two acts was undeniable. Where Aerosmith would usually never go to the side of the stage and watch any of the bands that opened for them, with G N' R it was different; they were there just about every night. There were always one or two members of Aerosmith watching eagle eyed from the wings, and sometimes the whole band would be gaping into the inferno Guns' would create on stage.

The Gunners were visibly enthused but equally nervous with their idols watching them but true to form they managed to carry off their remarkable standing with consummate ease and merely used their new found friends to guide them to further heights. The bands would not only watch each other play but they would hang out (minus the use of recreational drugs) together and create something of a family vibe. Slash recalled: "I did a guitar solo one night – one of those finger picking slow blues things – and after the show, Tyler got me to one side and said, 'That was amazing!' I just stood there and said, 'Well, thanks', and couldn't think of anything else to say. I was blown away. Seriously, that's something I'll never forget... That, and a couple of other things he did, which I won't mention because it would get us both into too much trouble..."

The good time vibe would eventually give way to something approaching envy, at least from Aerosmith's manager. Tim Collins said, "By the end of the tour Guns N' Roses were huge. They basically just exploded. We were all pissed that *Rolling Stone* showed up to do a story on Aerosmith but Guns N' Roses ended up on the cover of the magazine. Suddenly the opening act was bigger than we were." Such was the risk in taking a band who had not fully reached their eventual success level and it seems either Aerosmith were not shrewd enough to think through what could happen (or they assumed they would blow their opponents offstage every night) or they were simply giving their own career the kick start it needed by taking a band who they knew would fit into most of their fans record collections quite easily as well as bringing a sizeable audience of their own to every show.

This is indeed what happened but Collins felt something approaching sympathy for the newly crowned media darlings of rock n' roll. "We felt sorry for them" he pined. "One, they were so fucked up it was ridiculous. Two their stupid manager had negotiated a bad deal for them and never bothered to renegotiate it or even complain. Three they were travelling like gypsies their old suitcases held together by twine and gaffer tape. At the end of the tour we bought them all new Halliburton cases which their manager took as an insult."

There are two ways to view Collins' comments but it is certainly easy to see where Alan Niven felt the opposition manager was being slightly pedantic in suggesting Guns' should need new suitcases. The band themselves were making enough money (despite their supposed bad deal) to buy new suitcases but it was something of a luxury for them to bother with such things. As long as they had enough money to indulge in their excess binges and get from A to B and occasionally eat, that was all Guns' required. It wasn't the only time the behind the scenes enforcers of the two respective bands fell out however.

When the tour stories emerged and Collins was quoted as saying that Guns N' Roses was very much like Aerosmith and that they would essentially have to do $2.5 million dollars worth of dope before they could get help, according to Collins, Guns' manager reacted by going into a "psychotic rage". Collins claimed "He came up and punched me at a restaurant on Melrose Avenue in L.A. a couple of weeks later, the moron. He's not in the business anymore. David Geffen asked me to manage Guns N' Roses and I thought about it for ten seconds and declined."

The most ramshackle famous band in the world had a guitarist who was still living out of a suitcase; staying in hotels in L.A. It was only later that year that Slash actually bought himself an apartment in North Hollywood. The abode was five minutes drive from the Roxy, the Rainbow and a whole host of other dingy clubs and bars he was apt to dwell in. By his own actions he may as well have still been living from an open suitcase. The whole experience was something new to Slash who had bought his first ever apartment.

He reasoned, "I can't live off everybody else forever; if I can afford to have a place. I can't just keep being, like, a total fuckin' gypsy all my life…" the gypsy mentality would have seemed to keep the band rooted in the doldrums as far as writing new material was concerned but Slash gushed that he had already started writing for the full follow up to *Appetite For Destruction*. He used an eight–track mobile studio to put down the best ideas on tape. For Slash, his dishevelled appearance belied his strong work ethic and it was a surprise to some that he actually worked on the band all the time and maintained a highly productive schedule.

A typical day for Slash involved waking early, around 8:30 or nine o'clock in the morning, visiting the Geffen Records office and handling the press for the bands increasing popularity, everything from interviews to promotional activities for whatever the office 'suits' lined him up for. "One morning they woke me up at 5:30 am to talk to some guy on the phone from a magazine in Greece" Slash complained, "But that's not every day. And it's a small price to pay, anyway – for not having to worry about your rent, and getting to work on time every day, and all these other horrors that our music has helped us escape. To pay for those privileges, you have to fuckin' be there for the few responsibilities you do have as a band member."

It was a typically humble statement from a man who as well as being able to sustain unhealthy levels of substance abuse also knew when to put the work in that he needed to do to keep Guns' afloat along with his mostly hard working band mates. As Slash observed at the time somewhat ruefully, "Anybody can sit around all day just getting out of their heads… and I should know. I'm still not very good at looking after myself in lots of ways, but I take the best care of my music I can, and my music takes care of me". That much was certainly true and 1988 was very much a good year in terms of musical creation and an increasing fan base. The band played a few, or in some cases, any shows which unusual as they seemed at the time helped garner Guns N' Roses a reputation that exceeded their humble back alley roots in simple rock n roll.

The media regularly questioned relations between Axl and Slash but there seemed to be invisible glue that held them together. Slash would comment "The relationship between most lead singers and most lead guitar players is very sensitive, very volatile – I could go on listing these things for hours. It's just very intense. It has major ups and major downs. But somewhere between all this intensity and this friction there's chemistry. And if the chemistry's right, like Axl and me are really tight, then there's something – a spark or, you know, a need, that holds it together. You fight too. The biggest fights are between me and Axl but that's also what makes it happen."

Making it happen was something of a Guns N' Roses specialty. When they didn't make the stage on time or sometimes at all, there was as much attention if and when they did take to the stage – something was always bound to happen when the riotous mix of personalities that was Guns N' Roses got together. Thus where Aerosmith and G N' R was a perfect match for each other it seems to often be overlooked by metal or rock historians just how unusual Iron Maiden and G N' R playing together actually was although only for a period of a few shows.

Of course at the time the entire scene was more straightforward – often if you wore long hair you were treated as outcasts and regardless of genre definitions within the metal scene, bands seemed to be able to stick together. The common enemy of virtually all other rock and metal acts seemed to be the glam scene. Utterly derided by the more coarse and distinctly underground thrash scene, glam was seen as a mainstream alternative to thrash – and a blatant attempt to make metal softer or more accessible. Where most bands wore make up and dressed as if they were women, Guns N' Roses soon broke out of this eventual stereotype and decided they would perform and walk around more naturally – and when they did so it was to under-line their roles as regular rockers.

It was no advert for excess or for attempting to be something they weren't. They dispensed with the lip–gloss and hairspray as initial-ly it was something to get them noticed but it soon became redun-dant when their material was strong enough. At one point on the Aerosmith tour Axl was jailed for punching a Chicago businessman when he had called him a Bon Jovi look alike. Axl for one was intent on distancing himself from any 'hair rock' references.

In times where metal has been split into many other directions than it once stood – the memory of Guns N' Roses and Iron Maiden shar-ing a stage is all the more bizarre. For that to happen today would take promoters with the patience of Mother Theresa (not to mention the mothering skills) and the financial clout of Don King. So it is no surprise the bands seemingly did not gel so well. The down to earth geezers from stiff upper lip Britain – in the music business more for laughs and culture as much as the money, compared with the ever increasing circus and volatility surrounding the Guns' camp.

However much of Guns' notoriety spread from sources other than the band themselves or any direct action they took it is certain that it was somewhat frowned upon by the more regular touring schedule and clockwork precision with which the Maiden ship ran. Already tour veterans the band had begun to take impressive new bands as touring support acts for reasons that were as much to do with show-ing they could compete as it was about selling tickets.

When L.A. Guns were the ironic replacement for G N' R on a night when they cancelled rather late it was hardly going to distract the at-tendant Maiden maniacs from their devotion to Eddie and co. given Guns' notoriety it did not help when it was announced Axl could not cover a particular show and then Slash disappeared to seek help for his addictions, leaving for rehab in Hawaii.

Iron Maiden's rivalry before Guns N' Roses existence was more focused on fellow Brits, as Bruce Dickinson said later, "There was rivalry to a point. We were neck and neck in the States, but Leppard rapidly overtook us. At our peak, Maiden probably sold 2.5 mil-lion of each album worldwide, of which one million or so were sold in the States. But once you get a hit album in America, you just go through the roof. Maiden never made the breakthrough that Def Leppard did."

Nor would Maiden ever eclipse Guns N' Roses in their home-land and as the festival bill was announced for the Monsters Of Rock Festival at Castle Donington in Derbyshire, England – one surprise was the inclusion of the burgeoning Guns N' Roses. As Bruce Dickinson said of the Donington match up: "The European Monsters Of Rock shows were massive, even if the US tour that year was pretty average. But look at what we were competing with: Guns N' Roses were all over the place."

He wasn't wrong. Fifty seven weeks after entering the US bill-board Top 200 *Appetite For Destruction* had reached top position along with the issue of *Sweet Child O Mine* as a single – timed per-fectly to match *Appetite For Destruction*'s success, it had the charm of an instant radio hit as well as enough guitar to effectively keep G N' R 'relevant' to the masses of rock fans who felt they were one of their own and a band they wanted to keep hold of.

The video was equally stunning – captivating Axl's trademark swagger and the respective members' individual performances, from Steven twiddling his drumsticks with a mischievous grin, to Slash swaying with the assurance of a confident and well worn drunk. Then there was Duff and Izzy ably keeping the ship steady and rolling the backdrop to an entrancing scene that had been cap-tured in the Ballroom in Huntington Park California. The band shot the video on April 11th and by September it had topped the charts – thanks to heavy rotation on video channels worldwide and radio play. A cosmopolitan crowd picked up on the sweetly rasped cho-rus lines and Slash's evocative, distinctly memorable introductory guitar lick.

With such events in the bands favour they were placed dubious-ly low on the festival bill and in retrospection perhaps this was a contributory factor to the tragic events that followed. While attend-ance on the day was rumoured to be up to 120,000 (which would have been the largest metal attendance number ever in the UK) it was more like 100,000. However as anyone who has ever been to

Donington knows, the stage field itself is not as large as it would need to be to accommodate that volume of people and as the expectant throng surged forward fans began to get trapped or squashed painfully against each other.

However at the front of the barrier the chaos was at its highest. As G N' R took to the stage at their proposed time slot of 2pm with 'It's So Easy' the crowd was bathed in mud which clambered around everyone's feet in the first few hundred rows. 'Mr Brownstone' didn't ease on the acceleration pedal and the band picked up haste with Axl posturing in rapturous trademark style and with the band noting each riff and rhythm from the debut album the crowd was out of control, though the feet of the audience were obscured from view.

It took a more visible disturbance in the crowd to start the band into action. Midway through the semi acoustic version of 'You're Crazy' as Axl spotted the crowd growing increasingly rowdy and carefree he was instructed to make an announcement by security who could see first hand the dangers ahead if they did not start to ease the cramped effect of the crowd. As several audience members were ejected by security staff the scene was one of confusion and uncertainty with the band seemingly oblivious to its true scale or how to deal with it. In the interests of decency there were several attempts to grind the frenzy to a halt without ending the set, which would have surely caused greater problems. Who can say with hindsight whether any audience members were guilty of being unwittingly flagrant in terms of pushing or shoving but what is certain is the band were aware to a point of the melee and tried to deal with it calmly.

After pausing again through the following 'Paradise City' the expelling of bodies from the front of the crowd was clearly excessive and Axl responded, "Look! I'm taking time out from my playing to do this and that's the only fun I get all day". The retort seemed to restrain the actions of the audience visible to Axl and the band but there were problems ahead – as the band rounded off a turbulent set with first a mellow 'Patience' and then a somewhat subdued 'Sweet Child O Mine' (which was to receive the biggest cheer of the day as Slash carried out the intro) which promptly saw the end of the bands set. Axl remarked at the climax "Don't kill yourselves!" But the damage had been done much earlier – at the beginning when G N' R had first hit the stage and the excited thousands had pushed forward in their droves.

Two fans, twenty year old Landon Siggers and Alan Dick who was only eighteen had been crushed beneath the crowd and into the mud below. As the band played on unaware and the crowd atop only increased in their enthusiasm and verve nobody seemed to notice they were trampling on two of the audience and by the end as the crowd cleared Dick and Siggers were discovered. As they were rushed the long distance to the backstage emergency centre they were found to be beyond help and pronounced dead. The body of Landon Siggers had to be identified from his tiger and scorpion tattoos on his arms, as he was otherwise unrecognisable. Event organiser Maurice Jones later speculated that the incident could equally have happened with a crowd of 5–10,000 who did not respect their fellow human beings.

Steve Harris, Iron Maiden bassist would later talk of an event, which he fully expected, could happen. Despite none of the bands being told of the two deaths until the day had seen all bands finish their sets – Harris recalled crowd problems earlier in the day during David Lee Roth's set. Roth was indignant at security staff who had tried to appeal to him to calm the crowd and instead continued unabated. Consequently Harris assumed Dick and Siggers had perished during the set of Roth. Although it is pure speculation it was particularly a wise move by Guns N' Roses to distil their set with a blend of blues and acoustic numbers which reduced the surges of the crowd and perhaps made sure that more people escaped intact. Steve Harris had also mentioned to security the seriousness of the situation and doubtless prevented anything further happening.

Though many of the hundred thousand strong crowd had not even arrived at the point of Guns' set there were still a record number of people clambering towards the stage to participate in the crowd – the previous record of 66,500 when AC/DC headlined in 1984 was already bettered and although there was still free space behind the crowd itself, the main culprit was the mud which had begun to soften during opening band Helloween's set when the rain had started to fall.

The mud was so bad that people began to slip and it was just incredibly unfortunate two fans were unable to climb back up. The one triumph of the festival was that it forced the organisation to be much more focused and the crucial difference from then on was the audience cap of just 72,500 and the inability to buy tickets on the day itself. During 1988's festival there were roughly 35,000 who bought tickets on the day and increased the attendance to a figure far ahead of the organisers' expectation. It is without doubt many of those extra fans came because of Guns N' Roses and the fact that the bill itself was arguably the strongest in Donington's history. Along with the aforementioned acts were Megadeth and Kiss who along with perhaps Guns N' Roses themselves could easily have headlined the event at the time.

On either side of Guns' performance at the Donington festival were their shows on tour with Aerosmith. After Donington 'Welcome To The Jungle' was re–released as a single and came out in the same month as the latest Dirty Harry movie *The Dead Pool*. The Clint Eastwood blockbuster featured Guns' in a cameo role playing at a club in Miami. From then on the band could only increase in popularity and there was a desire from at least those behind the scenes to release some form of new material to keep the fans appeased before G N' R could get around to finally recording another full length album.

Everybody knew that the follow up was important to record and first write properly, it was also expected that time would be needed given the bands desire to play live everywhere they could. Perhaps those closest to the bands way of working also expected a certain delay in actually getting the record done not to mention released and then promoted. The resultant mini album was a well–timed stopgap.

Originally the title was going to be *Guns N Roses: Lies! The Sex, The Drugs, The Violence, The Shocking Truth!* While this would have made more headlines and corroborated the myth that Guns N' Roses were a result of the worst excesses of Led Zeppelin, Rolling

Stones and Spinal Tap all rolled into one, perhaps sensing problems with certain stores or radio stations Geffen decided on the abbreviated *G N' R Lies*. The cover image was parodied as a newspaper front page, espousing the rumours and mostly ridiculous stories involving the band.

Most like the British paper *The Daily Sport*, which prides itself on inane and often completely untrue headlines and features, the cover of 'G N' R Lies', was the band at its most humorous and vitriolic. Inside the record was further evidence of the bands interest in the way the British press had treated them, especially over the Donington incident. As well as a page three girl ("the loveliest girls are always in your G N' R LP") there was a reference to soap opera Eastenders with the headline, "Westenders star goes back to jail. Dinky Den in the pen." Not to forget the ultra English phrase, "Let the sods rot in jail!" Even the royal family could not escape a mention with the caption, "Heir to throne caught with trousers down in lurid lust pit."

There was a dig at those who believed Axl was the second coming of the messiah, or something equally beyond the truth. The headline squeezed into the bottom right corner of the cover asked, "Can Axl help you? If you've got a problem I'm here to help." The explanation to 'You're Crazy' was also a reminder of the bands angle – it stated the song was not something that had been done for any reason other than something to amuse themselves. "We do what we want" was the conclusion.

Indeed Axl further underlined this principle when he spoke of the supposed new direction of the EP, especially those who had stated it was an acoustic departure. He explained, "First off, we've been talking about the songs as 'acoustic', but on three of them there is electric guitar. That's the way we've tried to get people mentally prepared for the songs. We've written some mellow songs that seem to grab people's hearts. It's just something we planned on doing for a long time. We wrote some of the songs during or before the recording of Appetite and revised them until we felt they were strong enough to put out. The reason we did it is because we wanted to."

The recording was so casual, verging on the careless, that it sounded as if many of the second sides' cuts had been recorded in one take, and certainly in a very live type environment. You could even hear guitar picks dropping on the floor and the band members talking and counting the songs in, as with the unmistakable Duff introducing 'Patience'.

With copies of the ultra limited edition Uzi Suicide release of *Live ?!*@ Like A Suicide* selling for upwards of $75–$100 Geffen hit upon a clever compromise to accompany 'new' Guns material. As well as including the four live songs ('Reckless Life', 'Nice Boys', 'Move To The City' and 'Mama Kin') from that original EP the record, along with the alternate version of 'You're Crazy' and the pastiche of 'Used To Love Her' ("she broke my heart so I ripped hers out") would feature two new 'acoustic' songs, the emotional and maturely focused 'Patience' and the barrage of low slung redneck glory that was 'One In A Million'.

This song alone propelled the band into (many unwanted) areas of notoriety amongst press the world over. In short they had a field day with the lyrics, which featured the usual Guns N' Roses profanity as well as potentially inflammatory words such as 'niggers', and 'faggots' which did indeed inflame many peoples opinions and comments regarding Axl Rose.

The live tracks, for those who had not heard them before were good enough to have appeared on *Appetite For Destruction* and it is no wonder the EP sold so well. Given the inclusion of the Aerosmith cover of 'Mama Kin' that had being played live only a few months before this was enough of a selling point but there was even greater glory in the lesser known Rose Tattoo cover version of 'Nice Boys (Don't Play Rock n' Roll)' which was more suited to Guns N' Roses than the band who had originally performed it. 'Move To The City' was a tale of a fictional character that was very much like the Axl Rose youth offender – essentially the story was of a young teenage tearaway who was always in trouble with the police and constantly fighting with their parents. To escape small town confines the only option was to go and follow the bright lights and a chance of redemption.

The opening 'Reckless Life' was as much a statement of intent as anything Guns N' Roses had previously put their name to – the lyric "I lead a reckless life and I don't need your advice, I lead a reckless life and you know it's my only vice" was spat so convincingly by Axl it was difficult to imagine him and the band ever changing. The opening salvo to the live tracks was that of the typically manic MC Guns' would often employ, screeching in a slurred drawl worthy of Slash and Duff put together, "Hey fuckers! Suck on Guns N' Fuckin Roses!" There was then a split second before Steven Adler's cowbell prompted the drum roll and the lead riff instantly grabbing the listeners' attention. With Axl in venomous vocal mood, he sounded inexperienced and unprepared but still confident in appearing on stages the world over. One could certainly imagine the band swerving boundless around the small stage.

Yet of course they showed their more emotional, or 'soft' side as some felt, within the second part of the record. Aside from 'Patience' the lyrics on the B–side were more 'punk' than the music of the A–side. The incendiary 'One In A Million' was a tale of the same young kid speaking in 'Move To The City' actually moving to the big bad city and singing on the subject of what he sees. Much like Axl when he appeared in the video for 'Welcome To The Jungle', 'One In A Million' was the verbal accompaniment to his first sight of the city.

"Immigrants and faggots, They make no sense to me…
They come to our country and think they'll do as they please
Like start some mini Iran, Or spread some fuckin' disease
They talk so many goddamn ways. It's all Greek to me
Well some say I'm lazy And others say that's just me
Some say I'm crazy I guess I'll always be
But it's been such a long time
Since I knew right from wrong" 'One In A Million'

His misguided use of expletives, racial and homosexual slurs did not sit well with many however, who couldn't believe their ears at hearing such words uttered calmly and forcefully on a mainstream record. The media, both in the rock world and the broader press went delirious at the bringer of bad tidings immediately castigating Axl Rose for having such sentiment. Axl gave mixed explanations as to his intentions lyrically in the song and to its original meaning.

He said greatly contrasting things to explain himself and whether these were either misquotes, he was just fooling with the press or simply that he had several different meanings in his own mind we will probably never know and as time went on the interest in the song's intentions was helpfully sidelined by the part black member of the band, Slash. It was he who admitted he felt somewhat uncomfortable with Axl saying the word 'nigger' given his own origins but also confirming Axl's innocent intentions and his lyrics being merely a story of something every country boy must feel when stepping into a completely alien environment where he is immediately accosted by vagabonds, thieves and basically several experiences beyond his realm of understanding.

As far as being possibly homophobic Axl even partially admitted this. He told *RIP* magazine "I don't understand it. Anti–homosexual? I'm not against them doing what they want to do as long as it's not hurting anybody else and they're not forcing it upon me. I don't need them in my face or, pardon the pun, up my ass about it." Amusing as this was Axl did give cause to peoples grievances when he also revealed "The most I do is, like, on the way to the Troubadour in "Boystown," on Santa Monica Boulevard, I'll yell out the car window, "Why don't you guys like pussy?" I'm pro heterosexual. I can't get enough of women, and I don't see the same thing that other men can see in men. I'm not into gay or bisexual experiences. But that's hypocritical of me, because I'd rather see two women together than just about anything else. That happens to be my personal, favourite thing." His comments were somewhat juvenile in many people's eyes and only served to fuel the fire regarding the intolerant nature of 'One In A Million'.

"Radicals and Racists, Don't point your finger at me
I'm a small town white boy. Just tryin' to make ends meet"
'One In A Million'

There was however one deeper explanation to his opinions on why he would prefer gay people to stay out of his way. "I've had some very bad experiences with homosexuals," he revealed in the same magazine. "When I was first coming to Los Angeles, I was about eighteen or nineteen. On my first hitchhiking ride, this guy told me I could crash at his hotel. I went to sleep and woke up while this guy was trying to rape me. I threw him down on the floor. He came at me again. I went running for the door. He came at me. I pinned him between the door and the wall. I had a straight razor, and I pulled the razor and said, 'Don't ever touch me! Don't ever think about touching me! Don't touch yourself and think about me! Nothing!' Then I grabbed my stuff and split with no place to go, no sleep, in the middle of nowhere outside of St. Louis. That's why I have the attitude I have."

As much as those who claim women can almost be inviting rape to dress provocatively, some wondered was Axl not asking for potential trouble to go into an unknown room with a strange guy he did not even know? There were a myriad of views on Axl's explanations but one thing was clear. Anyone who had previously believed the singer was homophobic did not have their views changed by the rambling and defiant rationalisation of his words. And the line in the song which refers to 'faggots' in America and feeling free to spread 'some fucking disease' was surely a reference to the AIDS epidemic which had initially spread from Africa. He sounded confused when he remarked, "I don't know what to think about gays. They're in a world of their own. I'm not too happy about AIDS. When I say I'm a small town white boy, I'm just saying I'm no better than anyone else I've described. I'm just trying to get through life, that's all."

Where the use of the word 'nigger' was involved, in the line "Police and niggers, that's right. Get out of my way, no need to buy none of your gold chains today" the justification was even harder to supply and Axl spent many an interview trying to do exactly that. However innocently the words were spoken on record it was certainly clear the band did not expect the level of reaction they received. The only good thing from it as far as Guns N' Roses were concerned was the hype produced further record sales and certainly greater notoriety for the band albeit one they would prefer to be able to distance themselves from. Axl it seemed in particular, learned a great deal from the press following the release of *G N' R Lies*.

The varying accounts of 'One In A Million's actual meaning were as follows: "'One in a million' is about…I went back and forth from Indiana eight times my first year in Hollywood. I wrote it about being dropped off at the bus station and everything that was going on. I'd never been in a city this big and was fortunate enough to have this black dude help me find my way. He guided me to the RTD station and showed me what bus to take, because I couldn't get a straight answer out of anybody. He wasn't after my money or anything. It was more like, "Here's a new kid in town, and he looks like he might get into trouble down here. Let me help him get on his way." People kept coming up trying to sell me joints and stuff. In downtown L.A the joints are usually bogus, or they'll sell you drugs that can kill you. It's a really ugly scene. The song's not about him, but you could kind of say he was one in a million. When I sat down after walking in circles for three hours, the cops told me to get off the streets. The cops down there have seen so much slime that they figure if you have long hair, you're probably slime also. The black guys trying to sell you jewellery and drugs are where the line 'Police and niggers, get out of my way' comes from. I've seen these huge black dudes pull Bowie knives on people for their boom boxes and shit. It's ugly."

There was an alternate revelation to the somewhat unexpected story, which featured a helpful black person (unexpected as the public wondered why was this guy helping out and then referred to in the same breath as 'nigger'?), especially as this story was only spoken of very rarely. More common as an explanation was that Axl had written 'One in a Million' sitting in the apartment of his friend West Arkeen, it was written whilst watching TV and a little bored. Axl would just play the top two strings of a beat up guitar he was using, writing a small part at a time. The idea came to Axl to sing about wanting to get out of Los Angeles.

The Greyhound bus station in downtown L.A. was the setting for the song and Axl would later state: "If you haven't been there, you can't say shit to me about what goes on and about my point of view. There are a large number of black men selling stolen jewellery, crack, heroin and pot, and most of the drugs are bogus. Rip off artists selling parking spaces to parking lots that there's no charge for. Trying to misguide every kid that gets off the bus and doesn't quite know where he's at or where to go, trying to take the person for whatever they've got. That's how I hit town. The thing with "One in a Million" is, basically, we're all one in a million, and we're all here on this earth. We're one fish in a sea. Let's quit fucking with each other, fucking with me."

How could such an explanation fit in with a black person who had helped him when he initially arrived at the station? Or was he simply merging two separate stories into one overall fictional song? Either way, given either the various magazines decisions to print what Axl later claimed were misquotes or at least 'different' quotes, it was more difficult to find clarification of the bands views on racism other than their denial and championing of their part Mediterranean guitarist. Axl was indignant at the fact of not being able to use the word 'nigger' as much as anything else and perhaps viewed the whole situation as somewhat laughable. If he knew he wasn't a racist then he felt he could use the word in another context and if people took it the wrong way it was their problem.

He said a year after, the record had sat in 5 million homes worldwide, "I used words like police and niggers because you're not allowed to use the word nigger. Why can black people go up to each other and say, "Nigger", but when a white guy does it all of a sudden it's a big put down? I don't like boundaries of any kind. I don't like being told what I can and can't say. I used the word nigger because it's a word to describe somebody that is basically a pain in your life, a problem. The word nigger doesn't necessarily mean black. Doesn't John Lennon have a song "Woman Is the Nigger of the World"? There's a rap group, N.W.A., Niggers with Attitude. I mean, they're proud of that word; more power to them. Guns N' Roses ain't bad, N.W.A. is baad! Mr. Bob Goldthwaite said the only reason we put these lyrics on the record was because it would cause controversy and we'd sell a million albums. Fuck him! Why'd he put us in his skit? We don't just do something to get the controversy, the press."

As if to solidify his own statement, Axl could often latterly be seen sporting an N.W.A. cap and it was certainly within his character to say something purely because he was told he couldn't. And many would have to concede he made a valid point – just one to which mainstream America and the rest of the developed world could not possibly defer.

The chorus itself seemed to refer to a friend or close relation experiencing drug problems – with the line "we tried to reach you but you were much too high" which was certainly at odds with the other lyrics, again pointing at a potential mixture of events in the story. Where the homophobic content had been presumed there was an equally incendiary word used in the same line, in fact all the words in this sentence were very reminiscent of another band who whether Axl was familiar with them or not certainly spouted the same rhetoric.

Axl sings, "Immigrants and faggots, they make no sense to me. They come to our country and think they'll do as they please. Like start some mini Iran or spread some fucking disease. They talk so many goddamn ways it's all Greek to me." This was akin to the hardcore/thrash crossover band S.O.D. (Stormtroopers Of Death) whose *Speak English Or Die* album caused grievances and questions but on a much smaller scale because of their more underground status. However their own statements regarding lyrics such as "you don't know what I want, you don't know what I need, why must I repeat myself? Can't you fucking read? Nice fucking accents why can't you speak like me, what's that dot on your head do you use it to see?" Centred on the tongue in cheek embodiment of a racist character, not necessarily their own views.

Axl was more straightforward in describing his use of the words and decision to sing them. He explained: "When I use the word immigrants, what I'm talking about is going to a 7–11 or Village pantries – a lot of people from countries like Iran, Pakistan, China, Japan et cetera, get jobs in these convenience stores and gas stations. Then they treat you as if you don't belong here. A six–foot tall

Iranian with a butcher knife has chased me out of a store with Slash because he didn't like the way we were dressed. Scared me to death. All I could see in my mind was a picture of my arm on the ground, blood going everywhere. When I get scared, I get mad. I grabbed the top of one of these big orange garbage cans and went back at him with this shield, going, 'Come on!' I didn't want to back down from this guy. Anyway that's why I wrote about immigrants. Maybe I should have been more specific and said; 'Joe Schmoladoo at the 7–11 and faggots make no sense to me.' That's ridiculous! I summed it up simply and said, 'Immigrants.'"

It was typically scathing comment from Axl who was clearly aggrieved at such a fuss being made of lines he'd written flippantly with little regard for potential offence. He could not understand why there was such an adverse reaction to words he could use every day without cause for concern. It was also fitting for him to admit being scared made him mad. This explained a multitude of situations where he had lost his temper after losing control, perhaps a consequence of his abuse as a child.

Axl further dug himself a hole when he revealed he took offence to immigrants taking advantage of their newfound freedom in America to castigate him. He reasoned, "I don't have anything against someone coming here from another country and trying to better themselves. What I don't dig is some 7–11 worker acting as though you don't belong here, or acting like they don't understand you while they're trying to rip you off. "What? I no understand you". I'm saying, "I gave you a 20, and I want my $15 change!" I threatened to blow up their gas station, and then they gave me my change. I don't need that."

Besides the slurs within the song on either races or minorities there were lines such as "Some say I'm crazy I guess I'll always be, but it's been such a long time since I knew right from wrong it's all a means to an end, I keep it moving along." These lines seemed to pre–empt the potential reaction by explaining at first that he knew he was doing wrong but either didn't care or couldn't stop it. There were clues to Axl's mental frame of mind even within the songs where he exercised his rage to crass proportions.

Trying to understand the Guns' front mans' state of mind was the last thing on some people's minds however. In March of 1989 a festival, which was eventually cancelled, scheduled Guns N' Roses for an appearance. Rock And A Hard Place was an AIDS benefit gathering in New York but gay activists in the city and elsewhere were unhappy at G N' R's inclusion given their use of the word 'faggot' in 'One In A Million'. It was also only a matter of time before the other incendiary lyrics received criticism in a more high profile manner. Black rock artists Living Colour along with the Black Rock Coalition joined the gay activists in denouncing the band for their use of the words 'immigrants' and 'niggers'. Axl explained the song was merely a reflection of tensions between one race and another on the streets of downtown Los Angeles though this fell inevitably on deaf ears.

One thing often overlooked by the furore surrounding 'One In A Million' however is just what a superb song it is, musically. Had the lyrics been different and been more of a sentimental lament such as 'Patience' it is likely it would have become a live favourite. Instead the band has only very rarely played the song live.

"I been walkin' the streets at night just tryin' to get it right
Hard to see with so many around, you know I don't like being stuck
in the crowd" 'Patience'

Despite the negative opinions surrounding certain lyrics on the mini album, the band sold millions of copies and far outweighed both their own and the record company's expectations. The EP was only supposed to fill the void left by *Appetite For Destruction*, which despite still being at the top of the Billboard chart was already considered Guns N' Roses 'old' album. Instead of simply making up the numbers the band had the honour of becoming the first for fifteen years to have two records simultaneously in the Billboard Top 5.

One of the biggest factors in the EP doing so well was the success of *Patience*. Though it seemed to garner as much press fervour for Axl being recorded whistling as much as any inherent song writing quality it was nevertheless one of the bands strongest tunes, showcasing their more emotional side. Unlike other exponents of the time however, (bands such as Extreme would follow with *More Than Words* being something of a one hit wonder with housewives worldwide as would the otherwise unknown Mr Big with *To Be With You*), Guns N' Roses would not stop at one song making the headlines or the higher reaches of the charts.

In a year where things were almost as expected, Axl was arrested several times and Duff married Mandy Brixx from the Lame Flames. There were also achievements beyond the bands initial expectations and not merely limited to record sales. Quite unusually for bands of their ilk they toured such extreme places as Australia, New Zealand and Japan, developing a steady fan base in all countries, which has remained to the present day. In a year where so many things went wrong for the band and could have easily seen them disband, this was an incredible achievement.

"We toured for so fucking long, and by the time the tour was over we were told we were mega – Spinal Tap, you know. You're great! And there's all this stuff going on around you, all these people treating you like you're on a pedestal even if you don't feel that way. So we went from nowhere to being this really huge band, not feeling any different only having people tell you that and react to you a certain way" Slash 1988

ABUSE YOUR ILLUSION

1989 was something of a year of respite for Guns N' Roses. After touring for what seemed like forever in support of their two record–breaking releases it was time to take stock and replenish the batteries in order to make a new record. There were few gigs in the year following but it seemed the band could not stay out of the headlines. Already people were talking about the follow up to *Appetite For Destruction*, and the pressure was on to complete it. In truth this was the last thing on the various members minds. The touring for *Appetite For Destruction* had brought the band to the point of burn out and drug problems were spiralling.

Both Slash and Axl felt at odds with comments they had made in *RIP* magazine about drug use. Slash had admitted heroin was his favourite. In hindsight he felt paranoid the police might be after him and could turn up at his door at any moment. Slash would always claim to be in control of his usage, assuring everyone he was not addicted.

Axl too always carried the air of a sensible substance user, if such a person can exist. He voiced his concerns over his previous confessions in *RIP* magazine, "I'm not and never have been a junkie. The last interview in *RIP* Magazine got taken out of context about me talking openly about my drug use. That was over two years ago and was only for a few weeks when there was nothing to do. I was also very safe about it. That doesn't mean that at some point I won't get really sick of life and choose to OD. Then people will go, "He was always a junkie." That's not the case, but you can believe what you want, I don't give a fuck. No one's really going to believe anything I say anyway as far as what I do or don't do with drugs, 'cause it's such a taboo subject. Lately I've been drinking champagne for fun, a few beers, you know. Right now drugs get in the way of my dreams and goals. I really don't want drugs around me now, I'm not necessarily against the use of drugs, they just don't fit in my life right now. Then again, I could be out on tour for six months and a blast might be what cheers me up that night."

There were early signs of Axl's distaste for the lifestyles of the other band members. He commented, "I don't want to see drugs tear up this band. I'm against it when it goes too far. Right now, for me, a line of coke is too far. A line of coke puts my voice out of commission for a week. I don't know why. Maybe it's because I did a lot of stuff before. Maybe it's guilt and it's relocated in my throat. All I know is it's not healthy for me right now. And if somebody goes, "Oh, man, he's not a partier anymore, "hey, fuck you! Do you want a record or not?"

Clearly the record company and the public wanted a record, though everyone seemed to delight in discussing the bands problems with substance use. It wasn't as if the band could not still function. Videos were still being filmed; Guns' went against the grain with their personal favourite, *It's So Easy*, a lo–fi 'live' performance that was almost deliberately low budget in order to go against the MTV music video rhetoric. It featured Axl's then girlfriend Erin Everly in a submissive bondage role, more of which is explained in Chapter 11.

1989 was also a year where the Guns' members realised that although beautiful women regularly flanked the band it was mostly because they were a famous rock act. As Slash explained: "the situation with women is all fucked up. The girls you tend to run into – the ones that are only interested in you coz you're in a band – they tend to be pretty low I think. There's just a bleak kind of aura around them".

Although it did not seem apparent to the band members at the time, the last few years had taken their toll as much as they had brought success. Relationships were fragmented between the core members, what had once been closely bonded brotherhoods seemed to subside with the appearance of more money than could be spent all at once. It split those members who could live without the trappings of success such as Slash and Duff, from Axl who in their view took the power and control of fame and fortune far too seriously. It also gave members like Steven Adler an appropriate method of getting regularly blitzed in order to escape the pressures of being constantly in the public eye. Where Axl thrived in some ways on the attention, those who were always shy individuals had more difficulty using their natural personality resources to cope.

"Sometimes there's these girls backstage going 'I love you'. I feel like telling them, 'Honey, if you knew me, you would hate my fucking guts'" Axl Rose

Therefore what was recreational substance use before, turned into an addiction needed to survive. Slash tried to rationalise his obsession by saying: "If you were to ask, as a therapist, why do I drink? – The simple thing is you do it out of boredom and to relax. The worst thing is it's for people who are so volatile and so shy – because that was always my biggest problem, to be able to deal with everything that's going on, especially when you're in the public eye so much and then being a very reserved kind of person. You end up drinking a lot to come out of your shell. In that way it's a vicious sort of drug because it really works."

There were memories of earlier comments where Slash had the English press believe everyone in the band woke up with their hands shaking like windmills. Slash knew he would "get into these really ridiculously bitter fights" whenever he drank alcohol and the vicious circle was compounded; by doing cocaine the appetite for alcohol became even more pronounced.

Situations ranged from the bizarre to the ridiculous. As Slash recalled "I lost somebody's car the other night. I borrowed a car to drive myself home from a friend's, and I was so drunk that I parked it somewhere, but I can't remember where. It's just gone, kaput! I have the keys sitting on the table in my living room, and I don't even know where it is. And the thing is, I always want to drive when I'm drunk. It doesn't really interest me as much when I'm sober. I get drunk and I want to drive fast, and I just know it's going to get me into big trouble one day if I don't watch out..."

There were bad memories of other rockers who had already experienced that kind of trouble, such as Motley Crue's Vince Neil who had killed Hanoi Rocks drummer Razzle (real name Nicholas Dingley) after driving under the influence. One thing is for certain Slash's comments did nothing to dispel the myth that the members of Guns' were stupid irresponsible rock stars with more money than sense. Though Slash it seemed had learned a lesson from a previous experience. He remembered, "I've been through the experience once already of hitting somebody in a car... I hit a van; it was when we were recording the album. I realised pretty quickly then that one drunken night just isn't worth years in jail, or being responsible for somebody else's misery..."

For some, there was confusion at Axl's stance on the dangers of substances. He always seemed to be perfectly lucid (despite temper tantrums) yet had clearly gone through his own problems, and was sometimes alluded to by others as having just as much of a problem as Slash and Steven. In 1989 he told *RIP* magazine: "After leading a life of girls, drugs and whatever, people draw a certain picture about me. I've toned it all down, because I have other things I have to do. I can't be doing drugs every night because, after selling six million records, the business I have to deal with is a lot more intense than most people's. Slash probably wouldn't drink so much if it wasn't for the fact that that's the way he's able to deal with all these people. He's able to quietly drink his bottle and talk. Me, if I'm drunk, I'll tell everybody to get the fuck outta my house. I can't get wasted because I react differently. As soon as I'm drunk, I realize 'Ya know, this past week of doing business has been really boring'. I want to fucking kill something!"

"This band will do its thing until each of us is dead" Izzy Stradlin

It was as if Axl had discovered the secret to living life – to accommodate those who can help get you where you want to be. His comments suggested therefore he knew where his problems lay and by using substances they would be exacerbated far more than any of the other band members'. Indeed in the same interview Axl commented that he had a "different physical constitution and different mindset about drugs" than anybody he had known in Hollywood.

This was he said "because I don't abstain from doing drugs, but I won't allow myself to have a fuckin' habit. I won't allow it. When I'm high, I'll analyse the shit out of everything that's happening in my life and why things are going wrong. That's not enjoyable. And if I have shows to do, I won't touch drugs because it fucks up my throat. My advice is don't get a habit, don't use anybody else's needle and don't let drugs become a prerequisite to having a good time. Do things in moderation, and just be careful."

It was thereon a case of following his own advice as Axl forsook the pleasures the band once enjoyed as a unit. As the money flowed in, the other members of G N' R saw greater opportunity to excel in drug usage and drinking. Axl saw the danger he could do to himself if he carried on in the same manner. It was a realisation that in the past getting high had been an escape from either childhood anxiety or general life pressures, but Axl now seemed to decide that he should not be in a position where he needed to escape and consequently wanted to try and handle life as relatively clean as possible for as long as he could.

APPETITE FOR SUSPICION

"I like being successful. I was always starving on the other side. When it came to people with money, it was always "The rich? Fuck them!" But I left one group and joined another. I escaped from one group where I was looked down on for being a poor kid that doesn't know shit, and now I'm like, a rich, successful asshole. I don't like that. I'm still just me, and with a lot of people's help, the group was able to become a huge financial success. None of us were the popular kids in school – we were all outcasts who got together and pooled our talents" Axl Rose 1989

The two Guns N' Roses records in the charts had already sold over twelve million copies combined. This led to comments, which were taken out of context. Though Axl would at one point be quoted as saying "we were all sitting around with bits of paper trying to figure it out. Everyone came up with different numbers, but basically we stopped counting after we got past $100 million" (thus fuelling much of the rancour which caused his eventual 'Get In The Ring' media outburst) he more sensibly opined after the bands success of two products in the Billboard Top 5: "We're not millionaires. The world, people outside of the music industry, seems to think that if you go platinum, one million copies sold, you're a millionaire. It doesn't work like that...You have to pay the people that work for you – management, lawyers, accountants, roadies and so on. Out of the buck we make, we're paying all our debts back. Everything we've borrowed, used, broken or had on loan comes out of this."

It seemed to be a sore point for Axl who was at pains to confirm that although the band might be getting paid well it didn't merely go into their pockets. He stated, "After doing a tour, there's a lot of past debts that need to be paid. To go out and do anything for less than $1,000 or $1,500 a show means you're paying to play. If you headline and go past eleven o'clock, then you're talking paying major overtime and fines."

Money was an increasingly important issue for the band and they needed every piece of advice to be steadfast, for by their own admission they weren't well schooled in business or understanding exactly who got what money wise. A recurring name in interviews around the time was that of Vicky Hamilton, the ex band manager. Or so she claimed.

There was an insistence on the part of the media to let Hamilton have her say and it turned into her word against the bands. The band was against giving her any credit for managing them professionally. In their explanation they said Hamilton had promised to give them $25,000 in order to purchase decent equipment earlier in their career, but that she didn't ever give them anything. In the end they had to get a $35,000 'memo deal' with Geffen meaning that the band didn't have to sign with them but had to pay the money back.

According to Axl, Hamilton claimed that "she invested $100,000 and she should be party to any of the money we make. She says we all get along, but in reality nobody likes dealing with her. Nobody trusts her. She managed the band? We – Slash, Duff, Izzy, Steven and Axl – managed the band. A year later she sued us for one million dollars. We didn't want to go to court, pay lawyer fees, court expenses and shit, especially when I don't trust the law and judicial system. I don't need the hassle. I don't believe in the fuckin' law system. I don't believe in the fuckin' government. We settled out of court for $30,000, 15 of which Geffen paid."

It seemed viable and from a neutral perspective it seemed likely that if one had invested a hundred thousand dollars they would not accept a mere thirty thousand in return. Either way, the name of Vicky Hamilton will always remain synonymous with Guns N' Roses and for her it is perhaps both good and bad luck given her reputation.

"I'm very sensitive and emotional, and things upset me and make me feel like not functioning or not dealing with people, the band or anything. I went to a clinic, thinking it would help my moods. The only thing I did was take one 500 question test – ya know, filling in the little black dots. All of sudden I'm diagnosed manic–depressive. "Let's put Axl on medication". Well, the medication doesn't help me deal with stress. The only thing it does is help keep people off my back because they figure I'm on medication" Axl Rose

In Axl's view the Hamilton debacle was just another symptom of a fickle world where being famous suddenly brought all comers out of the wood work to either contact those in the band or speak to the press about what they knew from the past. It was a downside many who experienced sudden fame found to their cost but it seemed to really hit Guns N' Roses and particularly Axl Rose harder than most.

He was responsible for smashing up his own apartment in many cases, sometimes in the company of the press, which in hindsight he would surely concur was a nonsensical thing to do. When those outbursts were witnessed or told in private to writers of worldwide magazines the temptation to betray Axl's confidence for the sake of selling three times as many copies was too much to resist, though in the long run it would irreparably damage the relationship between G N' R and the media. "When I was growing up, I was never really popular," Axl said in *RIP*. "Now everybody wants to be my friend. I like my privacy, to live alone in my own little world. I live in a security building, and all my calls are screened. I don't even know my own phone number." Come the period of the 'Chinese Democracy' sessions Axl would change his phone number regularly, sometimes twice a month.

He had also developed a passion for firearms as both a means of curiosity and a way of protecting himself. He owned an Uzi semi-automatic machine gun and a 9–mm pistol. His house was decked out entirely in black. According to Axl he wasn't paranoid and his description of his living circumstances was typically brazen. He claimed, "This is how I choose to live. This is comfortable."

Perhaps it was comfortable for Axl at the time but it was secretly leading to a distance between him and the other Guns' members, which would linger despite their eventual reconvening to record a new album.

Rumours were rife of a new G N' R album and the talk was of an expected covers EP surfacing before any new material. Songs that the band had interpreted from their early days had apparently been recorded in the studio, though the public saw this as just another convenient delay in giving them any truly 'new' material. Even Axl laughingly admitted that he had been "jacking off" as opposed to working seriously on new material. He did say however "We're trying to regroup. I'm ready to work. I'm creating, and finally I have an environment in which I can work. I haven't had that for a long time, since three years ago, when we all used to live in one room, sitting around writing songs."

In truth the adulation suddenly experienced by G N' R, specifically Slash and Axl had not gone to Slash's head. *Kerrang!* readers voted him 'best rock guitarist' which he found a proud accomplishment but he was philosophical about life in the public eye. He said, "There are people I know that walk around believing their own hype. Then all of a sudden it turns to the next flavour of the month and they get left standing there looking on wondering what the fuck happened."

It seemed Slash understood that both praise and criticism were relative to where it came from and he wasn't about to let the distraction of being one of the most recognisable and admired guitarists in the world stop him from being himself and believing the heehaw surrounding the G N' R camp. It is in truth an attitude that remained with all the original members throughout their stay in the band and perhaps is one of the reasons to explain why they are all still around; some more prominently than others.

APPETITE FOR COMMOTION

"It seems to me that we're a spectacle, a freak show. Magazines are more interested in who fell over last night than the music. I'm to the point where I'm tired of being a spectacle. One of the things that make this band so controversial is that we tell the truth. We tell what really happens. I like being honest with the press. What bugs me is after reading something about me; people don't have the slightest clue as to what I'm all about. Isn't that what doing interviews is about? From now on, interviews will be very limited. That must sound like, 'Oh, he's being a rock star', but the truth is, I don't need the headache of not getting things across to the public the way I feel they should be" Axl Rose

On August 30th Izzy Stradlin was arrested on a flight from Los Angeles to Indianapolis. Not only did he verbally abuse a stewardess when ordered to stop smoking in the non–smoking section but he also urinated on the floor of the US Air plane. His explanation was that he was tired of waiting to use the bathroom and an official source quoted that the urination was simply Izzy's "way of expressing himself". This incident caused much conversation but it was something of a minor incident in the grand pantheon of Guns N' Roses activity. Nevertheless it paved the way for a dramatic end to the year.

In September the band were special guests to the Rolling Stones for a sequence of four shows at the 70,000 capacity L.A. Coliseum. Guns' previous detractors Living Colour were third on the bill at the shows. Guitarist Vernon Reid made a speech on the first night saying "Anyone who calls somebody else a nigger whatever the situation, but particularly in the mass media context of a popular song is promoting racism and bigotry, no matter how hard they try and explain it away."

Reid received a warm reception and large areas of the crowd erupted in appreciation. It is unknown whether Axl had heard this speech before going on stage himself, though it is to be expected someone may have passed on the information. It certainly seemed beyond coincidence that Axl threatened to quit G N' R midway through their set. His announcement was to the effect that unless certain members of the band didn't stop "Dancing with Mr. Brownstone" he would quit. The reference to heroin was specifically pointed at Slash and Steven. It was a shrewd move by Axl, to draw attention away from the racist issue. A large percentage of the crowd, and backstage artists were most probably awaiting Axl's reaction with baited breath. He instead, rightly or wrongly, selfishly or otherwise, spun the situation into a purely Guns N' Roses issue.

It was left to Slash to restore confidence in Guns' line up lasting to the end of the Stones shows by meekly announcing from the stage he would clean up his act. Thus Axl returned to the stage the next night, resplendently watched from all corners of the globe where people wondered what he might say or do next.

On New Years Eve Duff was involved in a fracas with a person who he said just wanted to "fuck with him". It caught McKagan at the wrong time. Only the night before he had split with his wife Mandy Brixx of which he commented that it was generally for the best as things hadn't been right for some time. Of the New Years incident he puffed, "Check it out, it was my first night out since I busted up with my wife and all I wanted to do was have a good time. We were there to see Bang Tango. But within twenty seconds this guy comes up to me and says, "Where are you from?" I said I live here you know. He said, "Well don't ever touch me again!" I mean I haven't even been near the guy; I've just walked through the door! I just saw red all of a sudden cos of the shit I've been going through." The loyal friend of the band, Del James was with Duff and he was asked by an incandescently angry McKagan to hold his wallet for him. "Then I turned back to this guy" Duff continued, "and this guy was big man, and I just went HUURRRGGG! And I fuckin hit the guy. It's the first time I've ever seen it in real life but his eyes went cross–eyed, like in a movie, and then he went down."

In October Izzy pleaded guilty to a public disturbance charge relating to the airplane incident. A Phoenix court ordered him to pay a $2,000 fine and $1,000 for cleaning costs. Izzy was put on probation for 6 months and ordered to seek counselling. Much was written of the band suddenly travelling separately from each other. Axl it was reported, now travelled alone from his G N' R buddies but he was relatively angry at this insinuation that this was due to his forceful personality or individual insistence.

He said, "First of all, it was Izzy's idea to get a separate bus, and secondly, after shows I can't afford to party out like the other guys. We all used to live together, but we've outgrown being crowded in together. Not because we don't like each other, but because we have different lifestyles."

The difference in the relative band members' new ways of living did not manifest themselves until later on but the acrimony caused from varying public disturbances was the beginning of the end for the original Guns N' Roses.

"Slash once said that God didn't want us to happen" Axl Rose

"When they dropped us off at the airport after the tour was over, I had nowhere to go. It kind of runs in the family with us – maybe not with Axl but definitely with me – where if I'm not busy and focused, I get loaded to pass the time. So that's what happened. I went through a phase of that and then I cleaned up and we tried to rehearse and write new material." So said Slash in 1991 of the incredible feeling experienced when finishing a tour of the length Guns N' Roses had just completed.

Slash seemed somewhat perplexed. "The worst thing of it, though, was because of no longer having to live in one room, the band got separated, getting their own homes. And that was the hardest part. It's like Slash is here, Axl's here, Izzy's over there, Duff's here, and I don't even know where Steven lives, right? Like, Duff, can we come over? "Well, the gardener is coming today..." That was a whole huge experience that really took a while for me to adjust to."

The anticipation for Guns N' Roses to follow up *Appetite For Destruction* was immense. Although fans had been somewhat appeased by the 'G N' R Lies' Mini Album there had still been no significant amount of new material. Life was somehow a continual struggle for the band and things rarely moved quickly. After touring and various shenanigans the band had somehow prepared over 30 songs for recording. The title *Use Your Illusion* came from a painting Axl had spotted in an art gallery by Mark Kostabi. The painting title became the album title(s).

Initially the idea had been to release *Use Your Illusion* as one set, amounting to four LPs and four cassettes all under the same banner. However as the phrase 'commercial suicide' entered the heads of several Geffen executives the far more sensible and financially viable option seemed to be to release the albums separately, as Parts one and two. The absolute certainty of the matter was that the band wanted to release all the songs they had recorded. Although one review (and several in agreement) would later state: if the best songs from each part had been released on one record it would have been the greatest rock record of all time.

Without understatement Guns N' Roses had almost managed this on the strength of the songs they had put out and when compiling the potential best of each album it is hard to see which tracks could be left off. *

There had been plans to record an all 'x–rated album' or another EP featuring cover versions of The Damned, Sex Pistols and other punk material but this was to come later and rather than go the easy route by taking further time off after a shorter recording session the band instead travelled to the place they had recorded *Appetite For Destruction,* Rumbo Studios in Canoga Park. Steven Adler was just about with the band after they had secretly worked with both Sea Hags and The Pretenders sticksmen.

"You may not like our integrity...we built a world out of anarchy"
'Get In The Ring'

In the meantime Axl heard of the Farm Aid IV show in his home state of Indiana and called the organiser Harry Sandler to book the band at short notice. At 8:15 pm the band took to the stage to per-form new song 'Civil War' and UK Subs cover 'Down On The Farm'. The rumours concerning Adler's dismissal were already rife in the press and as Adler tripped on his way to take the drum seat it seemed he was still chemically dependent. Axl finished the short set with a rousing "Have a good fuckin' night everybody!" and was promptly sneered at by producer Dick Clark who had been the same poor unfortunate in charge at the American Music Awards that Slash had cursed at.

However lucid the band appeared to be at the Hoosierdome show, according to Slash Steven's timing had been way off. As Steven took Slash to task over a contract he had been made to sign promis-ing he would stay straight for shows and rehearsals it was still clear he had no choice but to enter rehabilitation before work could con-tinue on *Use Your Illusion.* Plans for reformation were scuppered however when Steven walked out of the Bryon clinic to score drugs again.

Slash commented at the time: "I moved into an apartment, the cheapest apartment I could find…but it was such a long period. And I got so wrapped up in dope and coke and all the fucking scum that goes along with it that finally it just got out of hand. So I cleaned up and bought a house. I went and cleaned up and then it was Steven's turn."

Axl however seemed to be happy as he finally tied the knot with Everly Brother Phil's daughter Erin Everly. The couple had been living together since 1986 while Erin worked as a model. According to Erin Axl had proposed by coming over to her home and threatening to kill himself unless she married him the next day. So the next day (April 28th) they travelled to the Cupid Wedding chapel in Las Vegas for a low rent wedding. At the time Erin was 24 and Axl 28. Less than a month after the wedding Axl filed for divorce, though some reports claim it was Erin who made the first move to separate, amidst the charges of physical abuse she claimed to have suffered from Axl.

However Axl soon changed his mind about divorcing Erin and later in the year she became pregnant although tragically suffered a miscarriage. By the end of 1990 Axl and Erin had split up for good and in January of 1991 the marriage between them was annulled. This was forced by Axl's hand, probably because Erin was not entitled to a huge financial settlement after an annulment whereas she would have been if the couple had divorced.

(In 1994 Erin filed a multi–million dollar lawsuit against Axl citing domestic violence as the reason. She then went public with her tales of how Axl had both physically and mentally abused her while they were together. She was also subpoenaed in a lawsuit against Axl by his following ex girlfriend Stephanie Seymour. Both lawsuits were later settled outside of the courtroom. In an interview since the break up Erin stated that she had to sell her wedding rings for cash and relied heavily on the support of her family for financial sustenance. She also remarried an Atlanta man and gave birth to a son named Eason in 1998.)

"When I get stressed, I get violent and take it out on myself. I've pulled razor blades on myself but then realized that having a scar is more detrimental than not having a stereo. I'd rather kick my stereo in than go punch somebody in the face. When I get mad or upset or emotional, sometimes I'll walk over and play my piano" Axl Rose

Back in professional surroundings things were running as smoothly as could be expected for Guns N' Roses. The band had several songs on tape, including the Bob Dylan cover 'Knockin' On Heaven's Door' used for the *Days Of Thunder* movie released in June. However they were still experiencing problems with Steven and after considering both Adam Maples and Martin Chambers for the almost vacant drum seat, settled on The Cult drummer Matt Sorum. The band had played with The Cult several times and knew Sorum well enough as a reliable and solid performer.

Slash would later state in an interview with *Musician* magazine that "Steven's chops were all over the place and he was lying to us about his drug use on a daily basis". He expanded "At Rumbo, Steven would nod out to the point where he would be on a stool, but his head would be touching the floor. He'd say, 'I'm tired. I'm sleepy,' and he couldn't play. That was basically it. We gave him so many chances to turn around. When the sex and drugs and the whole bit started to get out of hand, he went right along with it. But there's a certain time when you really have to control your life. As far as the rest of us, we bounced back we straightened up. Steven never did. We always told each other when it was getting real bad. Everybody was there for the individual who needed help. That's how we're survived as a band. But Steven would never cop to anything, as far as telling us how bad it was."

Axl felt aggrieved at more than simply Adler's inability to play. According to Axl, "at one point, in order to keep this band together, it was necessary for me to give him a portion of my publishing rights. That was one of the biggest mistakes I've made in my life, but he threw such a fit, saying he wasn't going to stay in the band. We were worried about not being able to record our first album, so

I did what I felt I had to do. In the long run I paid very extensively for keeping Steven in Guns N' Roses. I paid $1.5 million by giving him 15% of my publishing off of *Appetite For Destruction*. He didn't write one goddamn note, but he calls me a selfish dick! He's been able to live off of that money, buy a shitload of drugs and hire lawyers to sue me. If and when he loses the lawsuit he has against us, and he has to pay those lawyers, if he has any money left, it'll be the money that came from Guns N' Roses and myself."

"We couldn't get any work done at Rumbo. Steven cost us a fortune. We had to edit the drum track to 'Civil War' just so we could play to it" Slash

There were further revelations that caused much aversion from Adler's point of view, but Axl was indignant. "At this point I really don't care what happens to Steven Adler" he puffed, "because he's taken himself out of my life, out of my care and concern. I feel bad for him in ways, because he's a real damaged person, but he's making choices to keep himself in that damage. There's nothing we can do at this point. We took him to rehabs, we threatened his drug dealers, and we helped him when he slashed his wrists. I even forgave him after he nearly killed my wife. I had to spend a night with her in an intensive–care unit because her heart had stopped thanks to Steven. She was hysterical, and he shot her up with a speedball. She had never done jack shit as far as drugs go, and he shoots her up with a mixture of heroin and cocaine?"

According to Axl he had been nothing but a good friend to Adler. For someone like Rose who prided himself on not being taken for a fool he felt Steven had gone far enough and tested his loyalty beyond reasonability. Axl illuminated "I kept myself from doing anything to him. I kept the man from being killed by members of her family. I saved him from having to go to court, because her mother wanted him held responsible for his actions. And the son of a bitch turns on me?"

"Steven is scared to death of me. If he sees me in public, he just turns into a grovelling heap of defeatism. Until now I haven't said a word about Steven to the press. I haven't attacked him; I haven't insulted him. I felt sorry for him. I didn't want to hurt him. We gave him a year to get his shit together. He couldn't play any of the new shit anyway. It got to a point where the material was way beyond him. I can't believe this little fucker. I read the shit he said about us in Circus. He said in that article he's sober now, but every time I've seen him, he's been wasted. I lost all concern and feeling for the guy" Slash

Duff was more plaintive but also seemed to be of the opinion he had helped Steven much the same way Axl had. Duff recalled in 2002, "We were saying to him, 'Steven, you're fucked up. We said: 'Me and Slash, we're fucked up, but you're really fucked up'. I remember saying to him: 'if me and Slash think you're fucked up, think about who's saying that. The truth is I probably fought a little harder to keep him in the band, because I wasn't working with him on a daily basis like the other guys were. I've read interviews where he's saying that he's straight. Most of the time he isn't. He's the type of person who wants everything handed to him, and he did get it handed to him. He got it handed to him from me."

Adler later said, "Believe me, it wasn't *me* that was doing the heroin. I did it *after* they kicked me out when I was trying to kill myself for ten years from that happening to me. I mean that was *my life,* me and Slash worked at it since we were twelve." By the time Steven Adler had been out of the Guns' set up for a while, his chemical dependence worsened, and it is alleged that this was why he suffered a stroke and a slight heart attack. According to Adler, his speech was completely indecipherable for the first two months after his stroke, and he will now forever talk with a minor slur.

Adler's departure was the mark of a revised G N' R line up utilising a 'fuller' sound which Axl was particularly interested in. This meant the inclusion of varied instruments like horns, banjos and even a sitar. Dizzy Reed was also enlisted as a full time keyboardist. Axl, began to utilise his own experiences with playing piano and he seemed most sold on the emotional and ballad like material on the album to be.

"We didn't even have a set list for Rio. We have this 'pick list' we like to use. We tell Matt, three minutes before he goes onstage in front of 140,000 people, that he's gotta do a drum solo. And he pulled it off! Right before we went onstage, the whole band – and this hadn't happened for a long time – got together in one room. You could just feel the electricity" Duff McKagan

He commented: "The most important songs at this point are the ones with piano, the ballads, because we haven't really explored that side of the band yet. They're also the most difficult songs to do – not difficult to play, but to write and pull out of ourselves. The beautiful music is what really makes me feel like an artist. The other, heavier stuff also makes me feel like an artist and can be difficult to write. But it's harder to write about serious emotions, describing them as best as possible rather than trying to write a syrupy ballad just to sell records."

While he was eager to confirm the bands progression in terms of straightforward rock he was equally quick to dispel rumours the band were selling out in any way. He told *RIP* magazine, "We're not getting away from hard rock. Our basic root is hard rock, a bit heavier than the Stones, more in a vein like Aerosmith, *Draw the Line* type stuff. We love loud guitars. George Michael was telling me he really loved our melodies and wondered why we covered so much of it up with loud guitars, and I said because we love that. I told him he should put some more loud guitars in his music. He has such beautiful melodies, and it'd be nice to hear some loud guitars in there. At the same time, I have my favourite symphony pieces, orchestra pieces if you will."

An old friend of Axl's Monica Gregory remembers an emotional side prominent in his music even early on. "There was one really cool place called the Stabilizer and David Lank's front porch; in Axl's bedroom because he just had mattresses sitting around and drawing pads and his piano and you could get really artistic in whatever way you wanted to. He got a piano and put it in his bedroom and practiced. He would just sit down and play the most beautiful things – I mean, beautiful. He turned me on to Elton John 'cause he used to do a lot of Elton John. The creative side he had was so intense and I think it grounded the little group of people that was there for I don't know how many years even before I entered the picture."

Axl was also succinct in admitting his other influences outside of usually acceptable spheres. One such influence was the early Elton John records which gave Axl a different spin on rock music. Along with ELO and Queen, Elton John was responsible for Guns N' Roses progression by keeping simple song structures but supplying them in an emotionally charged or heartfelt manner. The success of Guns' earlier output allowed Axl the luxury of freedom to make the record he wanted.

He was able to write as he pleased and what satisfied him was approaching work in a way his heroes had. He said, "my favourite record by Queen: 'Queen II'. Whenever their newest record would come out and have all these other kinds of music on it, at first I'd only like this song or that song. But after a period of time listening to it, it would open my mind up to so many different styles. I really appreciate them for that. That's something I've always wanted to be able to achieve. It's important to show people all forms of music, basically try to give people a broader point of view."

The album was in part controversial for some at least, in branching out beyond the Guns' blueprint and endorsing instruments such as piano but Axl was quick to justify its use and importance to him. "I've been playing piano my whole life" he explained. "I took lessons, but I only really played my lesson on the day of the lesson. All week long, I'd sit down at the piano and just make up stuff. To this day, I still can't really play other people's songs, only my own. I haven't had a piano for years. I couldn't afford one. I couldn't figure out where I was sleeping at night, let alone try to have a place for a piano. So I had to put it aside and have the dream that I'd get into it. Now I really want to bring the piano out." The piano was indeed brought out and gave depth to the skeleton songs the band had created.

"Gonna rest my bones an' sit for a spell, this side of heaven this close to hell" 'Right Next Door To Hell'

Eventually G N' R had recorded 35 songs instrumentally and all that remained was for the vocals to be completed. But Axl was fighting with Erin. Even though he called the Howard Stern Radio Show to announce the couple were back together there were several arguments at home, with Axl calling Erin a 'bitch' on a regular basis. After one sordid dispute Erin threw her wedding ring out of the window. The next day saw Axl scanning the front lawn with a rented metal detector.

Axl also got himself arrested and taken to the West Hollywood Sheriff's Station in November for a 'public disturbance' charge. It stemmed from an argument with next door neighbour Gabriella Kantor when Axl broke a wine bottle over her head. The troublesome woman next door was forever immortalised in the opening track on *Use Your Illusion 1*, 'Right Next Door To Hell'.

In between recording with the album almost completed in January 1991 the band played two sets at the Rock In Rio II festival in the Maracana stadium in Brazil. They debuted new material such as 'Estranged', 'Pretty Tied Up' and 'Double Talkin' Jive' as well as the 'Knockin' On Heaven's Door' cover version. At the festival the press were heavily slighted by the refusal of the band to do interviews with anyone who did not sign an agreement which manager Alan Niven had drawn up stating that no interview could be published without the bands consent and approval. Attached to the contract was a $100,000 for failure to adhere to the terms. Unsurprisingly no one took the band up for a conversation. Guns N' Roses stuck to their task, played their set (on time) and left the building.

SO FINE

"'Use Your Illusion' is a cross between 'Physical Graffiti' and 'The Wall'. It's a record that's going to amaze and frighten at the same time" Alan Niven

"One thing about this album," Slash said, "is that a lot of these songs were written during different time periods for us – some of them even before we met one another. So what happens is, you have lyrics to a song and some music that on of the other guys wrote a long time ago, and you go in to record it, and you can't catch the vibe he had at whatever time he wrote it". A perfect example was the track 'Don't Cry.' The song first appeared on G N' R's first demo tape in 1986. It was also a firm live favourite causing a different kind of ripple in the crowd as the band laid its emotions bare to offset the snarling menace of tracks such as 'Welcome To The Jungle'. In the end were three versions of 'Don't Cry' – the original demo, the finished version, and an adaptation featuring alternate lyrics.

"When our record comes out, I know it's going to be really different – whether it's accepted or not I couldn't give a shit" Slash

During the time of recording at The Record Plant in Hollywood Axl physically moved his bed into the studio beginning a tradition where he often worked at night and slept during the daytime. To offset tension and to avoid damaging any equipment, Axl invested in a punching bag and for recreational purposes, two pinball machines, one of Kiss and one of Elton John.

With recording going well Axl and his friend Del James were driving around Beverly Hills, pumping new mixes of 'Back Off Bitch', 'New Rose' (a Damned cover version the band had recorded for possible B–side use) and 'Right Next Door To Hell' at stupendous volume. Due to Axl's enormous car stereo (which was actually featured in *CarAudio* magazine) the pair drew the attention of the local police department. Axl smiled at the officer and turned down the voluble music. "Hey, we ain't like the West Hollywood cops," one of the officers shouted from his car window. "We like it loud!" After raising a hand to the officers, Axl and Del drove away.

Further up the same road, Axl once again raised the volume, again inviting police attention. This time they asked Axl to pull over." I was just about to shit a cow," remembered Axl, but the officers simply wanted an autograph for their fellow officer, who happened to be a big fan of Guns N' Roses.

"It's taken a lot of time to put together the ideas for this album... we're not gonna put out a fuckin' record until we're sure we can! So we've been trying to build it up. I think that the audience will have gone through three years of shit too, so hopefully they'll be ready to relate to some new things. Now I think there's enough different sides of Guns N' Roses that when the album is finally released no one will know what to think, let alone us! Like, what are they tryin' to say? Sometimes I don't fuckin' know...."Axl Rose

Behind the scenes there were management negotiations as the band decided they were no longer to be represented by the Stravinski Brothers firm and Alan Niven. Niven's partner Doug Goldstein had recently split from him and Guns' took Goldstein (an ex security guard), as their sole manager with Tom Zutaut handling A & R. As such Alan Niven was not even mentioned in the liner notes for the album.

What would have to be given a mention however was the 'offensive' language that would be contained within the album. As was par for the course a sticker was an essential requirement stating that the language within was indeed likely to cause offence. In a typical G N' R twist of rebellion the sticker which was eventually plastered on the album read, "This album contains language that may be considered offensive. Fuck off and buy something from the new age section instead".

In April 1991 a rough mix of a new G N' R track flooded several radio stations until it was discovered the copy was an illegal version of 'Bad Apple' and the stations were threatened with legal action for playing a pirate tape. The A.S.C.A.P. sent 800 letters to radio stations warning that playing the song would render them liable for a lawsuit.

The band officially began their world tour at the Alpine Valley Music Theatre in East Troy, WI on May 24th and 25th. At this time Axl met up with Arnold Schwarzenegger who told him he had long been a fan of G N' R and with the upcoming 'Terminator 2' movie due Schwarzenegger suggested the band use one of their songs in the film. He also agreed to appear in the video for the song at Axl's request.

This was to be lead single *You Could Be Mine* which did indeed set the tone for G N' R's return. In June the premier for the *You Could Be Mine* video was shown on MTV at 9am, 2pm, 6pm and Midnight. Parts of this had been shot at The Ritz show in New York where Axl hurt his foot and subsequently had to wear a special brace for the first weeks of the *Use Your Illusion* Tour and there were also parts which were shot at the Roxy nightclub in Los Angeles where the band met up once again with Schwarzenegger.

One of the most pertinent occurrences of the year, at least for Axl was playing in Indiana. It had been three years since he had performed in his home state and his hometown of Lafayette. Axl was in the mood to come out all guns blazing and barked at the crowd: "This stage here, in Indianapolis, Indiana, this time around, is the finest fucking stage in the world that I could ever walk...It seems to me that there are a lot of fucking scared old people in this state and for two–thirds of my life these motherfucking old people tried to hold my ass down."

The homecoming show was one of Guns' finest and set a precedent for the year ahead. A few months later the band set a new ticket sales record at The Starplex Ampitheatre in Dallas, Texas and played to a brimming stadium whose public were still awaiting the touted new album along with the rest of the world.

PATIENCE

One track on the album was a recollection of a supposed Axl over-dose. 'Coma' was an emotional epic, which was to end the first part of the *Use Your Illusion* twin set. Slash co–wrote the song with Axl. He said, "I like 'Coma' a lot. It's got a defibrillator in it you know, the instrument that starts your heart when it's stopped. And there's some EKG beeps too. We were just fucking around, but the song is heavy, and Axl's vocals are gorgeous I mean really amazing".

According to Slash it was he who was plying the references to drugs at the time of composing the song. "I wrote some really cool shit when I was high" he laughed. "There's a song called 'Coma', a long song, really heavy, and I wrote that loaded. And it's not some-thing that I can really see myself writing right now. And then me and Izzy wrote a song called 'Dust And Bones' in a similar kind of state." This echoed comments in earlier years by Slash who felt whatever he had to go through was worth it to get a good song in the end.

Axl was so determined for songs to be right that he had threatened to quit the music business altogether if one particular song did not turn out the way he wanted. 'November Rain' was a discreet musi-cal paean to Elton John and it was a song, which had been in exist-ence for a number of years. Now Guns' were party to a big budget, Axl felt he could tackle the song appropriately. He admitted he had considered quitting if the song didn't match his desires.

"That's the fuckin' truth, alright" he said, "but the worst part of it is, like, if you wanna look at it in a negative way, I've got four of these motherfuckers now, man! I don't know how I wrote these, but I like 'em better than 'November Rain'! And I'm gonna crush that motherfuckin' song, man! But now I've got four of 'em I gotta do, and they're all big songs. We play them and we get chills."

* How many of you agree with my perception of the ultimate 'Use Your Illusion' album?

You Could Be Mine
Civil War
Yesterdays
Knockin' On Heaven's Door
Get In The Ring
Don't Cry (Original)
Back Off Bitch
Breakdown
November Rain
Estranged
Don't Damn Me
Dead Horse
Coma

"Well, as you can see, being a fucking psycho basket–case like me does have it's advantages" Axl Rose

Though Guns' would eventually finish recording *Use Your Illusion 1 & 2*, the problems were just beginning during the bands world tour. The band would regularly show up late to gigs, which usually prompted some kind of negative audience response. When the band did not show up at all the results were often catastrophic.

Axl tried to explain his problem with timekeeping, "I don't mean to inconvenience the crowd by being late" he said regrettably. "I don't want to get onstage unless I know I can give the people their money's worth. I'm fighting for my own mental health, survival and peace. I'm doing a lot of self–help work. People say that I'm just spoiled. Yeah, I am. But the work I'm doing is so I can do my job."

It was typical of Axl to be so self–depreciating and yet justifiable of his actions. Once again, he felt his explanations fell on deaf ears despite going into considerable detail of his mental problems. He further elucidated, "I've learned that when certain traumas happen to you, your brain releases chemicals that get trapped in the muscles where the trauma occurred. They stay there for your whole life. Then, when you're 50 years old, you've got bad legs or a bent back. When you're old, it's too hard to carry the weight of the world that you've kept trapped inside your body. I've been working on releasing this stuff, but as soon as we release one thing and that damage is gone, some new muscle hurts. I've had work done on me – muscle therapy, kinesiology, acupuncture – almost every day that we've been on the road."

The work was part of a gradual plan to become not only clean, but a human machine capable of dealing with the irregularity of life on the road. Unbeknownst to many fans Axl had such deep–rooted worries and fears that he was taking a growing entourage of carers and helpers to whichever venue Guns' was playing in.

"He lost his mind today, he left it out back on the highway"
'Dust N' Bones'

When G N' R played at the Riverport Amphitheatre in Maryland Heights a riot was caused by the leader of a local biker gang. Stump, of The Saddle Tramps, was harassing fans in the front row. Axl asked for the security men to remove him. But as the security were friends of the biker gang they refused. The biker proceeded to goad Axl by waving a camera. Axl again asked the security to extradite the biker. Once more they ignored his pleas. After several fans managed to get to Axl and grab both his ankles (including the ankle which had still not fully healed after his accident) and two bottles were thrown at Duff, Axl took matters into his own hands; during 'Rocket Queen' Axl jumped into the crowd to confront the biker.

"Thanks to the lame ass security, I'm going home!" Axl shouted when he returned to the stage. However the band did intend to come back to finish their set, as long as Axl could locate a contact lens, after one had been lost during his encounter.

"I went backstage and found a new lens. It was getting crazy, and we decided we were going to go back out and try to play, because we didn't want people to get hurt..." Axl said. But before Axl and the band could return, the crowd had destroyed the drum set. There was a resultant riot, which led to damage in several areas, not least of which were breakages to equipment that caused another three shows to be cancelled. "We were backstage, watching cops on stretchers all bloody and shit, and it was like, 'Fuck! How could this be happening?'" recalled a contemplative Slash, "I was so scared somebody was going to die. It was completely out of hand. The kids had a field day. I lost all my amps, my guitar tech got a bottle in the head, someone got knifed, our stage and video equipment and Axl's piano were trashed. It shouldn't have happened... but it did."

Sixty fans managed to injure themselves and sixteen were arrested. They caused $200,000 worth of damage. The venue sued Axl. Slash tried to put the farcical event into perspective. "I feel bad for what happened, but I can't just say it was our fault. And I won't blame the kids of St. Louis, either. It just happened. I'm not putting the rap on anybody."

"G N' R is like a living organism. It's not an act. Even if I'm doing the same jump during the same part of a particular song, it's not an act. That's the best way for me to express myself at that point. I get there, and I let it out. It's like, how can I give the most at that without giving up my life? We don't go onstage like Guns N' Roses used to thinking that if we don't make it to tomorrow, that's okay. Now there's a lot of things depending on tomorrow and G N' R. It's like, how can we give the most and turn around tomorrow and give that much again? It takes a lot of work, a lot of effort and a lot of maintenance" Axl Rose

After the St. Louis incident the band received a lot of flak and from then on many promoters were nervous about endorsing a Guns N' Roses gig. A concert due to take place at Lake Compounce Amphitheatre in Bristol, Connecticut was cancelled because the residents living near the venue were afraid of a riot breaking out.

It was behind the scenes where problems were really beginning to bubble however. After Adler's termination things had not been quite the same between the remaining band members and one in particular was fed up with Axl's reactions on stage and equally unimpressed by Guns' high profile. Izzy Stradlin was simply not cut out for the level of stardom he had attained and was nonchalant about playing in large venues. A show that the band played at Wembley Stadium in London, England on August 31st 1991 was to be Stradlin's last.

"I feel like shit all over me, and I wiped it off and ain't too happy that it happened" Axl said of his old friend. "There are certain responsibilities to Guns N' Roses that Izzy didn't want to face. He basically didn't want to work as hard at certain things as we did. He pretty much just showed up before we went onstage, would get upset that I wasn't on time, played, then split. There were times when we'd get off stage, and five minutes later he was gone. He didn't socialize with the band on any level, and he had a real problem being sober and being around us…he wasn't able to do the things re-

quired of him in Guns N' Roses." This, if true brought a certain justification to Axl's earlier statements as to why he travelled separately from the band.

It was ironic that Izzy, who had kept the band afloat creatively and
managerially early on, was now the person who couldn't be bothered making an effort since the band had gone beyond his fragile
expectations. It was the turning point for Axl who was indignant at
the lacklustre group of reprobates Guns' had become. The split with
Izzy fuelled his desire to make Guns' an institution. Beyond a band,
Guns N' Roses would now be an act that no lawsuit could touch. No
one member was indispensable, except Axl who he had decided was
the only one capable of running the band properly. When Izzy left
much of Axl's innocence and the past went with him. From the departure, a new Axl Rose emerged.

Rose pulled no punches when talking of his ex comrade. "I'm glad
we got the songs out of him that we did, and I'm glad he's gone"
he spat. "You wanna know how he really hurt me? When he came
up here to my fucking house and acted like, "What's wrong, man?"
It's really weird; I knew he was coming. I could literally feel his car
driving up as I was getting dressed. I went outside and sat down, because Izzy couldn't come into my house. I couldn't act like he was
my friend after what he'd done to me. He came up and acted like he
hadn't done anything. Izzy called up members of the band and tried
to turn them against me by saying that I pushed him out. He said a
lot of shit behind my back. He tried to make a power play and damage us on his way out, and that's real fucked up."

According to Axl, now the real truth could emerge, Izzy just hadn't
been committed to Guns' work on the *Use Your Illusion* albums. Axl
elaborated, "Getting Izzy to work on his own songs on this record
was like pulling teeth. When Izzy had 'em on a four–track, they
were done. I mean, I like tapes like that, but we'd just get destroyed
if we came out with a garage tape. People want a high–quality album. And it was really hard to get Izzy to do that, even on his own
material. Sometimes I've been massively wrong, and Izzy's been
the one to help steer me back to the things that were right. But I

know that I wanted to get as big as we possibly could from Day One,
and that wasn't Izzy's intention at all."

The final nail in the coffin was the letter Axl received when Izzy
was supposed to be filming with the band for the *Don't Cry* video.
"We got this letter saying, "This changes, this changes, and maybe
I'll tour in January." Axl said, "and they were ridiculous demands
that weren't going to be met. I talked to Izzy for four and a half
hours on the phone. At some points, I was crying, and I was beg-
ging. I was doing everything I could to keep him in the band."

After Izzy left the band and became a solo artist in his own right,
he released an album with a band known as the Ju–Ju Hounds and
despite his protestations as far as touring had been concerned with
Guns N' Roses decided it was ok to go on tour himself. He took The
Wildhearts in support but it seemed they were too good for Izzy
and his manager to bear. Wildhearts front man Ginger commented,
"We got asked to do the Izzy Stradlin tour in 1992 and after the first
show in Nottingham Rock city we got kicked off the tour. The reason seemed to be, apart from smoking pot backstage, that we'd sold
too many t–shirts. And the next night after we were off the tour we
went to pick up our t–shirts and sold them at the bar while the new
support band was on. So we out sold them that night as well." The
band created a humorous retort which both apologised to their fans
for not being able to play the remaining shows and threw a double
talkin' jibe at the ex Gunner. The poster read:

IZZY STRUGGLIN

SORRY BUT THE WILDHEARTS

WILL NOT BE APPEARING ON ANY OF

THE FORTHCOMING SHOWS

BECAUSE WE BLEW THEM AWAY AT NOTTINGHAM

AND IZZY HAS KICKED US OFF THE TOUR

WE APOLOGISE FOR GIVING VALUE FOR MONEY

Guitarist CJ recalled, "we printed this up to give to people outside to let them know we weren't playing. I remember having an argument with Izzy's tour manager who was saying, "next year we'll be up here (*motions high with hand*) and you'll be nowhere."

The day after Stradlin had vacated Guns N' Roses, Axl flew from Finland to Paris to see a specialist for throat problems he was having and the band began to look for a touring guitarist. After apparent consideration, Dave Navarro, once of Jane's Addiction (later the Red Hot Chili Peppers and solo artist), was out of the running. Eventually the suitable candidate was found. Gilby Clarke who had been in My Life With The Thrill Kill Cult was an acquaintance of the band, having plied his trade around Hollywood for the better part of a decade.

Once he had established himself as a Guns' member, Axl and Slash joined him on his first solo album, *Pawnshop Guitars*. "Gilby is awesome, and a pleasure to be around" Axl gushed. "He works the stage and the crowd really well. He has his opinions of what's going on with us, and it helps us get a different perspective. He's been putting himself through his own rock and roll education with his other groups for years. Now he's a part of Guns N' Roses."

Fans accepted the six–stringer unequivocally, after all despite writing many of the G N' R songs Izzy was something of a backseat member visually. Not only did Gilby look very similar to Izzy but also his analogous guitar style underlined the Guns' songs with the exact same languid technique. Gilby performed his first show with the band at the Worcester Centrum Centre in Worcester, MA on December 5th. Towards the end of the month the video for *November Rain* was filmed providing the band with a plateau that would render the name Guns N' Roses memorable long after their sell by date.

STANDOUT LYRICS ON THE 'USE YOUR ILLUSION' ALBUMS

"I would like to record for a long time.... I have to make this album. Then it doesn't matter. Our second album is the album I've been waiting on since before we got signed. But as much as it means to me, if it bombs, I'm sure I'll be bummed business wise and let down or whatever, but at the same time it doesn't matter. It's like; I got it out there. That's the artistic thing taken care of. Then I could walk away..." Axl Rose

The beginning of the Guns' comeback album double was a lead bass line from Duff before the music came crashing in to rampant bluster from Axl. 'Right Next Door To Hell' was his version of events that lead to his arrest following the altercation with his next door neighbour Gabriella Kantor. Kantor aged 37; claimed Axl struck her with a wine bottle on the head. After attending hospital she was released after 2 hours in "good condition". Axl said "It's really weird, she cranks my music all the time" in reference to the original complaint made regarding his playing music too loudly. There could have been a counter claim by Axl after he was threatened with a chicken bone from Miss Kantor!

"Right next door to hell, Feels like the walls are closing in on me"
'Right Next Door To Hell'

After spending four hours in a police cell Axl posted $5,000 bail and was not prosecuted due to "lack of evidence". After studying the evidence the District Attorney said "it doesn't appear Rose struck her with a wine bottle".

Supposedly on the day of the altercation, Axl had just learned of Erin Everly's miscarriage and was subsequently in a state of nervous anxiety and stress. Although the song makes reference to Axl living next door to someone who is clearly the subject of much distaste, the song delves deeper into his own mind state. The song flips between two seemingly polar story lines, from lines referring to "so many eyes" being on Axl, clearly referring to his spell in jail after such a minor quarrel, to phrases such as "when your innocence dies you'll find the blues". This reference is connected to Axl's latest revelations about his childhood, as borne out with the following verse:

"My mamma never really said much to me
She was much too young and scared ta be
Hell "Freud" might say that's what I need
But all I really ever get is greed".

In the end there was a cryptic message spoken by Axl asking, "Can you tell me what this means...huh?" This appears to be a veiled snigger at anyone who might not understand his state of mind, (probably the majority of people at the time!)

'Dust N' Bones' was one of Izzy's finer moments, showcasing his lead vocal abilities and song–writing prowess. It's one of the few songs on the *Use Your Illusion* albums to not feature an Axl Rose credit and the lazy stroking rock n' roll proves Stradlin's desire to mellow out musically (his later solo albums would also bear this out, such as the underrated 117° opus). The lyrics were a veritable shrug of the shoulders to the pressures of life, especially life in a famous rock band. Stradlin seemed to be indignant at the melee often surrounding him. His philosophical retort sums up his view perfectly:

"There's no logic here today
Do as you got to, go your own way
Time's short your life's your own
And in the end
We are just

DUST N' BONES."

According to Axl, 'Don't Cry' was "the first song we ever wrote in Guns N' Roses." The track was co–written by Izzy and Axl and shows the early maturity of the band. The lavish production and in-strumentation gave Axl the chance to fully realise his ambitions for the song, evident in early shows the band played.

The heartfelt tribute to making concerted efforts in a relationship seemed ironic given Axl's latter problems with the women in his life and the lines were tell tale. "Something's changing inside you, and don't you know. Don't you cry tonight I still love you baby."

'Perfect Crime' was a confirmation of the volatile side of Axl's per-sonality. There does not appear to be a specific target for the vitriol in the lyrics but perhaps the warning within one verse of the song is the most pertinent. "You wanna fuck with me, don't fuck with me – 'Cause I'm what you'll be so don't fuck with me. If you had better sense, you'd step aside from the bad side of me. Don't fuck wit' da bad side o' me, stay away from the bad side o' me."

'Back off Bitch' was a track written by Axl and his friend Paul Huge. It was another old number, which had been written at the time of Axl, the band. Nevertheless whether the lyrics were added subsequently, or they were pre–existing, they spoke volumes about Axl's view of women. He said, "I've been doing a lot of work and found out I've had a lot of hatred for women. Basically, I've been rejected by my mother since I was a baby. She's picked my stepfa-ther over me ever since he was around and watched me get beaten by him. She stood back most of the time. Unless it got too bad, and then she'd come and hold you afterward. She wasn't there for me. My grandmother had a problem with men. I've gone back and done the work and found out I overheard my grandma going off on men when I was four. And I've had problems with my own masculinity because of that. I was pissed off at my grandmother for her problem with men and how it made me feel about being a man. So I wrote about my feelings in the songs."

The songs were none more applicable than 'Back off Bitch'. It was not merely a general feeling towards women; rather it was apparent-ly aimed at Stephanie Seymour. In the song Axl refers to a "pretty baby" who is obviously a female partner, yet the lyric "I ain't playin' childhood games no more", was a cleverly ironic quip at his younger days and an insistence that he refused to continue acting out his inner child. As he states, "I said it's time for me to even the score."

Towards the end of the song the lyrics become even more direct and the music sees a cascade of instruments backing Axl's parting refrain, "It's time to burn – burn the witch" before sarcastic comments from other band members, "Hey wha' d'ya think he's tryin' to say there, anyway?

"I think it's something each person's s'posed to take in their own special way" prior to the concluding line spat by Axl, "Fucking bitch!"

'November Rain' was the ultimate in contradiction. The 'other side' to Axl's nature, the most relevant on the album, his lovelorn epic that would propel the band into mainstream households around the world. Despite its eventual success 'November Rain' was an intensely personal song. It was based on the Del James' short story 'Without You' that had been sitting in the background for years, yet became a deeply delicate sentimental ballad most reflective of Axl Rose. So important was the song to the Guns' front man that he warned if it weren't recorded to his complete satisfaction he would quit the music business. At the time, of all the songs on the two albums, 'November Rain' was the most vital to Axl and he was serious when he suggested a prolonged break if it didn't match up to his expectations. Although he used piano synths to recreate a full orchestra the effect was identical.

Though the video to the song would appear cryptic and refer to a situation beyond a relationship problem, the lyrics were romantic and direct, Axl suppurating "So if you want to love me then darlin' don't refrain". This was an admittance that he required love as much as anyone and he felt together (with Stephanie, the subject of the song) he and his 'perfect woman' could "still find a way. 'Cause nothin' lasts forever even cold November rain."

"Don't ya think that you need somebody, don't ya think that you need someone. Everybody needs somebody, you're not the only one" 'November Rain'

'The Garden' was a duet between Axl and Alice Cooper who perfectly suited the sinister undertone of the song and subject matter,
which was just one of a number of unusual departures for G N'
R. Alice was drafted in after Axl had originally sung the song and
sounded so much like the shock rocker. And so Alice was asked to
sing half the song, which he did terrifically. The title seemed to have
been brewing around in Axl's brain for some time. In a 1990 interview with *Kerrang!* he stated, "Something always fucking happens
before the show. Somethin' always happens and I react like a motherfucker to it. I don't like to have this pot smoking mentality of just
letting things go by. I don't feel like Lenny Kravitz: like, peace and
love, man, for sure, or you're gonna fuckin' die! I'm gonna kick yer
ass if you mess with my garden, you know? That's always been my
attitude."

The lyrics spoke volumes about Axl's current mental state, "You
can find it all inside, no need to wrestle with your pride. No you
ain't losing your mind you're just in the garden. They can lead you
to yourself or you can throw it on the shelf. But you know you can
look inside for the garden."

Was "the Garden" a place of tranquillity hidden deep within the re-
cesses of Axl's mind, which he had long since lost the chance of finding solace within? Following the relative serenity of 'The Garden'
was a surely deliberate reference to another garden, in 'Garden Of
Eden'. However this form of control was perfectly summed up in
the final verse of the song, "Most organised religions make a mockery of humanity, our governments are dangerous and out of control. The Garden of Eden is just another graveyard. Said if they had
someone to buy it said I'm sure they'd sell my soul." The chorus of
the song, a pounding full on velocity number (featuring an equally vivid and frantic video with Axl taking supreme close up centre
stage) also sang of being 'out of control', "The fire is burning and
it's out of control, it's not a problem you can stop it's rock n' roll."

It seemed Axl was stating that as everything around him and society generally was so disorganised and chaotic then he would give
the public what they expected and live in a perpetual state of chaos
both as man and band. Or rather, as life is 'out of control' therefore

the music that reflects it must be. This would surely explain the intense nature of the 'Garden Of Eden' song itself.

"'Cause the pissed off rip offs 'R' everywhere you turn. Tell me how a generation's Ever s'posed to learn"

'Don't Damn Me' was fairly self explanatory and reflected Axl's predicament of 'damned if you do, damned if you don't'. As he speaks of in the song "don't damn me and don't idolize the ink or I've failed in my intentions, can you find the missing link". Axl did not want to be revered as the messiah (perhaps also a reason why he wore the 'Kill Your idols' t–shirt so often) but he did not feel he deserved constant chastisement either. As elsewhere it was also a statement by a man struggling to come to terms with his own status, an almost graphic explanation of his potential mind swings, "Sometimes I wanna kill, sometimes I wanna die, sometimes I wanna destroy, sometimes I wanna cry, sometimes I could get even, sometimes I could give up, sometimes I could give, sometimes I never give a fuck." Perhaps this verse more than any other on the album summed up where Axl Rose was at in 1991.

'Dead Horse' was an equally graphic revelation, another song whose topic was the childhood Axl was still learning about. Beginning with acoustic guitar played by Axl himself, the initial verse is almost spoken: "Nobody understands, quite why we're here. We're searchin' for answers that never appear." The song deals with his problems in attempting to explain himself to those close to him. He states he would have to "look real hard" to see "you're tryin' too." It's another emotional song that builds up into a powerful renouncement. The weary sentiments of a man who felt older than his tender years were best expressed in the lines, "I ain't quite what you'd call an old soul, still wet behind the ears. I been around this track a couple o' times, but now the dust is startin' to clear".

The last line is also a reference to the regressive therapy Axl had been going through and which seemed to give him basis for comprehending his behaviour.

"Please understand me, I'm climbin' through the wreckage of all my twisted dreams" 'Coma'

"Writing 'Coma' was so heavy I'd start to write and I'd just pass out. I tried to write that song for a year... I wrote the whole end of that song of the top of my head. It just poured out." So said Axl of the closing song on *Use Your Illusion 1*. It is certainly one of the most ambitious tracks the band has so far recorded, ten minutes and thirteen seconds of intense emotional trauma. Though the song was apparently linked to an actual drugs overdose Axl had lived through, which allegedly saw him in a coma, the far more likely description would be it is a depiction of an 'emotional' coma. During the song Axl has to be 'zapped' back to life by doctors, whilst in his mind a myriad of female voices reprimanding him are spoken incessantly. The women are referred to in the liner notes as 'bitches' and named, along with the genuine doctor who also contributes a sound bite, Dr. Michael Smolens. There are feelings of a physical coma evoked throughout the song, specifically the serene section of the song where Axl laments,

"No one's gonna bother me anymore
No one's gonna mess with my head no more
I can't understand what all the fightin's for
But it's so nice here down off the shore
…Not like the world where I used to live

I NEVER REALLY WANTED TO LIVE".

After this section the song comes back to life with the aforementioned memory clips, with Axl narrating, "ZAP HIM AGAIN, ZAP THE SON OF A BITCH AGAIN." Other factors point to a disturbing mind state which alludes to a potential life coma such as the penultimate verse:

"On your last chance ride
Gotta one way ticket

To your suicide
Gotta one way ticket
An there's no way out alive
…No you don't need a doctor
No one else can heal your soul".

The overall feeling is of needing help but not being able to find
it wherever he looks. The bitter paragraph asking for assistance
("HELP ME, HELP ME, HELP ME, HELP ME – BASTARD") is
in essence a look back at a member of Axl's past who could and perhaps should have helped him and didn't, conceivably his Father.

USE YOUR ILLUSION II

*"People out there don't know what's real or not. Things are always
going to get changed or taken out of context, but some magazines
will make up an interview just to sell issues. One's written that Slash
said I run over dogs. I think it sucks when a kid has three bucks and
he buys a candy bar, a soda and a magazine because he's really into
Guns n' Roses, and he gets bad photos and an interview that's not
true. It's not fair. Unfortunately, it probably will never change"* Axl
Rose

From *Use Your Illusion II* there were several moments of controversy; none more so than 'Get In The Ring' and 'Shotgun Blues'.
The latter was reportedly written about Motley Crue's Vince Neil
who'd already received short shrift from an incredibly infuriated
Axl Rose in April 1990. In an interview with *Kerrang!* he responded to a previous issue where Neil had claimed he had punched Izzy
and that both Izzy and Axl were nothing but a pair of pussies, or
words to that effect. Axl's own interview response set the record
straight and laid the gauntlet down. Axl began "The interviewer
asks Vince Neil about him throwing a punch at Izzy backstage at the
MTV awards last year, and Vince replies 'I just punched that dick
and broke his fucking nose! Anybody who beats up on a woman de-
serves to get the shit kicked out of them. Izzy hit my wife, a year be-

fore I hit him.' Well, that's just a crock of shit! Izzy never touched that chick! If anybody tried to hit on anything, it was her trying to hit on Izzy when Vince wasn't around. Only Izzy didn't buy it. So that's what that's all about.... "

Axl, evidently exasperated continued "But where Vince says our manager, Alan Niven, wasn't around, and that afterwards he walked straight past Izzy and me and we didn't do a thing, that's such bullshit! Vince Neil took a pot shot at Izzy. He's momentarily blinded, as always happens when you come off stage, by coming from the stark stage lights straight into total darkness side stage. Suddenly, Vince pops up out of nowhere and lays one on Izzy. Tom Petty's security people jump on him and ask Alan Niven if he wants to press charges. He asks Izzy and Izzy says: 'Naw, it was only like bein' hit by a girl!' and they let him go. And now I read this and I tell ya, he's gonna get a good ass–whippin', and I'm the boy to give it to him...It's like, whenever you wanna do it man let's just do it. I wanna see that plastic face of his cave in when I hit him!"

And then a direct threat "there's only one way out for that fucker now and that's if he apologises in public, to the press, to *Kerrang!* and its readers, and admits he was lyin' when he said those things in that interview. Personally, I don't think he has the balls. But that's the gauntlet, and I'm throwing it down. Hey, Vince, whichever way you wanna go man, guns, knives or fists whatever you wanna do. I don't care."

The lyrics to 'Shotgun Blues' were never actually confirmed as being directly related to the incident, however reading between the lines of the song it's clear they almost certainly were.

"An now you're blowin' smoke, I think you're one big joke…I'm still waitin' for your ass to burn, ooooh you want a confrontation, I'll give you every fuckin' chance, with your verbal masturbation, me I just like to dance." The final line was a nail into the prospective coffin of Axl's victim. "You think anyone with an I.Q. over fifteen would believe your shit – fuckhead. Nothin' but a fuckin' pussy."

Over the months following Axl's initial challenge to Neil in the press there were many forms of speculation regarding an actual fight taking place with cartoons of the two rockers standing in a ring with boxing gloves adorning certain magazines. The music channel VH1 also covered the possibility in a piece on the duelling front men. However as always in such situations the melee soon calmed down and although Neil never apologised it seemed to be forgotten about within time.

'Get In The Ring' was more directly confrontational; one particular verse gave the album notoriety beyond its classy veneer. The antagonistic slant reeled by Axl, was a reply to the endless reams of media speculation and lies. Axl attacked the words like an express train, steaming:

"And that goes for all you punks in the press
That want to start shit by printin' lies instead of the things we said
That means you
Andy Secher at Hit Parader
Circus Magazine
Mick Wall at Kerrang
Bob Guccione Jr. at Spin".

The damage was done after specific journalists and publications were named, and on the downside it immortalised *Use Your Illusion II* for the wrong reasons. A song originally penned by Duff, under the name 'Why Do You Look At Me When You Hate Me?' was tastefully shortened in title (the old title became the first line instead) but lengthened in snotty diatribe. The song was not complete without another Axl challenge, "You wanta antagonize me, antagonize me motherfucker, Get in the ring motherfucker, and I'll kick your bitchy little ass PUNK."

Much like 'Dust N' Bones' from *Use Your Illusion I*, the second track on the album '14 Years' was another Izzy led swaggering blues tinged number. Co–written with Axl, the front man joined in for the chorus and it was clear the lyrics were mostly his. Harking back to more childhood distress were lines such as: "it's been 14 years of silence, it's been 14 years of pain. It's been 14 years that are gone forever, and I'll never have again".

Though Axl tinkered on the piano almost casually and briskly there were serious points made within the good time song. In another rant at misunderstanding press were the lines, "Bullshit and contemplation, gossip's their trade. If they knew half the real truth, what would they say"? This was another frustrated sentiment surely written by Axl in which he barely disguised his aversion at the way he had been portrayed. The conclusion was that he was "past the point of concern" clearly referring to the decision to not give the press the freedom they had once been granted.

Though much of the second album was musically upbeat with songs such as 'Pretty Tied Up', 'Get In The Ring', 'Shotgun Blues' and perhaps one of the bands strongest tunes to date, *You Could Be Mine*, it was in many ways a darker album than its precursor. The lyrics were more contemplative and less rooted in sarcasm. Where previously, women were mocked in the derisive jibes of 'You Ain't The First', on *Use Your Illusion II* songs such as 'Locomotive' and 'Estranged' were sombre in their scope of love and relationships.

One of the only songs to actually refer to 'illusions' in its lyrics was 'Locomotive'. "I bought me an illusion, an I put it on the wall. I let it fill my head with dreams and I had to have them all" Axl mourned, cursing the bitterness of success. As he further sings, "But oh the taste is never so sweet as what you'd believe it is". Elsewhere the subject is certainly a relationship, and one not going swimmingly well, ("my baby's gone off the track...got ta peel the bitch off my back"). The end of the song features one of Axl's most poetic verses as he pleads, "I know it looks like I'm insane, take a closer look I'm not to blame" and then a parting entreaty, "If love is blind I guess I'll buy myself a cane". The music pans into the distance with the hushed understanding, "LOVE'S SO STRANGE".

'Estranged' was the crowning glory of *Use Your Illusion II* – an astonishing eyehole into the chasms of Axl's mind, which was followed closely musically just as on 'Coma'. From the whispered initiation, "When you're talkin' to yourself and nobody's at home. You can fool yourself you came in this world alone (Alone)" it was apparent 'estranged' described exactly how Axl viewed himself, not only because of problems in his youth but equally due to his ongoing relationship troubles. As the personal nature of the third verse indicates:

"Old at heart but I'm only 28 and I'm much too young to let love break my heart. Young at heart but it's getting much too late to find ourselves so far apart".

'Estranged' is one of the many songs that demonstrate Axl's tendency to converse in riddles. Rather than explain too clearly or write about one specific feeling, more often than not Axl tends to cover a multitude of subjects and emotions within the same song. As he himself said of 'Coma', it just comes pouring out. One imagines Axl writes much as he talks, with a hurried pace of mind and an evaluated sense of expression, fulfilling the criteria for exorcising demons through penmanship.

"When I find out all the reasons, maybe I'll find another way, find another day.
With all the changing seasons of my life maybe I'll get it right next time" 'Estranged'

Musically the song writhes and swathes through passionate waves, taking over half its length to approach the telling chorus, melodically cultivated and assisted by Slash's harmonious guitar parts (for which he was thanked by Axl in the liner notes). Axl howls, "'Cause I see the storm getting closer and the waves they get so high. Seems everything we've ever known's here, why must it drift away and die". Perhaps an indication of an end to a relationship he saw as potentially perfect. As he later says, "I'll never find anyone to replace you. Guess I'll have to make it thru, this time– Oh this time without you." With the phrase 'without you' Axl continued the theme from *Don't Cry* and *November Rain* as borne out by the trilogy of respective videos. Vocally the song was Axl's finest moment, covering the untapped bases of his unique voice.

I knew the storm was getting closer and all my friends said I was high. But everything we've ever known's here, I never wanted it to die"

'Breakdown' was another plaintive mini epic, which took a different route down the familiar path of abandonment. "Just like children hidin' in a closet can't tell what's goin' on outside" was a telltale line in a familiar Axl vein. He was the sole writer for both 'Estranged' and 'Breakdown' and it's no surprise given their sensitive nature. Axl speaks with sadness; "To think the one you love could hurt you now is a little hard to believe". Again given the tangents throughout the song it is difficult to know who he refers to, whether it is a romantic partner or a family member. However it is obvious at the time Axl believed no one neither truly understood him, nor cared enough to try.

He sings as if mentally wounded, "When I look around everybody always brings me down. Well is it them or me I just can't see...but if someone really cared well they'd take the time to spare, a moment to try and understand another one's despair. Remember in this game we call life that no one said it's fair."

There is also a veiled reference to life as it was before the bands success. Axl sings, "Fun how ev'rything was Roses when we held on to the Guns. Just because you're winnin' don't mean you're the lucky ones", in effect mocking their achievements and winking ironically at their togetherness as paupers, their separation as rich rock stars. Separation was a theme evident throughout Axl's lyrics but there was also an abundance of themes linked to the desire to change.

" 'Cause yesterday's got nothin' for me
Old pictures that I'll always see
Some things could be better
In my book of memories" 'Yesterdays'

"Look at me – T–shirt, jeans, boots, that's me that's all there is, that's all there's gonna be. Gimme a roof over my head and something to drink and I've got everything I need. What difference is this money going to make?" Slash

In 1992 Guns N' Roses sold 40,000 tickets for the first day of their Alpine Valley shows, a feat equalled only once before in history, by The Who. The band was scheduled to tour America first, before heading overseas. Australia, Europe, and Japan... no place was to be spared the G N' R experience. "Part of the reason I don't go to rehearsals is, I like to go all out. If the band's not going out at the same intensity – they're concentrating more on getting the music right – I feel like an idiot, jumping around, taking it so serious," said Axl, who trained with daily voice exercises alone or with his vocal coach, Ron Anderson. The rehearsals took place in an airplane hangar containing their colossal, state of the art reformed stage set up.

In May of 1992 Metallica's Lars Ulrich, along with Slash, spoke at a press conference to announce a duel headlining tour of Guns N' Roses and Metallica for the summer in the United States. This was without doubt one of the biggest tours of all time in the world of heavy metal. Despite the obvious difference between the two bands' style and their fans to some degree, they were at the time the two biggest acts in the world of rock and to see the two link up together in such an unprecedented event made fans thrilled and promoters hungry for a piece of the action. Lars Ulrich was by his own admission the one "closest to some of those guys" and spoke of "late night drinking babbles where we would speak about actually going out and playing some gigs together".

From simple suggestions by the men who actually mattered, it was still a spectacular feat for the management companies involved to negotiate a tour of such magnitude and to furthermore see it through to run smoothly minus riots or negative incident. As usual in the world of Guns N' Roses at least, the tour did not pass without occurrence of the worst possible kind. It may have been a mistake when

Metallica front man James Hetfield was burned by pyrotechnics from the stage and had to cut short the bands set to attend hospital to receive treatment (further dates had to be rescheduled while Hetfield recovered, when he did return Metal Church's John Marshall filled in on guitar while Hetfield sang).

When Guns N' Roses took to the stage the same night Axl began to strain over monitor problems, claiming he could not hear the music properly and promptly left the stage. With the previous few hours' drama of Metallica cancelling the show through no choice, to see Axl walk off stage unnecessarily infuriated the crowd. They reacted much like other audiences had. Chants of "Axl sucks!" were the backdrop to an intense riot, which saw several law enforcement officers and stewards injured, not to mention some fans themselves.

It was nothing short of a miracle that nobody was permanently or seriously harmed. Yet the bands rolled on and quite surprisingly with hindsight, Axl had this to say in 2002, "I was definitely excited about how that tour went as far as how it went for *us* and we got to see a lot of people back stage. We threw some really huge parties that were a lot of fun, we had a different theme in every city everything from go–go dancers to ice sculptures".

Axl seemed to have fond memories but was this simply a jaded response to something that happened so long ago and had become (at least by 2002) of little consequence?

Times have changed and there are no longer many surprises touring wise. Where Guns' can now share a stage with young pop metal upstarts such as Hoobastank or Linkin Park to mass indifference, the Metallica tour was something unlikely to repeat itself and was such a unique and band altering experience for all involved, the simplest thing to do is overlook it ever actually happened. However, with simple analysis it is no coincidence both bands sales' increased from their experiences of the tour especially Metallica who went on to conquer both the worlds of heavy metal and rock with their self titled fifth album. There was admiration at the way in which Hetfield and co handled themselves in the public view and their humble and respectful reaction to problems on the road were surely a factor in their growing popularity.

Guns N' Roses meanwhile enjoyed a greater deal of exposure for all the wrong reasons. It was par for the course for the band to create some form of bad blood at every show despite their knack of playing many a concert perfectly well and on time. Axl felt typically defensive when faced with the barrages of criticism. He said, "Negativity sells, and the media knows that. "Axl Rose is rock 'n' roll's bad guy." There were a lot of people who felt that the Rolling Stones shouldn't exist, who talked crap about them. Now we're huge, and it seems the people who are most vocal are the ones who don't like us. They'll pick up any rock to throw at us."

His self protective mechanisms were well and truly in place long before the Metallica tour, yet had he known James Hetfield's views on him things may have come to a head even sooner. On the Metallica video *A Year And A Half In The Life Of Metallica Part 2* Hetfield is filmed making derisive comments regarding the singer of their touring partners.

Whilst reading from the Guns N' Roses rider requirements, and those specifically of Axl Rose, Hetfield snorts, "Horrible truths. The piddly wants and needs of certain folks on the road. Axl *'Pose'* dressing room requirements." Sneering, Hetfield read from the list, "absolutely no substitutions. One cup of 'cubed' ham, it's got to be cubed so it can get down his little neck...one rib eye steak dinner, I didn't know the guy ate meat, looks like a fucking vegetarian...pepperoni pizza, fresh – I think that's just for throwing around. One can of assorted Pringles chips, that's the greasy shit so he can grease his hair back." As those onlookers in the Metallica camp sniggered at Hetfield's obvious distaste, he finished with "honey that makes him SING LIKE THIS!" rising with a squeal and imitating Axl's voice, "one bottle of dom perignon – hey that's where the money's at right there."

He then says "its just fucking crap" and throws the list into the air and steps on it when it lands, all the while being filmed. One wonders the reaction if anyone connected to G N' R ever got to see this unfortunate piece of film. One thing is for sure; given Axl's remarks in 2002 it is unlikely he either knew or cared what Metallica thought of him. Slash it seemed had more of a relationship with certainly Lars Ulrich and his retrospection about Guns N' Roses when speaking in Kerrang! in 2002 gave just another interpretation of the unique way of touring to which he found himself privy.

Slash commented, "I just like to play guitar. It wasn't about business, or trying to be cool on Sunset Strip, or getting the cover of fuckin' *Rolling Stone*, or any of that. It was about just getting together with a bunch of guys that could cause something. Even if we weren't all on the exact same page as far as direction goes, somehow we managed to make a band that was a mixture of everything – of attitude. At the time, the five of us were the only people who could have made up Guns N' Roses and that I'm proud of." The perspective of a guitarist who simply wanted to do his job, however remarkable that job happened to be, and remain away from the hustle and bustle of touring life was at odds with the off stage antics of every single G N' R member at the time. In one notable side issue G N' R were sued by 57,000 Metallica fans after the concert in Montreal, Canada. It was business as usual.

YOU'RE CRAZY

"I thank God for it, that I've managed to succeed at what I love doing. And I'd like to continue being good at it. You can't let the hype justify the whole band's existence...you don't even know how hard it is once you get here, to keep it together" Slash

In contrast to the other members' refusal to deal with the 'pressures' of being Guns N' Rose it was Axl, as stated elsewhere in this book, who was the one keeping the G N' R ship afloat in a 'business' sense and had he not taken care of this angle so early on, who knows when the end could have arrived for Guns N' Roses. Slash made reference to this alter ego speaking in the same *Kerrang!* issue. "The older you get and the more you do this, the more significant the 'Spinal Tap' movie becomes. The funny thing about it is its so fucking accurate! There was one time during the stadium tour with Guns N' Roses where we had the worst show I think we ever had. We were in the dressing room before we went on, watching that whole movie before Axl was ready to go on stage. Then we went out there, and I'll tell you that I would never watch 'Spinal Tap' before a show again...ever!"

1992 threatened to be Guns N Roses most shambolic year. After the highs of finally releasing the *Use Your Illusion* double set and beginning to tour in support of it, there was an imminent danger of the core of the band being disrupted. As Axl made reference to that year, the band was essentially run by him and Slash with the two deciding on any ideas before clearing it with Duff.

He then went on to say "Guns N' Roses is basically Slash, Duff, Doug Goldstein and myself, but there's a lot of other people involved that are a part of our lives and a part of our family. It would be nice if he wasn't. I love everybody in this band. It's kicking ass and feels really warm and really cool onstage. At this point it's the 12 of us that get onstage and fucking go all out. There's Teddy, there's Dizzy, there's Roberta, Tracy, Lisa, CeCe, Anne, Gilby, Matt, Duff, Slash and me. Slash put this new band together, did all of the groundwork. He did such an amazing job that I just can't believe it really happened. I'm glad to be a part of it. It's a pretty huge thing, and we might even add some dancers, like we used to have back in the old Troubadour days. It's something we've considered."

Dancers were not such a necessary requirement with all the 'extras' G N' R now employed on stage as many in the business considered them something of a cabaret rock act, including some in the band themselves. Of course, no one had yet complained about the varied instruments and eclectic nature shown on the *Use Your Illusion* records. However not everybody realised if Guns N' Roses sought to play the songs live, to do them justice, female backing singers and the exact same instruments played on the albums would be necessary.

This business oriented side of Axl was more than anything a basic musical one as well. He simply believed in either performing the best show possible or not performing at all, as his regular stage exits or lateness demonstrated. Doubtless there were serious changes afoot personnel wise and these were to be long lasting alterations to the Guns N' Roses make up.

"The reason I bought the Uzi is because this guy was going to rent me this house, then started dicking around, jacking up the price. He wanted more money than it was worth. I was so pissed off that I bought the Uzi. I've always wanted an Uzi. Everybody talks about machine guns and shit. I realized the only reason I didn't go for it was I thought I'd freak out with it. Now that I own a couple of guns, I also understand the responsibility that goes along with them. I never take them anywhere unlocked or loaded. Dig this: I saw this ad in Soldier of Fortune magazine that said 'When the going gets tough, the tough get an Uzi.' Let's get tough!" Axl Rose

In the middle of the disorderly break amid the Wembley show and the start of the second leg of the *Use Your Illusion* tour, it was an increasing problem for Duff to remain sober. He sought solace in a solo project, which was to emerge a year later under his own name and a title of *Believe In Me*. Produced and engineered by Jim Mitchell the album was a long time dream of McKagan's. He also shone playing several different instruments including drums, bass and rhythm guitars. He even contributed some lead guitar parts along with Slash and friend Snake (Dave Sabo, from Skid Row). There was also an appearance from another Skid Row friend, lead singer Sebastian Bach who sang on one song.

This was rather remarkable given the affable four stringer was sometimes unable to string a coherent sentence together. Duff was drinking way too much, and his health was certainly deteriorating. Nowadays after years of being straight and with a passion for martial arts and regular training and exercise Duff looks back with obvious distaste at his somewhat sordid past. He has said "What a sad place to be. Every day I woke up, I had a vodka bottle sitting next to my bed. It was like being in a cardboard box and I couldn't bend it. I could not stop, I tried to stop for a month and then I started drinking a lot. I was too far gone."

KIDNAPPED

Whether the following was a product of beleaguered minds in either Duff's or Steven's case is open to debate but it certainly gives a clue as to the whereabouts of the marbles at one stage of the G N' R timeline. The story goes, as a close friend of the band tells it, that Duff was somewhat certain that Steven Adler had been kidnapped by drug dealers, to whom he apparently owed a great deal of money. The last time Duff saw Steven was a few days before, trounced in the Melrose avenue gutter, resplendently wearing just one shoe.

Steven's is hardly aware of even owing money, let alone actually paying it back, whether he had any within his grasp at the time was also questionable. Especially when you consider the 'one shoe' hint. In Duff's perception, the dealers owed, in their Hollywood role of minor drug Mafioso, were less apt to allow one appallingly rich rock star get away with a money debt, lest the floodgates could open. Steven needed to be taught a lesson. According to Duff, the repayment would consist of Steven losing a limb of some description, far worse than a shoe and certainly something to act upon post haste.

As Duff is telling this to his friend, she suggests taking him to find the wayward drummer, despite not being exactly convinced of his tall tale. Nevertheless they set off towards Sunset Boulevard, on the way stopping at Duff's house. Duff speeds in and out of the house carrying a loaded shotgun upon his return, "Let's Go" he says.

Clearly inebriated by the power of the steel, Duff is excitedly waving it around, almost in clear view of walking bystanders, at which point his friend fearing for his notoriety and potential police intervention, asks him to be a bit more mindful of his weapon. Duff responds with a cry they must head out to the Valley and as they reach the upper echelons of suburban society, it takes only a few yards before the energized bassist shouts, "Stop!" He then races over to the house to be met by an old man who, upon meeting with a rather vicious looking gun wielding 6ft 4" maniac clutches his heart and falls into his aged wife's arms. Duff meanwhile, streaks past them both scanning all rooms of their house screaming the place down.

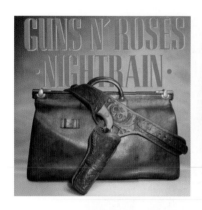

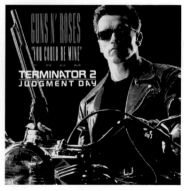

GUNS N' ROSES

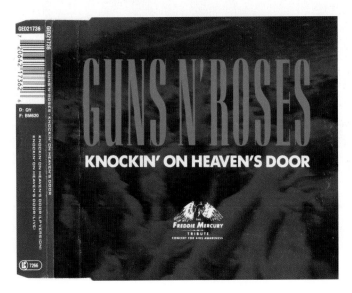

GUNS N' ROSES

KNOCKIN' ON HEAVEN'S DOOR

THE
FREDDIE MERCURY
TRIBUTE
CONCERT FOR AIDS AWARENESS

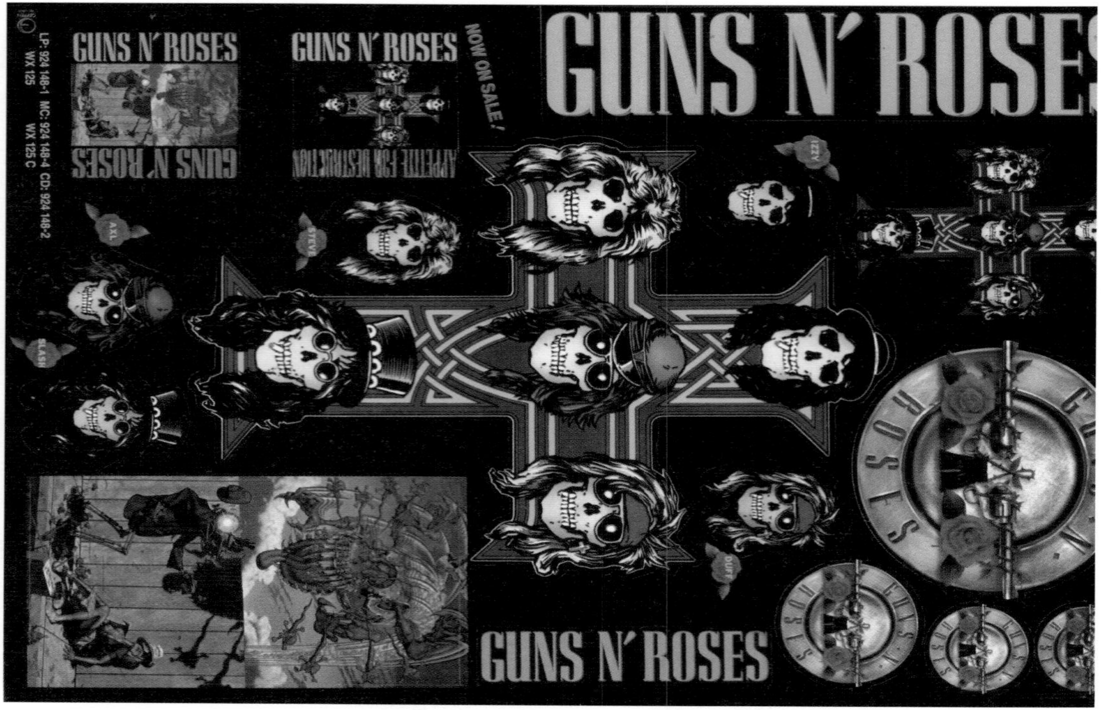
GUNS N' ROSES
NOW ON SALE !
GUNS N' ROSES
APPETITE FOR DESTRUCTION
GUNS N' ROSES
GUNS N' ROSES
IZZY
DUFF
STEVE
AXL
SLASH
GUNS N' ROSES
GUNS N' ROSES
LP: 924 148-1 MC: 924 148-4 CD: 924 148-2
WX 125 WX 125 C

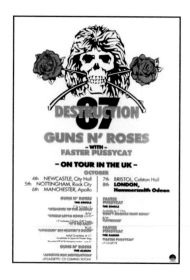

GUNS 'N' ROSES

Sat., Jan. 4th 11:00

Troubadour

"GET YOURSELF TOGETHER, DRINK TILL YOU DROP,
FORGET ABOUT TOMORROW AND HAVE ANOTHER SHOT!"

Happy New Year!

FROM THE BOYS WHO BROUGHT YOU THE MOST CHAOTIC SHOWS OF '85

SEND DONATIONS TO: GUNS N ROSES
KEEP US OUT OF JAIL FUND
9000 SUNSET BLVD., SUITE 900
HOLLYWOOD, CA 90069

$1.00 OFF WITH FLYER $1.00 OFF WITH FLYER

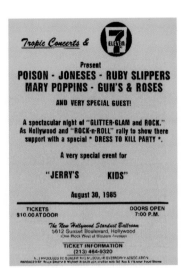

Tropic Concerts & **7 ELEVEN**

Present

**POISON · JONESES · RUBY SLIPPERS
MARY POPPINS · GUN'S & ROSES**

AND VERY SPECIAL GUEST!

A spectacular night of "GLITTER-GLAM and ROCK."
As Hollywood and "ROCK-n-ROLL" rally to show there
support with a special * DRESS TO KILL PARTY *.

A very special event for

"JERRY'S   KIDS"

August 30, 1985

TICKETS	DOORS OPEN
$10.00 AT DOOR	7:00 P.M.

The New Hollywood Stardust Ballroom
5612 Sunset Boulevard, Hollywood
(One Block West of Western Avenue)

TICKET INFORMATION
(213) 464-9320

ALL PROCEEDS TO BENEFIT THE MUSCULAR DYSTROPHY ASSOCIATION
PRODUCED BY: Bruce Smith & Michael Alago in conjunction with Bill, Ron & Connie Rose Stone

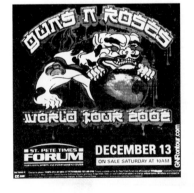

GUNS N ROSES

WORLD TOUR 2002

**ST. PETE TIMES
FORUM**   **DECEMBER 13**
TAMPA SPORTS AND ENTERTAINMENT CENTER   ON SALE SATURDAY AT 10AM

GNRontour.com

GUNS 'N' ROSES

LIVE AT THE MARQUEE
FRIDAY JUNE 19th · MONDAY JUNE 22nd · SUNDAY JUNE 28th
THE DEBUT DOUBLE 'A' SIDE SINGLE IT'S SO EASY · MR BROWNSTONE
4-TRACK 12" INCLUDES 2 LIVE SONGS SHADOW OF YOUR LOVE · MOVE TO THE CITY
ALSO AVAILABLE AS LIMITED EDITION 4-TRACK 12" PICTURE DISC

RockPower

LE MAGAZINE LE PLUS BRUYANT EN FRANCE

ANTHRAX
BLACK SABBATH
MEGADETH
JOE SATRIANI
EXODUS

WARRANT
UGLY KID JOE
SUICIDAL
TENDENCIES
POISON
ELECTRIC LOVE
HOGS

GUNS N' ROSES

POSTERS
IRON
MAIDEN
PEARL JAM

SKID ROW

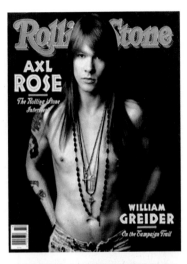

Rolling Stone

AXL ROSE

The Rolling Stone Interview

WILLIAM GREIDER

On the Campaign Trail

Interview

AXL

the Prisgrew

Rolling Stone

AXL ROSE
The Rolling Stone Interview

THE STONES
In the Studio

NENEH CHERRY
Pop's Unlikely New Diva

THE WHO
Tommy's Triumphant Return

KEITH HARING
An Intimate Conversation

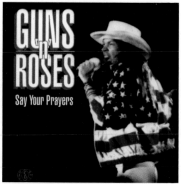

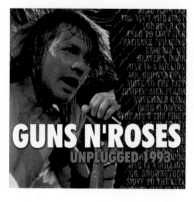

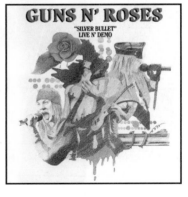

Leaving a baffled couple to contemplate what they had done to deserve such a confrontation, Duff is suitably frog marched back into the convertible car by his friend who gently persuades him it might be the wrong house after all. Back on the warpath Duff spots the actual house he's been looking for, or so he thinks. With a second cry to stop and check it out, the friend is once again forced to let manic Duff inspect his next point of call. This time he is met by a politely screeching Vietnamese lady, suitably struck by the size of Duff's piece and his urgency in wanting to use it, as he goes bounding into her house asking "where the fuck is Steven?" He decides to rummage around the ladies kitchen cupboards in his fruitless search, spewing cutlery and assorted household goods, much to the owners' dismay. It's at this point Duff is once again escorted back to normality by his friend. As they drive away the friend spots the lady owner talking into a phone. Finally the search seems to have proved ineffective enough for Duff to conclude "Fuck it, let's get a beer."

Perhaps unsurprisingly Duff was instructed by his doctor to completely cut out the vodka, which had been a staple of his diet up until that point. Duff planned to go a year without drinking but after another bout of alcohol induced illness McKagan woke up to his potentially serious problems. After being released from the hospital the doctor told Duff, "if you go and have even one more drink, you will die. Just have a beer, and you'll be dead." Duff realised the perils of his lifestyle but the revelation came too late to save his Guns N' Roses career.

Though he did not leave until some years later it seemed the band could not go back to its former comradeship with so many disasters befalling its members. Duff however underwent a personal revolution. He claimed he was fortunate in the doctor telling him one more drink could kill him. Before that happened, he had been trying to cut down his drinking but simply could not find the necessary resolve or commitment to do so.

In an eerie coincidence McKagan, being from Seattle himself just happened to be on the same flight to Seattle in early April 1994 as Kurt Cobain, who was flying home after escaping from a California drug rehabilitation facility. Heroin addict Cobain was found dead just days later of an apparent suicide. It was another act of fate for Duff who knew Cobain and many other junkies famous and non–famous, most of whom succumbed to the inevitable chemical over–dose and are now dead. As Duff himself would eagerly certify, there are not many junkies he could look at and seriously believe they could kick their habit.

In complete contrast to his time in Guns,' Duff now regularly gets to bed before 11 pm and has said "So much has gone on in my life over the last few years. Having to battle against the ravages of my lifestyle was really difficult, but overcoming my dependencies was the best thing that ever happened to me. It opened my eyes it turned my life around. It made me realize what was really important to me. I was offered a lot of money to stay in Guns N' Roses, and I was very honoured by that. But I realized that I had never gotten into making music for the money in the first place so why should I start now?"

With some affection remaining for his former lead singer, Duff was clearly the member who least wanted to step out of the Guns' circle but in the end could not stay any longer. His summary of the reasons that Axl kept going against the grain and eventually forced the original members out involved a critique of the hangers on in the Guns' camp many of whom Duff claimed would constantly tell Axl he was right and managed to maintain Axl's ruthlessness by under–lining what Rose himself believed – that he *was* Guns N' Roses and it did not matter if the others were to leave. So it proved.

According to Duff many of the business associates of Guns N' Roses feared Axl because they were scared they were going to lose their jobs. Duff now states, "I'm honest with myself and with the people surrounding me. Had I stayed with Axl, I would have act–ed against my personality. And nothing worse could ever happen to ME. In this story the real losers are the fans unfortunately."

The reality marker comes in the differing views of Axl and his former band colleagues. While Duff has been quick to state that he always felt Guns N' Roses was slightly unreal and never felt com–fortable in its cocoon Axl has been accepting of the G N' R pattern however bizarre or extreme, and simply shunned the limelight in response to its surrealism.

It might be with a wry smile one thinks of the irony in heavy drinkers and drug users such as Duff McKagan stating that life in Guns N' Roses felt surreal when they were experiencing several different levels of reality on a daily basis in their own minds. However insane or unreal the G N' R entourage and front man made the whole experience, the idea of adjusting to its excess by indulging in chemical overindulgence to cope with it clearly only fuelled the dreamlike experience. Though the whole band had emerged from far humbler beginnings, they were all able to sheepishly accept its benefits whilst bemoaning its negative aspects.

THE PERILS OF ROCK N' ROLL DECADENCE

"A reason I've been laying low is that I've been trying to take the time to survive our success and assume responsibility for where we're at" Axl Rose

Axl was more philosophical when he spoke to *RIP* magazine in 1992. He said, "This is music, this is art. It's definitely a good business, but that should be second to the art, not first. I was figuring it out, and I'm like the president of a company that's worth between $125 million and a quarter billion dollars. If you add up record sales based on the low figure and a certain price for T–shirts and royalties and publishing, you come up with at least $125 million, which I get less than two percent of." It was a bearing on Guns' sudden business oriented standing, which Axl felt was at odds with his own mission. Nevertheless he knew he had to swim with the tide as much as possible despite managing to equally stand against it when necessary – taking liberties with those who eventually grew tired of dealing with him (as well as the perils of rock n' roll decadence).

Of the 'member' situation Axl said it was "quite interesting" when referring to an interview where Matt Sorum remarked that if he could not be a full–time member of Guns N' Roses then he wasn't going to be *in* the band. Axl said "The truth of the matter is, Matt's a member of G N' R, but it doesn't really mean anything. It's kind of like a clubhouse/gang thing. We're all members of this gang. What it boils down to is, whose yard is the tree house in? Matt's a member of G N' R, and his opinions are taken into consideration. As far as that's concerned, Gilby is a member too; Dizzy is a member of the band. With all the background singers, horn players, and keyboardists – we look at it like we're all Guns N' Roses. But the bottom line is, the business is basically run by Slash and myself." The business would have alarming repercussions to Slash himself though at the time Axl balanced the turbulent relationship he had with the guitarist. He stated the two of them hadn't argued for the past year and a half and that he loved Slash. According to Axl the two of them were "opposite poles of energy" who balanced each other out.

"From day one Izzy always wanted to be about the size of The Ramones and do 2,000 seaters so there was always a little battle there. And then the other guys had to be on so many substances to be able to deal with that crowd. To his credit Slash could play great guitar on a lot of drugs!" Axl Rose

However at the beginning of 1992 (on January 14th) there had been an altercation, visible on stage to the crowd at the Erwin–Nutter Center in Dayton, OH. After Axl sliced his hand on his mike stand he went to have it treated. Whilst he was offstage both Axl and Doug Goldstein thought Slash had made a "shitty" remark about him to the 20,000 strong crowd. Distressed at this and that fact he had cut his hand to the bone Axl took the comments, which he had said he'd heard on the backstage monitors, to heart. He then wrapped his injured hand up in a towel and re–appeared on stage threatening to "kick Slash's ass in front of 20,000 people".

The crowd and resultant reaction of fans who learnt of the incident unsurprisingly viewed this with some disdain and uncertainty. For a while at least the eventual statement from both sides seemed to calm the rumours. After distancing himself from the media however the rumour mill further spun at the expense of Guns N' Roses. Eventually the rumoured split between Slash and Axl did indeed take place. Meanwhile Axl spoke of his renouncing the press and made a topical comparison. He stated, "I didn't have enough energy to stay in contact with the media. I was watching this thing today about de–metalizing kids. All a parent knows is they see their kid listening to Ozzy Osbourne. The kid is doing acid and painting upside–down crosses on his wall, and they don't know what happened to him or her, so it's Ozzy's fault."

Axl's observation was a typically wry one. He shunned focus from himself, confusing readers with a remark, which was all too pertinent, to them. From the likes of W.A.S.P. and Twisted Sister in the 80s and Judas Priest and Ozzy Osbourne in the early 90s the growing concern amongst parents across the United States, or for that matter the world, was that their children were in danger from listening to 'satanic heavy metal.' It was full of backwards messaging and subliminal instructions for the listener to kill themselves or somebody else.

Court cases focused on this and in retrospect it is a surprise Guns N' Roses escaped such harassment from the courts and the listening public. Indeed one comfort to the band was at least when they were sued it was over acts that had either definitely or certainly not taken place. Their music never once seriously fell under the microscope of 'satanic' or harmful scrutiny.

However anybody reading Axl's words would have found the simile a familiar one and understood his point. What the media were attempting to do to Guns N' Roses was precisely what it had been trying to do to rock and heavy metal – destroy it. The same media that built both forms up to mass sales and lucrative placements the world over was now responsible for charting its downfall. Axl was aware of this and had no intent of complying with his bands fall from grace. Unfortunately it had already happened, perhaps there weren't enough people who understood his comments regarding 'de–metalizing' kids and were content to be de–Guns N' Roses themselves.

After all, the public was, it seemed growing tired of the endless failures to commit to time schedules, live shows or even a stable band line up. However Guns' way of surviving obstacles and documenting them in their songs still held enough sway for the consumer, and it was certain by the end of the *Use Your Illusion* tour you were either with Guns N' Roses or against them. Whilst it appeared the band did not care any more either way this was the pre cursor to the release of their most critically slammed work and an ensuing hiatus that still provokes questions in 2005.

"When I was in school there were all these stereotypes. If you liked The Rolling Stones you were a faggot because of the time Mick Jagger kissed Keith Richards on 'Saturday Night Live'. If you like the Grateful Dead you were a hippie. If you like the Sex Pistols you were a punker. I guess that would make me a faggot hippie punk rocker" Axl Rose

1993 was a year for change in the music industry, especially the rock and alternative scenes. Nirvana had virtually single–handedly transformed the entire business with their *Nevermind* album (iron-ically on Geffen). Almost overnight the desire for good time hard rock music vanished as the dreaded 'grunge' genre found success in themes more concerned with the harsh reality of everyday life.

Though Guns N' Roses sat somewhere within the hard rock cate-gory, they were equally fortunate enough to have covered the gam-ut of emotions, not to mention instruments and styles, on their last two albums. Where lesser acts such as Poison and Warrant fell com-pletely off the scale, Guns' retained their credibility. This was due in part to their astonishing longevity in the press; they always sold magazines. Since severing all contact with the media, Axl had creat-ed an aura of mystique around G N' R and people were still remark-ably concerned with Guns' movements. Therefore the follow up to *Use Your Illusion 1 & 2* was hotly awaited.

Where the early 90s undoubtedly belonged to grunge, there was soon to be a new punk movement. When it came (with The Offspring and Green Day releasing *Smash* and *Dookie* respectively) it killed the last vestiges of the commercial rock and metal scene. Quite co-incidentally Guns' had long been considering a punk revival, with a tribute album that was way overdue. The original plan was to pre-cede *Use Your Illusion 1 & 2* with the covers opus but instead the songs lay unused until the Guns N' Roses comeback was decided.

The idea was for each member to pick their favourite songs and the band to attack them in their own style. In much the same way as *G N' R Lies*, the covers album was really intended as a stopgap before the next 'real' album. Covering the dirty underside of music was a brave move at the time and the year was not the best to release such a set. Many of Guns' fans were too young to remember the originals and as such were rather perplexed or disappointed at the 'old school' feel of the album. Although in the liner notes the band advised, "A great song can be found anywhere. Do yourself a favour and go find the originals" it seemed there were not many who were interested.

"I wanted to do 'Hair of the Dog', T–Rex's "Buick Makane", and Fear's "I don't care about you". Those are songs that meant much to me. Axl always hums on 'Since I don't have you', and he loves 'Black leather' so those were his choices. Duff picked 'Down On the Farm', and we all wanted to a song by the New York Dolls. It became 'Human Being'" Slash

It was a great shame T*he Spaghetti Incident?* became something of a neglected release in the G N' R back catalogue. Whether it was the cryptic title, the staid artwork (literally a photo of tinned spaghetti) or simply the choice of relatively obscure songs the album became the bands worst selling. In some senses perhaps they appreciated the lukewarm reception. After Izzy had departed it was ironic the band essentially revisited their roots and stripped everything down. They forgot about orchestras and copious female backing singers, instead concentrating on guitar, bass, drums and Axl's adaptable voice.

The front man turned in one of his most outstanding performances when singing the likes of 'Raw Power' (originally by Iggy And The Stooges), 'Hair Of The Dog' (Nazareth) and the superb cockney imitation that was the UK Subs' 'Down On The Farm'. Elsewhere the Dead Boys mini classic 'Ain't It Fun' was appropriately tackled (Axl duetting with Michael Monroe) and used as a single. Duff's punk heritage came to the fore when he sang The Misfits' 'Attitude' and a rousing version of The Damned's 'New Rose'. He even paid tribute to Johnny Thunders with a heartfelt, 'Can't Put Your Arms Around A Memory'.

"When Izzy first came to L.A. I was one of the first guys who met him, because there was at first a very small clique of people who grew up

*on bands like David Bowie, New York Dolls, and more of the punk
stuff like The Clash, Sex Pistols, so there was a small crowd of people who were into rock but then got into the punk rock stuff. And
that's how Izzy and me clicked. So him and I were much more com-
patible with our music, Slash was more about metal" Gilby Clarke*

Perhaps the two most unusual pieces were the versions of 'Since I
Don't Have You' (originally recorded back in 1958 by The Skyliners)
and the hidden track, 'Look At Your Game Girl'. The latter was
placed untitled at the end of the album to avoid negative attention
but it didn't take long for people to notice its distinctiveness, the
song having been written by imprisoned Charles Manson.

When asked of his opinion of the crazed Manson, Axl said,
"Manson is a dark part of American culture and history. I wore the
'Charlie Don't Surf'' T–shirt to make a statement because a lot of
people enjoy playing me as the bad guy and the crazy. Sorry, I'm
not that guy. I'm nothing like him. That's what I'm saying. There's
a real difference in morals, values and ethics between Manson and
myself and that is 'Thou shalt not kill',' which I don't. I'm by no
means a Manson expert or anything, but the things he's done are
something I don't believe in. He's a sick individual. Look at Manson
and then look at me. We're not the same. I think people think I'm
crazy because I believe in telling the truth. I'll admit sometimes I
don't do a perfect job of it, but my efforts are true."

It was a somewhat messy statement but didn't disguise the fact
the song was a good one, handled perfectly by the band. Whether
it was intentional or not, Axl had unduly paid lip service to one of
the world's most famous criminals, after previously making t–shirts
with 'Charlie' eyes all the rage.

The notoriety the song achieved was not planned according to
Slash, "It was exactly what we wanted to avoid", he said. "That's
the reason why we didn't write the name of the song or Manson's
name. We didn't want to be related with him. But things never turn
out the way you want..." For Slash the attention wasn't warranted.
He didn't even play on the song, that honour went to Carlos Booy.
Axl sang one line as if he himself had written it. "There's a time for

living, time keeps on flying. Think you're loving baby, but all your doing is crying" he crooned, to a sinisterly melodic backdrop. The conclusion was, even crazed killers can write nice pop songs.

"It would be cool if our fans discovered the bands that meant so much to us. Most of the records are hard to find and several of the musicians are dead, almost everyone are broke. It didn't go well for our heroes" Slash

The beautiful Jennifer Driver, model for Guess Jeans was the subliminal subject of *Since I Don't Have You* and she is the lady in the video the band made for the song. She and Axl dated each other but didn't last long as a couple. The song itself was a fairly ambitious attempt by a band like G N' R, placed at the beginning of the album. It was an unassuming initiation to an otherwise barnstorming listening experience and could well have distanced the band from potential new recruits, despite Axl's suitability for the laid back ballad. He used one of his many voices to take on lines like "I don't have love to share and I don't have one who cares. I don't have anything since I don't have you". Although difficult to find The Skyliners original is markedly different to the Guns' interpretation, focusing less on a forefront vocal. It almost doesn't sound like the same song, which makes the G N' R version all the more commendable.

The true theme of the album seemed to be a mixture of fun and anger. Songs such as the rowdy 'I Don't Care About You' epitomised Guns' idiom. A predominantly 'punk' tribute album wouldn't have been complete without a Sex Pistols track, but the band chose a strangely sultry number in 'Black Leather'. "I met Steve Jones from the Sex Pistols at Matt's wedding" Slash said. "He asked when the record came out and if our version of Black Leather sounded better then the 'cover' the Runaways did. Absolutely, I said, it sounds better than your version too..."

The relaxed sounding album came from the stress free vibe the band enjoyed whilst recording. Gilby was a peaceful guitar player who always hit the right notes but didn't throw tantrums or question others' parts. As Slash remarked with a smile, "I love recording like this. During *Appetite For Destruction, G N' R Lies* and *Use Your Illusion* I had to put up with Izzy the whole time. I never liked playing with him. It was wonderful to escape him on this record. It sounds tighter and so much cooler than anything we've done before. I always got irritated over Izzy's way of playing. It didn't sound right. Before *The Spaghetti Incident?* we erased his guitar and Gilby put on a new one. It sounded perfect!"

It was always going to be difficult for Matt Sorum and Clarke to come into a well established band and try to replace its resident fixtures. They had their work cut out introducing their own style into the G N' R camp. In truth it was harder for fans to accept them and some felt the new members had pushed the band in the strange direction of a covers album. Nothing could have been further from the truth to those fans who knew the band inside and out.

The one downside to the album was its inconsequence in 1993. Nirvana had not only dominated the airwaves for two years, they equally had made an impression on Axl Rose. The 'Skin N' Bones' tour G N' R undertook could have been even more of an event. Axl asked Nirvana to be his support act for the tour. Kurt Cobain gracefully declined. Axl also asked Kurt to play at his 30th birthday party. Again he refused.

In an interview with *The Advocate* in February 1993, Cobain was asked two questions about Guns N' Roses:

Q: Is there anything about Guns N' Roses' music you like?
A: "I can't think of a damn thing. I can't even waste my time on that band, because they're so obviously pathetic and untalented. I used to think that everything in the mainstream pop world was crap, but now that some underground bands have been signed with majors, I take Guns N' Roses as more of an offence. I have to look into it more: They're really talent less people, and they write crap music, and they're the most popular rock band on the earth right now. I can't believe it."

Q: Didn't Axl Rose say something nasty to you at the MTV Video Music Awards in September?

A: "They actually tried to beat us up. Courtney and I were with the baby in the eating area backstage, and Axl walked by. So Courtney yelled, "Axl! Axl, come over here!" We just wanted to say hi to him – we think he's a joke, but we just wanted to say something to him. So I said, "Will you be the godfather of our child?" I don't know what had happened before that to piss him off, but he took his aggressions out on us and began screaming bloody murder. These were his words: "You shut your bitch up, or I'm taking you down to the pavement." Everyone around us just burst out into tears of laughter. She wasn't even saying anything mean, you know? So I turned to Courtney and said, "Shut up, bitch!" And everyone laughed and he left. So I guess I did what he wanted me to do – be a man".

Axl barely had an opportunity to respond to Cobain's comments, but it was surely remarks such as this, which contributed to Guns' dwindling popularity after *The Spaghetti Incident?*

Interest may have been somewhat curdled by an album without new material but the band was still experiencing its fair share of notoriety. Earlier in the year, before the show at the Estadio River Plate in Buenos Aires, Argentina, 50 police officers raided the bands dressing rooms searching for a large quantity of cocaine, allegedly stashed in one of their rooms. A squad of drug officers was also dispatched to the stadium where they searched through the band's equipment. Axl released a press statement stating all allegations were false and that the police found nothing.

Still in Argentina the band played its final show of the tour at the same venue and after the gig, Axl, Dizzy & Slash went to the hotel bar where Axl played the grand piano. The impromptu get–together continued until 5:30 a.m.

"I guess I like who I am now. I'd like to have a little more internal peace. I'm sure everybody would" Axl Rose 1992

The character of W. Axl Rose post 1993 is more complicated than ever before. When those he has known for years misunderstand and find him intolerably difficult, what chance the buying public who have helped put Axl where he is now? Faced with hearsay, speculation and a forever spinning rumour mill, is it any wonder Axl feels more comfortable retreating in all but a live environment.

The vicious circles are endless…if Axl wishes people to know the truth why doesn't he talk to the press more? But then, the whole reason he doesn't talk to the press any longer is because of the suspicion and controversy, which has dogged him since 1987. It is far easier to be a hermit trusting in the sanctity of a legal writ rather than an emotional expectation. Axl once said "I trust everybody until they fuck me over. When they do, I don't trust them any more, but I like to give everyone a fair chance at that trust."

There are those who argue it was his paranoia, which led to ousting band members in order to be in control. The megalomaniac was in effect responsible for the downfall of remaining members because he wanted control for himself all along. This was evident in the early nineties when Axl decided he would either be given complete ownership of the Guns N' Roses name, or quit the band. In hindsight Slash and Duff, who signed this agreement were somewhat upset at themselves for being so naïve. Slash said, "I was blindsided by it, more or less a legal faux pas. I'd be lying to say I wasn't a little bit peeved at that – he can actually go and record a Guns N' Roses album without the consent of the other members of the band." But it seems that Axl had always anticipated sole control – his master plan was in effect back when *Use Your Illusion* was merely a chimera.

In fairness to his band mates why would they suspect the singer would ever need to use the sole ownership against them? Could he really have planned solo work under the guise of Guns N' Roses, so long ago? Perhaps it was merely advice given from well meaning associates who had by that time geared Axl towards a more business–oriented approach? As The Doors' Jim Morrison was infamously once tempted – 'ditch the other guys, you're the real star'.

In 1987, had Axl been told this (and who is to say he wasn't from the very start) he would doubtless have snapped the neck of the plotter. Axl is loyal when he deems it right to be so. If he sees loyalty and brotherhood from his friends he will show them the same honour. Up until at least 1991, Guns N' Roses was a band of brothers with a closeness bordering on an insular family. For such a massive act, there was plenty happening behind closed doors of which no one will ever learn. This is partly because anyone who was back in the dressing rooms, hotel rooms, rehearsal rooms or anywhere Axl was housed should fear a particularly virulent lawsuit if they ever provide any information. It is not a new revelation that anybody who was associated with the band in the past tends to keep their memories to themselves.

In this aspect Axl was clearly very sensible, and whether acting on impulse or outright business advice he at least has retained dignity and the ability to keep himself as private as possible given his status. Had the band always been together in its original guise this would surely have been impossible. Painstakingly and gradually Axl has discarded ex friends and musicians like relics for which he no longer has a use. The sheer amount of new blood drafted in, and then usually out, has been staggering.

Whilst some believe it is a new Axl who has taken this approach it is stretching the truth somewhat. Over a decade ago Axl made the comment that "What I'd tell any kid in high school is "Take business classes." I don't care what else you're going to do, if you're going to do art or anything, take business classes. You can say, "Well, I don't want to get commercial," but if you do anything to make any money, you're doing something commercial. You can be flipping hamburgers at McDonald's, but you're a commercial burger flipper."

Even in earlier interviews Axl confessed the band were not "the most intelligent bunch", but he was quick to state, "as far as street sense – hanging out, doing drugs, partying, girls and shit like that – we know and understand a lot. It's like we purposely put ourselves through street school. We learned how to survive, we learned who's who in the music business. We learned how to tell when someone's full of shit. We've learned some hard lessons and had to pay some out–of–court settlements."

"He's incredibly loyal and totally has your back if you're straight with him and are loyal back. Which is why him and I have gotten along so well. I'm the same sort of person. I don't fuck around or waste my time with people who waste my time, and I don't really take up people's time if they don't want it" Tommy Stinson

In keeping with a supposed 'techno' oriented new direction, Axl brought in Moby for a short while in 1997 to work as producer on *Chinese Democracy*. The diminutive artist states that he found Axl "emotionally reserved and a little bit suspicious, he seemed a little bit like a beaten dog". This image is one hardly difficult to believe, almost giving way to the delicate human being Axl has often been perceived as. Yet would such a fragile person have the wherewith-al and sustenance to act as Axl has? He abandoned the entire band (with one keyboard playing exception) in a matter of a few years, relying on himself to carry the G N' R name. It's Guns N' Roses but not as we know it.

It harks of the paradox that is Axl Rose. Yes he can be emotionally frail, a loner. But he would rather be alone until his dying day than not stand by his convictions or discover the secret to life. Why there is still a Guns N' Roses at all is somewhat confusing. For all Axl's soul searching and desire to escape previous confines, why exactly did he retain the Guns N' Roses name? What was the reasoning be-hind clinging to the vestiges of a band he has otherwise complete-ly distanced himself from? Axl might be able to answer at any given time but the answer would often be different. It's not that Axl contradicts himself or is in any way misleading the truth, rather that his mind changes and twists itself with alarming regularity.

"Oh my distorted smile" 'My World'

However he now sees no point in talking candidly when the core of the message is swept into a tide far removed from his original intentions. Axl's mind changes so quickly sometimes he'd prefer to withdraw a comment than stand by it, yet he is so fiercely proud and defiant he stands by it nevertheless. The lyrics and comments surrounding 'One In A Million' were tantamount to this uncertainty yet outward boldness.

TREATMENT

To see where Axl resides mentally in 2003 is difficult given others' perceptions of him. Some never speak of their experiences, like the newer ex members Josh Freese and Robin Finck. Others have opinions they are willing to share but working within Axl's implanted studio practices could well have tainted these viewpoints and perhaps they are not seeing him as naturally as Slash, Duff and Izzy once did. Far more convincing is the comment from a friend that "Axl is looking for anything that will give him happiness." From 1990 onwards this is fully borne out in how the singer has (re)acted and continues to act.

Axl once said "I definitely get my share of sticks and stones and rocks and stabs from people trying to bait me into something for whatever reasons. I have a lot of damage and I'm not saying that like "Oh, pity me," or anything. Instead of being myself, I was definitely a product of my environment, and that was something G N' R has thrown back in the world's face. When you feed someone shit, and they have the balls to tell you what it tastes like, most people have a problem with that. As a child I was beaten a lot. People can't handle a troubled child who doesn't know how to accept help." This was typical of Rose in the post *Appetite...* days when he had fully experienced the perils of rock n' roll decadence. Whilst all the members

of the group experienced the same things Axl dealt with it differently, dredging up his inner self and attempting to heal his physical and
mental deficiencies.

Guitarist Tommy Stinson has had a long time to assess Axl's personality and says, "maybe he still thinks too much of what people
are expecting of him. Maybe he could try just fucking exist, and not
worry about the way people want him to be? Maybe a little bit of
that? Might be hard for him, because he's got a lot riding on it. I've
hung out with him so much to know that it's hard to be him, just because people are rabid. They get pretty weirded out. He's got some
crazy fans, and people that have been there for a long time. He's a
huge fucking rock star, man. He can barely go down the street without someone fucking throwing some curveball at him."

One of Axl's protracted beliefs and ideologies (from the *Use Your
Illusion* sessions to the present day) centres on homeopathic medicine. Like Michael Jackson, Axl has become more interested in pre-
serving and prolonging his health than destroying it. Although not
quite to the same extent of Jackson, Axl is nevertheless a somewhat
paranoid individual in both physical and mental affairs. From the
heady days of vodka, heroin and cocaine binges, a refreshed and
health conscious individual emerged, seemingly further at odds with
his ex band mates. This can be traced back to the benefit for Freddy
Mercury in 1992, which gave Axl food for thought.

He stated in a 1992 interview with *RIP* magazine "I want to learn
more and start helping people. Freddie Mercury's death is a marker in my life that says there's no turning back, and I'm going to do
whatever I can to inform the public about certain things. We can't
sit idly and hope someone will change things and hope things will
be alright. There are alternative forms of medicine that are having
high success rates in treating AIDS victims. There are things like
vibrational medicine, oxygen–ozone therapy, there are homeopathic medicines, and there are Chinese medicines and different forms
of vitamins. The government is denying the public this information.
Over the last 50 years there have been different cures for different illnesses that have been kept from us. Freddie Mercury's death
made me want to fight for people to have the right to know about

these alternative treatments. Everyone has got a God given right to health, and it's being denied by power hungry, greedy people who want control".

"You know...I've been the beggar...I've played the thief. I was the dog...they all tried to beat" '14 Years'

In the same interview Axl spoke more specifically of his own approach to health. "I'm on very specific, high tuned vitamins. My body needs these vitamins. I'm also involved in extensive emotional work to reach certain heights with myself. I'm doing several detoxing programs to release trapped toxins that are there because of trauma."

Though ex G N' R musicians may claim to be 'cleaner' than in the past they are certainly not quite as attuned to self–preservation as Axl. Given his past history of throat problems it is perfectly understandable he would use homeopathic medicines to look after his voice. He has therefore introduced Echinacea and protein shakes into the G N' R world.

"I've had a mutated form of polio, a mutated form of rubella, the swine flu, scarlet fever, and strep throat in my heart," Axl told *RIP*. "It's mostly respiratory stuff. Air conditioners in hotels circulate the same air, and on the plane everyone's breathing the same air. So if anyone's got anything, my tonsils grab it. That's one of the reasons I've never liked touring. I also found out it is supposedly some kind of mental thing having to do with me punishing myself for expressing myself. For 20 years of my life I was beaten by my parents for expressing myself so part of me believes I should be punished for that expression. I do this by lowering my own resistance. Turn that around, and there you have it – self punishment. Other than that I'm pretty healthy." A health conscious regimen which in 2005 includes kick boxing.

It would seem probable Axl would look down upon anyone who interfered with his adopted healthy lifestyle. Thus it's likely those who dabbled in narcotics would receive a typical Axl tongue–lashing. At the bands live show in Paris in 1992 Axl introduced 'Live

And Let Die' with the following diatribe. "I'd like to dedicate this song to those who try to control and manipulate you, the powers that be, the government, your family, your friends or anything else that chooses to fuck with you. You can even try to talk to some of these people you can try to be friends, you can try to work it out, but you can't save nobody else you'll be lucky if you can save your own ass. But we'll dedicate this to these people. This is called 'Live And Let Die'..."

It would be easy to dismiss the statement as representative of the verbose Axl Rose, who enjoyed nothing more than to attack the establishment at any given opportunity. Yet within his veiled criticisms of authority and opposition – it was clear he faced a battle to save himself and had given up on trying to change anybody else. Announcing he'd retreated into his own shell was simply another indication that Axl had indeed decided to concentrate on himself.

"Right now I don't want to have a child, because I can't give it enough time. But I'd want him to talk about what he listened to with me, and have him show me new things, and me show him new things. He could play me the Screaming Banshees From Hell, and I could play him Jimi Hendrix or something. We could talk about the music. We'd talk about things together. I think it's a parent's job to raise their child" Axl Rose

His mission nowadays centres on finding the elixir of life. Despite this Axl still maintains his lyrics are "worded in a way that a great number of people will be able to relate to the experiences; it's not so personalized that it's only my weird, twisted point of view." This is certainly the case and from reading particularly the newer lyrics there is no indication Axl is in a depressive mental state. He did admit however, "the next record will definitely be much more emotional. I try to write so the audience can understand what emotions I was feeling." The question is, can Axl's fans ever fully understand the emotions he feels?

Sharon Maynard, (also known as Yoda) has been the catalyst for his new found sense of self. At the time of *Use Your Illusion*, Maynard and her husband Dr. Elliott formed a close association with Axl. The Asian woman who runs a business called Arcos Cielos Corporation is based at Maynard's home in Sedona, USA (just over a hundred miles north of Phoenix). It is a non–profitable organisation that calls itself an 'educational enterprise'. The company, whose name translated from Spanish means Sky Arcs has assets somewhere in the region of $300,000.

Despite the force of Axl's convictions, which lead him to almost ruthlessly control his life he has seemingly been able to accommodate Maynard's opinions and influence for well over a decade. The downfall of the original G N' R line up coincided with roughly the time Axl brought Maynard and her 'New Age' friends on the *Use Your Illusion* tour. One crew member described them as "aliens", unable to fit in and "dressed in funny shoes".

"Yesterday, There was so many things I was never shown, Suddenly this time I found I'm on the streets and I'm all alone" 'Yesterdays'

Maynard was even responsible for a cancelled date on the bands tour with Metallica in 1992. The Minneapolis date had to be rescheduled after it was announced the magnetic fields in the area were not conducive to a harmonic environment. Is it any wonder fans have rioted and people have complained so bitterly of G N' R's treatment of its fans? Is it any wonder that Izzy, Slash and Duff walked away after revelations, which bothered Axl but no one else?

As everyone is fully aware, no Axl no G N' R show so it is perhaps unsurprising that Sharon Maynard and her 'crew' were looked at with disdain by those who depended on the G N' R ship sailing smoothly to earn their living. Simply stating that the strong magnetic field concentration meant cancelling a scheduled date does not offer justifiable explanation in most people's eyes. Deeper into the published reasons however is a more understandable explanation. It has been rumoured that Axl has undergone new scientific treatments for depression.

As of 2003 psychiatrists have been developing and conducting trials based on theories that electrical magnets can be used for treatment of mild to severe depression. Specifically the research is to target those who fail to respond to conventional drug treatments and therapy. For the minority of patients who do not improve with drugs theirs is a frustrating cycle of endless trips in and out of hospital to avoid doing themselves permanent damage. It is estimated that between 10 and 30 per cent of depression victims are in this minority. When a patient is still untreatable then, as a last resort electro convulsive therapy will be used. The method is to use electrical currents to bring on a brain seizure. This serves the purpose of restoring normal electrical brain activity.

However, doctors at the Maudsley hospital in South London have recently begun to try a more serene approach and this fits in with Axl's purported methods. Transcranial Magnetic Stimulation (TMS) targets the smallest areas of the brain where depression triggers are centred, and uses magnetic energy pulses to treat and restore them to normality. TMS has been shown to work on 50 to 70 per cent of the people who took place in trials and therefore is as effective as ECT but far less dangerous. One of the main benefits of TMS is it's a simple and painless procedure, which poses no risk of the patient having a mental seizure or fit. The image of Axl in the 'Welcome To The Jungle' video, where he is being electrocuted in a chair conjures up realistic images of his terrible past experiences in attempting to beat this depression.

The treatment for TMS might sound similar but it's a far gentler approach. A coil is lined up with the left frontal lobe (the area of the brain which is responsible for mood disorders and is only the size of a small coin). A magnetic field is sent to the brain via the coil. The treatment lasts for around 20 minutes with 10–second pulses applied with brief pauses. Usually a patient will be treated daily for two to three weeks before being assessed to determine if there has been any improvement. Side effects are mild if present at all – some patients experience mild headaches, or a sensation of a heartbeat in the head itself.

"His world is very insular, he doesn't like many people" Doug Goldstein

Ex Gunner Duff McKagan said in *Hard Force* magazine in 1999 "I am still friends with Axl, but it doesn't mean we agree on everything. But he's got a problem: too many people around him confusing his mind. To be honest, he probably doesn't live in the same world as you and me. I hope Axl won't feel like I let him down. I was just honest. I didn't wish to go on that way."

Before one scheduled show in Tokyo, at The Dome – Maynard had to gather information about the magnetic forces and atomic power sources that would be in existence whilst the band was there. There would always be trouble when Axl was under the jurisdiction of strong magnetic fields. While many people would find this amusing perhaps and at the worst deplorable – it is necessary to understand the psyche of Axl Rose and see his viewpoint of the world and the harm it can bring.

Axl trusts Maynard partly because unlike the reams of supposedly authentic psychics and healers who charge for their services and list themselves in every available business pages, Sharon Maynard retains her privacy and is so low key that the rest of the local psychic community know nothing of her or her work. These days it is customary for potential employees of G N' R to have a photo of themselves and also their sons and daughters, examined by Maynard in an attempt to hijack those with a bad aura before they taint the singers life in any way. Those who could potentially harm Axl are spurned and this in some way explains Axl's bizarre choice of hired musicians – who on the surface resembled a complete hotchpotch of personalities.

Where G N' R was once a collective, today it's a stream of multi dimensional characters who represent no threat to Axl or his enterprise. Nobody with a personality too forceful or controlling is accepted and this filter floods down into crew members, record company executives and anyone loosely connected to the band. After Axl and Stephanie Seymour broke up, in 1992, the model began dating Peter Brant. Axl sought to obtain a photograph of Brant's wife, Sandra so he could take it to Maynard.

A former Geffen employee stated: "Axl wanted to cast a spell around Sandra to protect her from Peter, because he felt that she, too, had been cuckolded as he had been, and he had a great deal of sympathy for her." Seymour was 26 at the time, and Brant (publisher of *Interview* magazine) was 48. They married in Paris, 1994 and as of 2005 are still together.

As a mark of the trust Axl puts in Maynard he once carried various gifts he had been given across the desert to Maynard for apparent psychic review. One present was a hand blown glass sphere that Axl was so worried about Sky Harbour International Airport security breaking or damaging he lost his temper. The Phoenix Police Department states Axl shouted, "I'll punch your lights out right here and right now. I don't give a fuck who you are. You are all little people on a power trip. I don't give a fuck. Just put me in fuckin' jail". The police duly obliged and Axl spent several hours behind bars. A year later Axl pleaded no contest to a misdemeanour charge and paid a $500 fine.

Axl's personality quirks are easily traced back to childhood. According to Axl his real father is now dead. He said in 1992 that his father was "A very unsavoury character". Like so many products of broken homes and a father's negligence and/or abuse Axl Rose still felt or feels incredibly attached to the father figure whether it is a subconscious desire for acceptance or a direct plea for the help he has begun to crave, and had begun to seek back when the original members were still together. Axl said of his connection to his father "I've had a problem with not wanting to be him. I had to be macho. I couldn't allow myself to be a real man, because men were evil, and I didn't want to be like my father."

Such references to grieving as if he had indeed been deprived of a father were typical of Axl's comments surrounding child abuse. In fact he lifted a lid, which in the early 90s was left untouched by famous rock stars. Since the floodgates have opened it has been common practice to trivialise the abuse so called 'famous' people claim to have been victims of but it is certain that Axl's initial comments and subsequent behaviour are linked to actual and very intense disturbances he experienced in his youth.

He believes in and promotes self–healing. Despite counselling and support of the best child abuse organisations he is insistent that the

individual must change himself or herself and this stems from the
desire to do so in the first place. This is a typical psychosomatic tool.
As television star and psychologist Dr. Phil Mcgraw often states,
'you cannot change what you don't acknowledge'.

Axl's fundamental belief for a long time has been that he must accept what happened to him, deal with the effects of it and move on.
But, as so many find in such cases the trauma experienced and the
same disturbance that is re–discovered once investigating the problem doesn't just disappear. It appears Axl is still trying to cope with
the events he has revealed to the fans about his upbringing.

*"A family is what Axl wants more than anything in life. He wants to
find within himself the ability to show affection. He's really, really
incapable of showing gratitude and affection" Friend of Axl Rose*

Axl stated in 1992 that discovery was "more important to me than
Guns N' Roses, more important to me than anything I've done so
far. Because I can relate to that more than anything. I've had such
hatred for my father and for women." A discovery about his real father he made around the same time was that he had actually been
shot at close range and murdered.

It is no surprise Axl's hatred was further fuelled by his family's insistence on trying to conceal the information he was talking of and
suggesting that the family deal with it themselves or in other words,
ignore it as if nothing ever really happened. Rather than make legal
allegations or any such potentially life–draining procedures he took
the decision to deal with his pain himself, internally. Perhaps this
was a mistake given that he was not particularly well placed to take
a break from his job and begin to organise his life but it certainly reveals a lot about his decision to become so reclusive.

In Axl's revelations he also claimed his stepfather to be one of the
most dangerous human beings he had ever met and stated that it was
important for both he and his sister to be away from him in case
anything further happened. Indeed they may forgive but certainly
never forget or neglect to take precautions. That Axl was so afraid
of his father after becoming one of the most famous individuals in

the world underlines his vulnerability on the inside. Regardless of his social persona and public image his greatest fear was not only the things that had already occurred but the same things could take place again.

Such psychological revelations are typical of the inner child, one who will only take heed from his 'master'. It is reminiscent of a young Japanese soldier who during the second world war was hiding for his life on a desert island and remained there for 25 years as a hermit, whilst adapting to the island's demands and its peoples ways of living. However, nobody had the chance of returning him to his homeland, as the only person he would take instructions from was his superior officer. A quarter of a decade later that officer travelled to the island where the Japanese soldier habituated and informed him his duty had been performed and he could return home, which the soldier did.

For Axl at least, his father will not return and even when he was here no responsibility was taken and no apology given. In turn the child begins to blame himself and the vicious inner guilt produces extreme behaviour. Sounds familiar doesn't it?

In 1992 the public viewpoint seemed to be that Axl behaved the way he did with no justification or forethought. He was guilty of ruining lives and in justifying his behaviour with tales of child abuse he wasn't living in the real world. Perhaps not, yet what exactly is the real world for a child abuse victim who has been propelled to world fame?

Axl used to wear a shirt onstage sometimes that said 'Tell Your Kids The Truth'. This was centred on his insistence parents should take responsibility for their children's upbringing and whether they had made mistakes or not their job was to help the child through it, to deal with the fact that it happened and love the child thereafter.

Axl's discovered through past life regression therapy the abuse and psychosis at work in his minds underbelly. It is certainly more understandable he now acts the way he does. Nevertheless it might take a psychiatrist to fully explain the reason why Axl believes certain people are trying to possess him. The clues were in the video for *Don't Cry* in which several characters (all forms of Axl himself) play out various roles indicating the singer is essentially made up of these parts and is in some permanent vegetative state.

In 1992 Axl gave some clue as to the ending of the video. He said "I'm still experiencing anger over this situation, but I'm trying to get over it. Burying it doesn't work for me anymore. I buried it for too long. That's why there's a gravestone at the end of the *Don't Cry* video. I watched almost everyone in this church's lives go to shit because their own hypocrisy finally consumed them." This explained the religious theme to Guns' videos like *November Rain* and *Don't Cry* and the oblique references to religion such as 'The Garden Of Eden'.

"I don't want to go solo, but there are areas I'd like to explore – maybe movies – where I might not be able to stay in the band to do it" Axl Rose

In the *Don't Cry* video, a black mini skirted therapist who watches over Axl in therapy was a real life psychotherapist, Suzzy London who like Maynard and Elliott actually toured with the band. At the time Axl said of his psychological work, "With my therapist, I work on releasing my unconscious mind. Unless your true self is in pain, why would you want to be detached from it? Yet most people are detached. Who knows how to go back and heal their own pain? Having help and being able to accept it is a lot stronger and sometimes easier. I found someone I trust and can work with. It probably sounds very weird, but the important thing is that it's working. I have certain emotional, mental and physical problems that I don't want to have to live with any longer than I have to, so I'm obsessed with getting over them. The only way a person can tell if they need help is if underneath however happy you think you are, you know that you're miserable. I've been miserable for a long fucking time, and now I'm not so miserable."

Many, if not all who watched it considered the *Don't Cry* video nonsensical and ambiguous, but Axl was presenting his fans and detractors with a shrouded yet effective commentary into his soul. It was either a plea for help or a snigger at his own insanity but the certainty is he gave us all clues to his mental state. Part of the trilogy, which he promised would make sense of each individual video (the others were *Estranged* and *November Rain*) it featured a strong theme of rebirth and finished with an apologetic retort which simply read, "There's a lot goin' on". This made light of Axl's own circumstances and was as cryptic as the video itself.

Suzzy London was most probably the trusted therapist who oversaw Axl's past life regression during which he became convinced he had lived several lives before and that he and Stephanie Seymour had been together in fifteen or sixteen of those lives. His earliest conscious memory was of a feeling that he had been here before and that he had a toy gun in his hand. He knew it was a toy gun but wasn't sure how he knew. The regression back to the exact point of conception gave Axl the realisation that his birth was not exactly welcomed or planned. He was made aware of his mother's problems, which arose from the pregnancy. This along with the discovery that his Father treated both he and his mother badly gave Axl justifiable hatred for his father. According to therapy Axl had hated his father from birth because he knew deep down how his pregnant mother had been treated. Consequently he blacked out most of his childhood. Relentless nightmares would lead to him falling out of the bunk beds he and his sister slept in. His teeth would pierce through his bottom lip. The nightmares continued unexplained for years.

THE WOMEN

"I'm a person that has a lot of different relationships. It's really hard to maintain a one on one relationship if the other person is not going to allow me to be with other people. I have a real open, hedonistic, sexual attitude. I think love and lust go hand in hand, like good and evil. One without the other is not complete, but I don't tell someone I'm in love with them if I'm not. I never have" Axl Rose 1990

Axl allegedly told Erin Everly that he and Seymour were sisters in a past life and wanted to kill her. Erin sued Axl in 1994 and testified to this effect. She said, "Axl had told me that in a past life we were Indians and that I killed our children and that's why he was so mean to me in this life". Axl was also charged with assault and sexual battery. Everly claimed Axl had told her John Bonham, the late Led Zeppelin drummer who died in his sleep in 1980, possessed him.

There was the famed incident at the MTV awards in 1992 where backstage, Axl confronted Kurt Cobain and his wife Courtney Love. Later Axl confided in a friend he believed Love was trying to possess him, insistent that many people were constantly trying to find a window through his soul to try and control his energy.

"A lot of people hold their anger back for a few days. I just explode right away" Axl Rose

During his marriage to Everly, Axl went for an exorcism. "Mainly it involved getting some kind of herbal wrap," he admitted, "some work on my skin." Axl was charged $72,000 for the privilege, saying, "I ended up getting ripped off for a lot of money in the long run." It seems treatment is not always beneficial, though Axl it appears, is willing to try anything once, just as in his days of excess. What is the difference between trying to find the secret of life in varying forms of spirituality, and getting mindlessly high to escape life itself? The difference is simply a willingness to face up to your pain and try to banish it.

Slash's former girlfriend Meegan Hodges–Knight, was Erin Everly's roommate and at the court case testified against Axl. Hodges–Knight claimed she would "wake up to Erin saying, 'Please stop. Don't hurt me, don't hurt me,' and Axl screaming at her, and then all of a sudden he'd come out and he'd break all of her really precious antiques, and she would say, 'Please don't break them, please.' And trying to get them back from him. And he'd push her and he'd break everything he could get his hands on. I remember sleeping and waking up to crystal flying over my head, shattering on the floor."

There were times when Slash was witness to the couples huge arguments but according to his ex girlfriend he would suggest to her she should not try and calm Axl down or stop the argument as it would "make it worse."'

Hodges–Knight claimed that Axl had dragged Everly around by the hair one night when she was wearing a see through tank top and panties, threw a television set at her (which missed), kicked her with his cowboy boots and spat on her. She referred to him as a "pig" for doing so. Everly testified Axl had sexually assaulted her. Apparently he ordered her to remove a bathing suit she was wearing. He then tied her hands to her ankles from behind, put masking tape over her mouth and a bandana around her eyes, leading her, naked into a closet, where she remained for several hours while Axl talked to a friend of hers in the living room.

When the friend had gone Axl was alleged to have untied her, picked her up and tied her again, face down, to a convertible bed. "He forced himself on me anally really hard. Really hard," Everly declared. She was screaming while this occurred and when it was over Axl "took it out and stuck it in my mouth."

There is an unreleased video version of *It's So Easy*, which depicts Everly in bondage gear, with a red ball in her mouth as Axl screams, "See me hit you! You fall down!" It is alleged by one of Axl's former employees he was insistent on the master tapes for the video being destroyed once Everly went to court against him. There are several parallels with Mike Tyson, someone whom Axl is said to admire. Not only have they both had histories of personal depression but also their respective love lives have been torrid experiences involving one break up after another. In 1991 Axl stayed in the very same suite in the Indianapolis hotel where Mike Tyson raped Desiree Washington.

Lawsuits were becoming a large part of Axl's life. Stephanie Seymour claimed Axl had beaten her, though Axl claimed he acted in self–defence after she grabbed his testicles – in one incident he dragged her barefoot through broken glass after an argument where he had shattered several bottles. She alleged he had "repeatedly hit her about the head and upper body and kicked her abdomen."

"You better back off, back off bitch, Face of an angel with the love of a witch" 'Back Off Bitch*

The cases brought against Axl were eventually settled with an undisclosed fee passing to both women. A source close to Rose, 33, told *Parade* magazine the insurance company representing the rock star agreed to pay $400,000 to supermodel Seymour, 26, to settle the 2 year old case out of court. "The papers still aren't signed," said the source, "but Axl won't do any talking. He's concentrating on his work." Axl's lawyers told the magazine: "Both parties agreed to dismiss their claims against each other. The litigation has been resolved." There was a denial of any payment being made however.

It is difficult to know what really happened in each incident, there are those who will claim Axl is an easy target and is being taken for a financial ride. Perhaps the same people who might sympathise with the likes of Mike Tyson. Are these people savage animals who abuse others or are they innocent victims of fame and fortune? There were never criminal charges pressed against Axl after the incidents were resolved out of court.

When he and Stephanie were still an item Axl claimed she had helped him deal with his regression and revelations. He claimed they were simply very close friends with a romantic edge. In the *Making Of November Rain* video this closeness is evident behind the scenes when both he and Stephanie talk separately of their parts in the video and Seymour in particular elaborates on her vision for the future.

It was rumoured Axl would have married Seymour if it weren't for the young age of her son Dylan. Axl loved her son and took umbrage when Seymour threw a lavish cocaine party in Axl's mansion whilst Dylan was present. The suing followed Axl putting a restraining order on *her*.

Asked in 2002 whether he was currently in a relationship Axl laughed and replied somewhat tongue in cheek "no, I don't have any significant others as yet." Supposedly when Stephanie Seymour's birthday came around Axl appeared to shut down for weeks. A regular employee at the studio where Guns' have been working on *Chinese Democracy* says, "A lot of this record is about Stephanie: She was his perfect woman, at least his image of what she should be."

STEPHANIE SEYMOUR PROFILE

Height: 5'10"
Birthday : July 23rd 1968
Hometown : San Diego, California, USA
Occupation : Super Model, IMC Agency
Has Married:
Tommy Andrews (1989–1990)
Peter Brant (1994–Present)
Romantic Links:
Warren Beatty, John Casablancas, Axl Rose
Children:
Dylan Thomas Andrews, 1990
Peter Brant Jr., 1993
Harry Brant, 1997

At the age of 14, supermodel Stephanie Seymour began to model in San Diego. At 15 years old, she entered the Elite Look of the Year Contest but did not win. John Casablancas was then President of Elite Models, and he took a shine to Seymour and eventually started to go out with her. Success as a model then followed, but it was paired with stories of drinking and drug abuse. (In interviews, Stephanie has come across as a Jennifer Capriati type character, referring to a hard–partying lifestyle at a very young age.)

In 1989, Stephanie married rock musician Tommy Andrews, to whom she had a son named Dylan; however Stephanie had an affair with Warren Beatty and soon divorced Andrews. It was while dating Warren Beatty, that Stephanie met Axl and immediately ditched Warren for Axl (this is also why Axl Rose refers to Beatty in the televised Paris 1992 show). After the split with Axl Seymour married Peter Brant and they had two sons together. Seymour still actively models, and her most famous fashion alignment has been Victoria's

Secret. Stephanie's 10–year relationship with Victoria's Secret finished in 2000, and she is said to be pursuing "other opportunities."

November Rain Wedding Dress & Video facts:
Wedding dress: $8,000, Specially constructed coffin: $8,000, Renting a symphony orchestra: $25,000, Specially constructed chapel: $150,000, Total cost of the video: $1,500,000+

ERIN EVERLY PROFILE

Name: Erin Everly
Birth date: 1967
Occupation: Former Model
Romantic connections with:
Axl Rose, Matthew Nelson, Anthony Kiedis, Donovan Leitch Jr, David Arquette

"I cry every time I think how horrible we treated each other. Erin and I treated each other like shit. Sometimes we treated each other great cos the children in us were best friends but then there were other times where we completely ruined each others life" Axl Rose

In 1998 Everly gave birth to a son named Eason with her husband, an unknown Atlanta businessman. They live together in Atlanta where Erin has since shunned the public's eye. The song 'Oklahoma' from the *Chinese Democracy* album is inspired by a court date with Everly. Axl said "I was sitting in litigation with my ex wife and it was the day after the Oklahoma bombing. We had a break and I'm sitting with my attorneys with a sort of smile on my face, more like a nervous thing, it was like 'forgive me people I'm having trouble taking this seriously'. It's just ironic that we're sitting there and this person is spewing all kinds of things and 168 people just got killed. And this person I'm sitting there with, she don't care. Obliterating me is their goal."

THE BUSINESS

"I'm going to do what I want to do. That may be selfish, but it's the best way for me. I couldn't say I'm the leader, like "We're gonna do what I say." It doesn't work that way" Axl Rose 1989

"One side of me is experimental and the other side of me wants to make something that people can get into, and I Don't Know fucking why! Why Am I Like This? And I'm sitting there thinking, I've got 20 more years of...that to look forward to? I'm already like that...20 more years? What am I going to do?" Axl once remarked on becoming friends with David Bowie whom he felt some similarity with after an initial fall out. Afterwards he had long conversations with Bowie and discovered a dark side, which illuminated him at the possibility of him being even crazier than he already was, as he got older. This experience alone seemed to drastically change Axl.

Touring with the Rolling Stones undoubtedly sparked another influence. Although Axl had always been something of a control freak, when he witnessed Mick Jagger's ruthless business streak it seemed to stir something inside him. While he made comments that Slash should take note of regarding the Stones' work ethic ("after working with Jagger it was like, don't anybody ever call me a dictator again. You go work for the Stones and you'll find out the hard way what working for a real dictator is like!") He then subsequently became a very similar operator. From Axl's own insistence that Jagger literally walked off stage to immerse himself in paper work it seemed something he admired.

He stated that Jagger was "involved in every little aspect of the show, from what the backing singers are getting paid to what a particular part of the PA costs to buy or hire. He is on top of all of it." Co–workers would empathise rather than sympathise given that their end of the wedge was noticeably thinner than Axl's. In short he took on the responsibility of the Guns N' Roses name in every aspect.

Though Axl claimed that he "doesn't sit around checking the gate receipts at the end of every show" he did concede that somebody

had to take the responsibility of front man and that "the guitar player can't do it because he is not the guy who has to be communicating directly with the audience with eye–contact and body movements. He can go back, hang his hair down in his face and stand by
the amps and just get into his guitar part."

However much he loathed some parts of the business he was always quick to admit he was happy to be in the position his band had
reached. He once said, "Trying to handle success is a pain in the ass.
It's really strange and takes some getting used to. I've never had
my place to live before, never had to deal with the amount of money we've made and not get ripped off, never understood doing your
taxes and all these things. I hated it a few months ago, trying to get
organized and trying to get a place to live and to get a grip on everything. But now things are coming together. I've wanted to be here
my whole life."

Eventually all the band had achieved, including a gross profit of
£57.9 million dollars in the period of 1988 to 1992 was to be tam-
pered with and used in everything from court cases to recording and
making lavish video presentations. Not to mention paying for dam-
ages after riots or show cancellations. This kind of income was distinctly rare for a new band, the likes of Paul McCartney and David
Bowie might enjoy regular earnings in the millions bracket but only
after a sustained career and a back catalogue featuring scores of albums.

G N' R had three full–length albums to their name. In court Axl described the bands shrewd way of dividing their earnings between the
respective members, which came after the 17.5 per cent commission
paid to management. Axl commented, "Slash devised a system of
figuring out who wrote what parts of a song or part of a song. There
were four categories, I believe. There were lyrics, melody, music –
meaning guitars, bass and drums – and accompaniment and arrangement. And we split each one of those into twenty five percent. When
we had finished, I had forty one percent, and other people had different amounts."

"Axl's whole visionary style, as far as his input in Guns N' Roses is completely different from mine. I just like to play guitar, write a good riff, go out there and play as opposed to presenting an image"
Slash

There are often legal threats made, at the hands of influential and powerful lawyers to try and prevent, or control certain things being said about Axl. Ex manager Alan Niven has been threatened with a lawsuit recently for allegedly breaching a confidentiality agreement in talking to magazines. Niven was warned to withdraw comments he made in *Rolling Stone*. Failure to do so would result in "swift and sure legal action".

Yet is this Axl's own form of control or has it always been a case of the business controlling a band who were instantly far bigger than they could have expected? Even after Vicky Hamilton's tenure with the band was amicably ended, she had to sign an agreement, which essentially meant she could not give details of her time with the band. She joked "I could tell you about the old days, but I'd have to kill you first!" when I spoke to her regarding this book.

Axl's lawyer Bert Deixler is one constant business companion who is well equipped to handle whatever legal wrangling affects Guns N' Roses. Doug Goldstein is the only remaining employee from 1987 – a manager and friend Axl clearly trusts. It is not, as some have suggested merely because Goldstein does anything and everything Axl wants. There have been bust ups, for instance due to the confusion when Goldstein supposedly booked a tour without telling Axl!

To some, this was a convenient person for Axl to blame and was in fact simply because he did not want to tour that he pulled out. According to one industry resource Goldstein is lumbered with Axl and will do anything to please him. "If Axl says, 'Jump,' he says, 'Fine,' If he's in the air, he says, 'How much higher?' says the source. However there is another possible explanation that says the pair has an unbreakable bond. If anyone other than Goldstein had made such a mistake they might not have been around for too much longer.

Gilby Clarke was one of the most unfortunate members of the band in terms of his 'rolling' contract, which saw him regularly leave or get the sack. Eventually he was fired for good. His lawyer Jeffrey Light wrote in an April 14th, 1994 letter to G N' R lawyer Laurie Soriano "As you are aware, Gilby has been fired at least three times by the band in the past month and has been rehired at least two times". Clarke sued the band in 1995 after he did not receive his appropriate portion of band royalties. Clarke maintains he did not want to go to court but no one in the band or the management staff would return his calls. G N' R counter sued. Eventually the matter was settled with an undisclosed payment to Clarke.

After a reported advance from Geffen for $10 million Guns N' Roses were supposed to begin the recording for the follow up to the *Use Your Illusion* albums yet instead, they tinkered with cover versions due to be released years earlier. *The Spaghetti Incident?* met with confusion amongst many fans and was to be the commercial downslide for G N' R, though it sold well, especially for a covers album – it was nevertheless dwarfed by sales of the bands previous work and it coincided with Axl's personal circumstances deteriorating.

Axl was spending more and more time in court. He and Seymour constantly argued viciously at home in Malibu and promptly split up for good. Axl viewed Seymour as the only woman he wanted to marry and have children with so he was severely depressed by the latest in a long line of disappointments. "The split had an enormous effect on him," a friend commented. "That was the first time in his life had stability. And then he had nothing."

ANONYMITY

"There were people who used to go down on sunset behind Tower records in L.A. and would purposely go to get their pictures taken by paparazzi. You could do that if you wanted to. But it's just not my world" Axl Rose 2003

Part of Axl's desire to remain anonymous has doubtless been precipitated by the media's failure to portray him in the way he feels appropriate. Whether or not they will ever play by his rules is uncertain but one thing is; Axl rarely plays by theirs. He is no stranger to heartbreak and pain – that many fail to see this and simply label him as a whiny rock star with more money than sense is surely what fuels his reclusive habits.

He has in recent years lost friends close to him along with his mother; Sharon Bailey who died in May 1996 aged fifty one. Later in the same year there were local fires, which threatened the forestry housing Axl's property. In May of 1997, one of Axl's loyal friends (and sometime song writing partner) West Arkeen died of a drug overdose. He was thirty six years old. It's not the only friend Axl has lost. Another overdose, this time of alcohol, claimed the life of Jetboy bassist Todd Crew who had been a long time friend of G N' R. Axl felt tinged with despair. He said, "I regret not talking to Todd before he went To New York. I felt a massive need to talk to him out of concern for his well being. But I wasn't aware enough to realize I didn't have the time I thought I did. I thought I'd have time later…"

Axl, speaking in a radio interview in 2003 was indignant about pressures he experiences in the public eye. "I really only go to clubs where I know the people who work there, so I can have some privacy and hang out. It's hard when you go to a club with 600 people and you end up having to talk to 400 people. You have no time of your own to have fun. Maybe if I haven't gone out for a week, I'll go to the Cathouse, because I know some friends are going to be there. I just want to be around my friends, even if we don't talk about anything. I just need it. You have all these people asking you for an autograph, and it gets kind of embarrassing. I don't want to be a prick to people and go, "Get away from me." But I don't enjoy going someplace and just signing autographs all the time. It comes with the fame, but sometimes it gets out of hand and people can be very rude and obnoxious about it. I've had people break into my hotel room with cameras, waking me up and taking photos. People find out where I live and show up at my building. I've never asked anyone for an autograph."

Such comments were at odds with the personable character the general public have encountered when they've noticed Axl out and about. In September 2003 Axl was spotted in a coffee shop in Orange County, California. A drummer from a local band Tyranis, Adam Capilouto and his sister Alexis Tyranis, approached Axl and asked for a photograph. Capilouto asked if he was who he thought it was, Axl replied "Right on dude, you got it right."

"He was real nice," said Capilouto, "but he didn't want to draw attention to himself because he was eating lunch with a couple of friends. He didn't say anything about what he was working on – he wanted to talk to me about what I was doing and where I was from. We had a five minute conversation and he signed my shirt. He was cool."

Axl said in early 2003, "Basically I don't go looking to promote myself unless there's some kind of product to put out that I think is worth it. We've been working on this band and trying to get things right for a long time and if I do interviews it just gets turned around so much by people around the world who don't have anything better to do than try to shoot people down and that was just too draining to deal with anybody else. It's interesting in L.A. there are places that I go to all the time but suddenly after MTV Music awards I go to these places and suddenly there's paparazzi and it's like "Axl's out!" and it's like, I was here last weekend and you didn't care!"

Axl is happy to control his day to day existence, along with the final say in what Guns N' Roses actually does. This, it seems is enough for him. He has managed to circumnavigate the rumours and criticism to lead a life of a virtual hermit. As Los Angeles resident and writer Ruben Macblue says, "Axl lives as a recluse in Malibu, no one ever sees him."

Despite being spotted in coffee shops or at live shows, Axl is relatively alone when it comes to his dwellings. This is one of the reasons the *Chinese Democracy* album has taken so long, much like the time when Axl was late for a live show because he was watching a basketball game on TV. As he now is in sole control of the Guns N'

Roses name there is little anyone can do to make him work when he doesn't want to or when he's not in the right frame of mind. Not to mention, trying to release a record before it's ready. Most of Axl's G N' R business is conducted via telephone and though he owns a computer, it is not used as often. He believes the Internet is pretty much a "garbage can".

Axl resides in a Mediterranean type complex near the Point Dume area of Malibu, California. The property follows on from Latigo Canyon Road. Originally Axl saw the house as an ideal setting for he and Stephanie to raise their children. Instead he has become one of the world's most famous bachelors. Though many see him as a loner he is still comforted by those he trusts and loves. He is rarely alone (he even has a live–in home help) there is usually someone in the vicinity. Like his old buddy Slash, Axl keeps tanks full of snakes and lizards and his regular visiting human companions include friends and some of his close remaining family members.

Axl's sister Amy Bailey, who once ran the Guns N' Roses fan club, and his half brother Stuart Bailey have been Axl's guests on many occasions. Masseuse Sabrina Okamoto has also stayed with Axl. She was the official G N' R masseuse after meeting the band while they were touring with Skid Row but remained working personally for Axl after the various original members disappeared one by one.

According to Fernando Lebeis, who works for Axl, "everybody loves him, he's always willing to hear what you have to say. He pays very well, and always wants to know what's happening, but don't lie to him, if you do it he says: 'Well, if you're gonna lie to me, better do it in another place'."

"Axl gets angry when people feel pity for him, thinking he might be sad. He's happy!" Fernando Lebeis

Axl has a personal chauffeur named Beta Lebeis (either Beta or her son Fernando drive him everywhere) who used to work for Stephanie Seymour as a babysitter for her son Dylan. Wherever Axl travels Beta can often be found alongside him. According to those close to Axl, Beta is the closest he has ever had to a real mother. The

image is of a man living out his childhood due to being financially secured enough to construct it as he wishes. There are many parallels with the life of Michael Jackson. A life of abuse from a father
who wanted to consistently beat sense into his children and a mother who was too scared to intervene or just accepted it.

A resultant success in the music business only saw a growing up
session in public – unable to deal with the intense spotlight into
their respective lives they have shunned gatherings other celebrities would fall over themselves to attend. Where no one would suggest Axl is quite as 'Wacko' as Mr Jackson is in many people's eyes,
there are nevertheless enough similarities to be linked to the world
of show business, which can both make and break its success victims. As many do in the insular world of multi millionaire musical
self employment Axl tends to work at night and sleep during the day
– who's to say he wouldn't be found walking the streets alone many
nights, as he portrayed in the *November Rain* video?

As just one of many celebrities in the Latigo Canyon area (beach
volleyball star Gabrielle Reece is one of his neighbours) Axl finds
solace in living amongst a slew of camera shy personalities. He
guards his privacy with strenuous constancy making sure his four–
acre gardens are dwarfed by a succession of trees and a fence, which
shrouds the inner happenings. However, drivers on the Pacific Coast
highway are able to spot the singers dwelling quite easily, a lighted
star on the side of the house can be seen for miles.

His property is of a relative value to the area, a standard $4 million
(his mortgage has been being paid off since around 1992 at a rate of
approximately $15,000 a month).

The large grounds feature immaculate gardens, which are attended to regularly. Axl is not unique in owning a tennis court (which is
used as a parking lot for guests when Axl hosts a party) and his own
pool, whilst flowing water gives the gardens a peaceful effect.

Though you are unlikely to see him on 'MTV Cribs' Axl is not entirely antisocial, again much like Michael Jackson he retains a childlike innocence, which sees him happy to throw parties for friends
and their children. When Halloween comes around he is wont to
throw a costume party sparing no expense to fully 'theme' his gar-

dens and grounds. He even provides specially constructed forts and mazes for the kids to play in. He can often be found joining in. There are usually two kinds of parties, one for adults and another for the kids. Axl is good friends with Fernando who says of the parties: "He throws two kind of parties: the first one is during daytime, for children, friend's kids and poor kids, abused by their parents, blind... About a hundred kids attend and when they arrive at the house, they become amazed, he builds a kind of amusement park with toys and everything else. The other one is for adults. We serve the best tequila one can buy. We even rented a tequila fountain. This is one of the few parties Axl gives, people used to think his house is surrounded by booze and loud music, but that's not true."

In 2003 Axl "cancelled Thanksgiving" as it didn't fit in with his timetable. "I'm trying not to do that with Christmas, since New Years comes up right away" he remarked soberly.

THE FUTURE

"In interviews, anything that I would say, would turn around and be used against me in these various behind the scenes court cases and they were all very very complicated. Things lasted for years, in all kind of cases that the public doesn't really know about yet. And it's little, by little time for me to talk about those things, but I'm more interested in having the music talk first, then I'll say what happened later" Axl Rose 2002

In 2002 Axl issued a statement, which was written both in a legal manner, dismissing Matt Sorum as a "former employee" and also in Axl's more expected sarcastic and jovial tone. His parting line was, "Power to the people, peace out and blame Canada." In his own words the song 'Oh My God', "deals with the societal repression of deep and often agonizing emotions – some of which may be willingly accepted for one reason or which (one that promotes a healing, release and a positive resolve) is often discouraged and many times denied. The appropriate expression and vehicle for such emotions and concepts is not something taken for granted."

The words of the song are more poignant given this description. Sample lyrics include:

"What can I do when there's so many liars that crawl through your veins?"

And a reference it seems to his Father, "How long can you bear him to come back and haunt you. To burn past your feelings and cause you to suffer."

The final statement from Axl Rose and Guns N' Roses has yet to be heard but it should be well worth waiting for. There is no doubt when Axl speaks people listen and though they might not understand his intentions or his methods, there are those who want to understand. In typical style Axl pulled out of an agreement with *Rolling Stone* magazine to write an exclusive account of the Guns N' Roses break up. Although he had reportedly written a 10,000 word description of his version of events, the day after it was promised to the magazine, Doug Goldstein pulled out of the agreement and has since severed all contact with *Rolling Stone*.

As always the life of Guns N' Roses is an unpredictable one and a legend still lives on in the heart of a man who defines the rock n' roll spirit more so than any other contemporary star. He may not appreciate the incessant public eye, but it's here for Axl Rose anytime he wants it.

"There goes the challenger being chased
By the blue blue meanies on wheels
The vicious traffic squad cars are
After our lone driver
The last American hero
The the electric sintar
The demi–god,
The super driver of the golden west!
Two nasty Nazi cars are close behind
The beautiful lone driver
The police cars are getting closer–closer...

Closer to our soul hero in his soul mobile– yeah baby!
They about to strike, they gonna get him, SMASH! RAPE!
The last beautiful free soul on this planet

But...it is written if the Evil Spirit
Arms the Tiger with claws
Brahman provided wings for the Dove
Thus spake the Super Guru"

Recited by Axl Rose on 'Breakdown' from 'Use Your Illusion II'. (Dialogue originally from Cleavon Little in the film 'Vanishing Point').

Will Guns N' Roses Ever Reunite With Slash, Duff, Steven And Izzy?

"Writers have to understand where we're coming from and hopefully print it that way. I've tried to be very open. Everything's in pieces and distorted. I understand that everybody wants to print the dirt – that sells magazines – but you should first try to find out if the dirt is true" Axl Rose

Slash and Axl have not spoken to each other for half a decade. Relationships with other ex members and Axl seemed to be strained and whilst there is no direct animosity a reunion would all depend on Axl's consent. On evidence seen elsewhere in this book that scenario seems unlikely. The end of Axl and Slash as a partnership was effectively the end of the old Guns N' Roses. Work for the double live album *Live Era '87–'93* was handled by Axl and the ex members separately, with Axl and Slash only communicating via their respective managers Doug Goldstein and Tom Maher.

While Duff and Slash happily worked together, Axl would be sent CDs and worked on alternate shifts to the other members in the studio. It was the final admonishment for the old line up.

In 2003 the ex members of G N' R, Slash, Duff and Matt Sorum came in to public view with a new band called Velvet Revolver (and if ever there were a subliminal dig at an old band that name is it!) It is here we find a link that is tenuous to say the least. While there will always be those loyal to their favourite gunner from the early days it has to be said that Axl has kept the G N' R name alive (however meekly) for the last decade almost single handed and is therefore the only one relevant to G N' R at the present time. Whether it is simply a media habit or something the fans are genuinely interested in and curious of ever happening, the subject of a reunion with the original line up has long been a topic of conversation and the familiar G N' R subject matter of 'rumour'.

Regarding Velvet Revolver, Matt Sorum has stated, "This is probably the best thing I've ever done. Everyone just seems to be more focused and there aren't those same distractions like alcohol, drugs and chicks. We have a certain name to live up to I think and we have to represent that. That's why it took us so long to find a singer. We waited for years to do something together because there was either a lot of apprehension or a lot of nervousness because we never thought we could be as great as the thing we once had."

Interestingly an irony that seems to be at odds with Sorum's current opinion is the things distracting the G N' R camp have not only dissipated somewhat but really were part of the bands public appeal. How many of the public want to read about clean living healthy guys pretending to still be punks? Not quite the legends of rock. Whereas Axl himself has cleaned up to the point of being freakishly healthy, at least physically he still contains the spark which has always been there – his temper and his intense drive and passion. Not to mention selfishness. Without this all consuming self–preservation he would surely have cracked by now and given up Guns N' Roses as a bad job or indeed gone for the easy option, the only option Slash would have accepted.

"Hopefully some time soon the press will want to talk to him about the positive shit that is going on in his life now. Not just about drugs and drink like the way they always do. But when people come to see Guns N' Roses, they come to see one person, we know that" Tommy Stinson

With reverence to his ex band mate Slash states, "There will never come a time when we get all together and play under the name Guns N' Roses because it's too fuckin' tainted. If Axl had done the solo thing, then we could have gotten together and jammed for one show. Now it's like, over with. He screwed that up. We're not going to go and do every big Guns N' Roses hit. But we have no problem with our history as long as it's not pushing Scott (Weiland) into something he's not into."

Slash spoke of the bands concoction with candid and observational eloquence. "I had played on Izzy's solo stuff and on Duff's stuff and Matt and I had jammed together here and there. But we never formally joined up for a group until now because subconsciously we weren't comfortable with the idea of being Guns N' Roses without actually 'being' Guns N' Roses. The Guns 'thing' is bigger than all of us. The reality of it is I'll forever be known as 'Guns N' Roses' guitarist Slash'. But we just never hooked up until the sad fact of Randy dying brought me and Duff and Matt together and when we did that was a huge, powerful moment."

Whilst being very commendable as far as Velvet Revolver is concerned it is more or less the end of that bands association with Guns N' Roses. Ironically all the ex members long to escape from G N' R, despite it being the sole reason they have complete musical freedom in 2005. For the personal factors that are involved the ex members appear to be in a happier place in their new band. As Matt Sorum has said in reference to VR singer Scott Weiland, "Scott is a walk in the park compared with the other guy! I'll put it to you Scott's a sweetheart and not that Axl wasn't a sweetheart sometimes but…" Speaking of the bands then plans to record the follow up to *The Spaghetti Incident?* Matt Sorum reflected on the policy of revolving band members when reacting to the question of Gilby Clarke's firing from the band.

"We all got a phone call, he's out," said Sorum. "And we were kind of bummed out 'cause we really like Gilby. He's a really nice guy. Now he's suing us." After Slash took songs he claimed Axl had not wanted to use for G N' R Slash formed the band Slash's Snakepit, and toured for six months causing further friction for Guns N' Roses. Sorum said, "Axl got pissed 'cause he wanted to work. Then there was a bit of a problem between the two of them. That's been sort of ongoing for a while and then they just weren't getting along."

"When I tried to bring Zakk and Slash together, that didn't go too well. It was like watching a giant snake with a tyrannosaurus rex. So it was pretty exciting, I mean we had a good time, I don't know if they did" Axl Rose

With rather amusing hindsight it is intriguing to look further into Sorum's comments at the time of his side project with McKagan, The Neurotic Outsiders seemed on the verge of something special. After being signed by Madonna's Maverick label and attracting guests such as Iggy Pop and Billy Idol, Sorum stated his thoughts as this: "I think Neurotic Outsiders is single handedly responsible for Guns N' Roses being reunited. It seems like every time something good starts happening, I get a phone call from Axl, 'We're going to start rehearsing tomorrow.' But seriously, when Axl heard that me and Duff had gone out and gotten this multi million dollar record deal and we're going to go out on the road, he started getting a little nervous."

Perhaps the most obvious indictment of Axl came when Sorum said, "Basically our band is about no egos. All of us have been in bands with singers, lead singers, and they're difficult. Lead singers are just difficult. They just are. I'm sorry. If you don't hold an instrument in your hand, then you're just going to be a pain in the ass." It is not with much wonder that Sorum was soon to be left out of future G N' R plans. In Axl's view these kinds of comments were unnecessary displays of a man with an instrument in hand that had gotten too big for his boots.

"Looking through this point of view, there's no way I'm gonna fit in don't ya tell me what my eyes see, don't ya tell me who to believe in"
'Garden Of Eden'

When Axl spoke onstage at Rock In Rio in 2001 and announced to the crowd: "People worked very hard to do everything they could so I could not be here today. Fuck that. I am as hurt and disappointed as you that, unlike Oasis, we could not find a way to all just get along," he put paid to rumours that he was the cause of the break up and insinuated there was an inner circle gathering against his ways of doing things which he only believed were right for Guns N' Roses.

Slash, felt the complete opposite as he proved when speaking in 1996. He was of the opinion it was indeed Axl's own hand that had forced the others from the fold and commented "I just wish Axl

would get this Guns N' Roses record done so I can see what this tur-
moil was all about. What was the point? Realistically you have a
situation where it was all centred around one person; you're going,
'What is it you want to do so bad that you forced everybody out like
that?" I just want him to do what it is that makes him happy, because
he seems so frustrated."

His comments were almost confrontational suggesting Axl was
discontented and should therefore release either the record of the
century, or be forced to reunite with the original members. His
words suggested Axl must prove everybody wrong with *Chinese
Democracy*, it had to be better than anything Slash, Duff or Izzy
could have written.

Speaking with hindsight of the band in *Classic Rock*, 2002 Duff remarked, "Slash is having a baby. It's changed him so much already.
I have two daughters, a beautiful wife, and a house. So any kind
of reunion would have to be a real relaxed, family type affair, like
it was in the beginning. I talk to Izzy all the time, see him around.
So does Slash. We're friends. It's not worth screwing that up. You
know, Izzy had to leave last time to save his life, he got clean of heroin and he had to get out." His conclusion of the whole saga G N'
R wise was "We went through so much, I mean, not like war or anything, but a lot. There are things that I can only talk to them about.
Things that not even my wife, who I sleep with every night, knows,
because she wouldn't understand that stuff. It was pretty heavy stuff.
The 'Loaded' album deals with that. It's a little snapshot of a guy's
life. A guy who's talking about life after seeing some pretty heavy
stuff. I mean, in my 20s they were pretty fucking intense".

Of course, like many of his ex band friends Duff was talking whilst
playing with his Loaded project which like the others, people were
initially interested in only to lose momentum after the album itself
surfaced. Good solid rock n' roll material might sell a few copies but
it is certainly not going to raise the stakes publicity wise and without Axl involved or at the very least without the trademark G N' R
logo behind their heads, the remaining ex members seem somewhat
less out of the ordinary. Usually the public seem only to be interest-

ed in what they have to say about the G N' R days or the possibility of a reunion.

"I left Guns N' Roses because the band didn't correspond to me anymore. What's left of the band has nothing to do with what we had created. I even think what's left is not Guns N' Roses" Duff

You have to sympathise somewhat with members who (in their view) were ousted from a band they claim they wanted to stay remain part of; especially as since they have been subjected to constant comparisons with G N' R. Yet you also must admire the vision of Axl Rose who, if he gets it right when he emerges again publicly, foresaw the necessary action over a decade ago. He realised Guns N' Roses was bigger than all of its parts even at that time. A conclusion his then band mates were either too unaware to realise or perhaps blissfully ignorant given their personal situations at the time.

To become something other than an ex member of the world's most dangerous band would take a Godzilla sized new project and at the very least a charismatic new singer. In Scott Weiland, Velvet Revolver has certainly found a singer with huge public interest behind him but this is mainly given his drug problems and frequent trips to the jail or rehab clinic. The well worn story of excess and Slash, Matt and Duff is once again rearing its uncomfortable head.

Whilst no one could confidently suggest that this association with a proven media friendly front man was behind their reasons to join a band there are certainties involved in the Weiland scenario, for two minutes it just might stop people mentioning either Guns N' Roses or Axl Rose.

"I have nothing against the guys, that was thirteen years ago. We all were on drugs, you make mistakes when you are on drugs, you don't realize what you are doing. I was thescapegoat. I was just a nice guy, a fun guy. Axl was so insecure about himself, and I am so secure about myself. Like I've heard Axl say in interviews "after the show is over, Stevie wants to go get pizza, go meet the girls" Axl? What does he do? "I gotta go into the bedroom and get my head to-

*gether" From what? I was the outgoing person and he didn't like
the fact that I had a great time and wasn't afraid to go up to people" Steven Adler*

In equal measure one has to feel sympathy for the current G N' R
members who, as Tommy Stinson noted received short shrift from
some fans at the beginning of the personnel crossover. "There's people in the audience who have 'Where's Slash?' banners or 'We Love
Slash' or whatever, Y' know, all those people, they don't leave and
they must not be hating it if they don't leave. People seem to be
pretty jazzed by the show that we put on. No matter what we do,
there's going to be some people that are just not going to let go of
the old band. But the majority of the people I see out there are having a great time; they're losing their minds and dancing and singing
along. It doesn't seem to me like they miss the old guys."

One of the old guys is Dizzy Reed who despite not being a fully fledged 'original' member is still the longest serving component
under the current G N' R guise discounting his boss Axl. Reed has
made interesting comments regarding the G N' R he has the distinct honour of seeing from both angles. To the old members who
have supposedly linked up minus Axl (including Izzy) he says, "I
say good luck, and I hope they have a good time and they should
enjoy it 'cause Izzy will probably quit in a couple of weeks. I think
some of those guys really go complacent. I know Axl thought we really needed to change, and in their mind we didn't need to change,
we should just do what we do and everything will be cool. But you
look around and you see bands that did that, and they're trivial now.
They're nostalgia. We didn't want to be that way and one by one,
people started quitting. The old band was a little more hell bent on
self destruction; this band is headed upward as opposed to downward."

These were acerbic words from the keyboardist who is the only
one Axl can endure. He also draws two very astute parallels to Guns
N' Roses, the irony of which is not lost on Axl Rose. Firstly that the
bands of Guns N' Roses' ilk have all but drowned in their own nos-

talgic trip. The fact most bands had to realise is that the 80s are completely redundant as far as music is concerned, unless purely for reflective reasons. While bands such as Ratt and Poison can quite easily sell tickets for the small venues at the moment, on the back of their 80s catalogue, it would be with some relish most casual fans welcomed back a band that could truly transcend genres and categories.

The only band apart from 90s touring partners Metallica who could command such massive crossover appeal – Guns N' Roses. Indeed they are a very rare phenomenon and therefore lies the irony of the bands enduring appeal. In an age where stardom can be founded on nothing more than a quirky audition to become a 'pop idol' and real musical talent takes a backseat to the gimmicks one can conjure up, it is with considered reflection Guns N' Roses must and *has* viewed their subjective appeal to the world, as we know it.

Where their peers laid down and died it was G N' R's notoriety which served them so well, added to which their insistence on doing anything to a time scale all of their own (and the incredibly strong records that emerged from the chaos) simply created as strong a legend as only bands in existence for decades had achieved. This legend was created without question from the hype and classic songs that surrounded *Appetite For Destruction*.

"It is something I lived by before these guys were in it. And there were other people in Guns N' Roses before them, you know. I contemplated letting go of that, but it doesn't feel right in any way. I am not the person who chose to try to kill it and walk away" Axl Rose

However what keeps it alive is the ongoing speculation and uncertainty as well as a very real belief from those who have seen it happen before that Axl can and eventually *will* deliver the goods. The way the situation has developed is to only hint at a reformation at some point in the future. But this would very much depend on the Guns N' Roses comeback. As Tommy Stinson alluded to, when G

N' R play live no one seems to mind that Slash or Izzy are not there, as long as Axl sings the songs the same as memory serves then it can still be Guns N' Roses if you close your eyes.

However time and again from denials and new band mates who contend that things are much better 'now' than they were before, reunions often occur. It has happened with Iron Maiden and Judas Priest to name but two. Yet with both those examples there was a constant turnover of new material and the public was soon jaded with the respective new singers and began to demand reunions.

In 2000 Slash said, "If someone comes up to me and asks me if G N' R is going to get back together, I say that if it was the original band and if everybody could straighten their heads out enough to be in the same room to do it, then I would do one show if the situation was right. We've been offered millions of dollars to re–group. Originally, I thought, 'Shit! A couple of days of rehearsal and then go out and play in front of a really excited, enthusiastic audience? Might be fun.' But when we recorded 'Sympathy for the devil' Axl didn't even show up. So everybody lost interest. If it was the original band, and Steven Adler could get his shit back together, which I know he's been trying to do since time began, since I still talk to him all the time. But the chances of that happening are pretty much nil."

The demand for a Guns N' Roses reunion has not happened in the same way as other bands because Axl has cleverly manipulated the press and been honest with the fans; the basic premise is the record will not come out until it is as perfect as it can be and for that Axl is to be admired. He has not rushed onto the bandwagon when it would have been much easier to do so. In taking the long road he may well have the most rewarding prize at the finish line.

And you can be assured wherever they are at the time, and whatever their opinion of Axl Rose and the carnival that has long been Guns N' Roses, messrs Duff, Izzy, Slash and Steven (not to mention Gilby Clarke et al) will be straining their eyes and ears to view and hear the *Chinese Democracy* record when it drops into record stores the world over; they and 50 million others.

"'Cause I see the storm getting closer and the waves they get so high. Seems everything we've ever known's here, why must it drift away and die" 'Estranged'

"Now, I'm thinking that God, he wants this band to happen"
Axl Rose

In 2003 most people believe the new Guns N' Roses album will never be released. Despite official statements to the contrary and confirmation from Axl Rose himself, it seems hard to convince the world *Chinese Democracy* will ever surface. "I'm not sceptical about 'if' the record comes out or not" Axl has assured fans "but the 'when' thing is when we decide it's completed. There's a lot of ideas we come up with as we go and it is a really slow process." Why does everybody remain so sceptical about the album being released? If it's just the small factor of time, then don't let that bother you. How many gigs have Guns' shown up late for? How many gigs were cancelled, rescheduled and then honoured? Did the *Use Your Illusion* albums eventually come out?

These questions are important and for all interested in G N' R, good news. One thing is certain; the band has not let its followers down in terms of quality output. Even the somewhat haphazardly compiled *Live Era '87–'93* album was a timely reminder of Guns' talents. Though it focused on old material, there was enough spark to suggest G N' R are still relevant. The album did not sell well. Less than a million copies in fact, small fare for the Guns' of the nineties.

Promotion of the record was limited to television and print advertising. It has been rumoured Axl forbade ex members to promote the record in their own way. Surely the reason for its poor sales figures centres more on the fact it's a live album taken from various venues and was seen by many as Geffen's shoddy idea of a 'greatest hits'. The sticker on the album bragged of the inclusion of 'Sweet Child O Mine' and 'Paradise City', both great songs, but somewhat out of date in 2003.

Though the album was steadfastly compiled and featured interesting band photographs, it is not what the world wants. What everyone wants is *Chinese Democracy*. Only the hardcore G N' R gig attendees will have heard the likes of 'Madagascar' or 'Silk Worms' and perhaps including these songs on *Live Era '87–'93* would have at least given a taster for the album, and perhaps an assurance it *will* surface. The longer it takes, the more it must deliver. Though the bootlegs in existence of the recent G N' R shows are of poor quality, they certainly hint at the grandiose appeal of the new songs.

"Stylistically speaking, there's a lot more going on. And I would say lyrically, definitely there is a lot more going on than old Guns'. There's a lot more introspection, a lot more social commentary involved" Tommy Stinson

Brian May, who joined the band at one stage describes the material he worked on as "fantastic. I was shocked that they didn't put it out straight away. Maybe its perfection on Axl's part – the desire to make it THE album of all time. I played on three tracks, I don't know if they'll be used. I don't wanna ask!" Not since The Beatles has a band truly transcended worldwide boundaries and garnered complete respect. Could Axl possibly achieve this with *Chinese Democracy*?

"It has to be the best in Axl's own mind," May thinks, "and an expression of his personal feelings. He's very passionate about it – every single word and note is very personal."

Another hired guitarist, Zakk Wylde (of Black Label Society & Ozzy Osbourne fame) claims, "There were never any melodies. There were never any lyrics." What Wylde heard over several months sounded like "Guns on steroids!" As for Axl, Wylde laughs, "The poor fuckin' guy's got every fuckin' cunt trying to sue his ass. I'd be on the phone with him. He'd be telling me about all these strategic moves his lawyers were making. I was listening to him playing Axis and Allies on the fuckin' phone."

"Putting this thing together I've had to do way more jobs in it than I'm supposed to" Axl has said. "I've had to be manager, A & R man and producer. Sole lyric writer. And to me what I worked really hard with Guns N' Roses on doing was making it a collaborative effort and there were a lot of people involved. This is a collaborative record with the players but the players aren't exactly sure what it should be to try and win the world over Guns N' Roses style so that's kind of my responsibility." Such comment was fitting justification of the time factor. In fairness to Axl, carrying the burden of one of the world's biggest bands alone cannot be easy.

"Slash told me, 'I don't want to work that hard' " Axl Rose

As he says somewhat matter–of–factly, "It took a long time but now it's working and I think we'll have the right record. When we do drop the record the plan is to drop the record, have a bunch of extra tracks. After a year or so drop another album then after a year a third record. This is a three stage thing and we'll be touring for a real long time." Such comments have only lead to increased uncertainty from fans. The official Guns' site is rarely updated with any concrete news. Whether this is because Axl is lazy or those maintaining the site have no idea where he is remains a mystery.

Former Nine Inch Nails drummer Chris Vrenna, joined the band in the spring of 1997 for sessions which lasted from 10 P.M. to 6 A.M but eventually left to pursue his own record. "It was going to be a long commitment," Vrenna says. "There was no firm line–up. Axl had a definite direction he ultimately wanted to head toward, but at the time there wasn't even a song."

Axl hired among others: Dave Abbruzzese, Pearl Jam's former drummer; Dave Navarro and solo guitarist Stevie Salas. There was room for Axl's friend (basketball player and rapper) Shaquille O'Neal, Josh Freese of the Vandals, plus eventual permanent members Tommy Stinson and old Lafayette partner Paul Huge. Slash and Duff couldn't accept Huge's involvement. "Nice enough guy," says a friend of the three musicians. "But they're Guns N' Roses for God's sake – great band, great players. He's not that good. Doesn't have the chops."

In 1996 Slash departed. Matt Sorum was fired. Duff lasted to the end of 1997 before quitting. According to a source, "Duff reached a point where he said 'I don't need this in my life anymore. This is too insane. This is rock n' roll. It's supposed to be fun'".

"It's not an Axl Rose album, even if it's what I wanted it to be. Everybody is putting everything they've got into singing and building. Maybe I'm helping steer it to what it should be built like"
Axl Rose

Of the complex where G N' R worked at night one observer says, "It's a musical instrument convention. Axl has more knobs and keyboards and strings and wire and wood in there than you could possibly imagine could even be manufactured." It is not hard to imagine Axl Rose pursuing the ultimate technology for the ultimate album. With his financial power it was natural he would experiment.

As Dave Abbruzzese recalls, "You could hunt buffalo with his rig. It had a lot of lights, a lot of blinking lights, a lot of things that you stepped on. It sounded like a freight train that was somehow playable." According to Rose, "educating myself" about the technology that's come to define rock in the nineties has been partly to blame for the delay. "It's like from scratch, learning how to work with something and not wanting it just to be something you did on a computer," he says. "There is the desire definitely to do it, to get over the hump of people trying to keep you in the past."

It was not only musicians who came and went like the postman. Producers too were introduced in a revolving door policy. Roy Thomas Baker, Youth, Moby, Mike Clink and Sean Beaven all attempted to oversee the Axl extravaganza. Apparently none could truly capture the spirit Axl hoped to get on tape. Rose is now himself co-producer. "I found it difficult to chart a linear development of the songs that they were working on," recalls Moby. "They would work on something, it would be a sketch for a while, and then they'd put it aside and go back to it a year later."

With regards to singing, Moby also saw Axl in defiant mood. For a long time vocals were not even mentioned. "He became a little bit defensive when I asked him about the vocals. He just said that he was going to get to them eventually," Moby continues. "I wouldn't be surprised if the record never came out, they've been working on it for such a long time." Axl is more insolent regarding the diminutive artist, "I appreciate all the publicity he's been getting us, but shut up already!" he laughs.

The song 'Oh My God,' released as part of the *End Of Days* sound-track, was a strange taster of new Guns' material. It seems to be at odds with the other planned songs. "It's Guns N' Roses music. There are rumours about it being a techno record. It's what Guns N' Roses has always been: diversified" Doug Goldstein says.

Tommy Stinson remarks, "it touches on a lot of different elements of old Guns N' Roses in some ways; in other ways it touches with more current sounding music. We wouldn't be doing this if it weren't going to come out. If it works out, it could be history making, 'cause no one's ever done this before. A lead singer's never taken the band name and continued on with an entirely new line up successfully. I kinda got into this for exactly that reason; if you're gonna try to do something really whacked, this would be the way to do it. I really don't think about the consequences either way; it's either gonna work or it's not, and in the meantime we're all having a good time trying to make it happen."

Many were indignant at the 'new' sound Guns' purported but Axl was defiant. "The reality is, go buy those guys' solo records" he said referring to ex members. "There are neat ideas and parts there, but they wouldn't have worked for a Guns N' Roses records. There are people that I thought I was friends with who are all of a sudden in the magazines, going, 'They'll never get anywhere without Slash.' Thanks a lot. Like I made this happen, you know. I basically figured out a way to save my own ass. There was only one way out, and I found it. Otherwise, you know, I believe my career was just going down the toilet. I figured out how to save my ass and then tried to bring everybody with me."

"I just wish the fucker would get the fuckin' record out so I could see why he took something so cool and systematically, destroyed it. I want to hear where he was headed, and what he was trying to communicate that none of us in the band could relate to" Slash

Rose describes Slash as "negatively seductive" and is clearly adamant he tried all he could to keep Guns' afloat in the manner it was accustomed to. The fact is, perhaps the G N' R 'manner' is so bizarre whatever happened next was bound to be problematical. In August of 2002 guitarist Robin Finck quit G N' R returning to Nine Inch Nails. Axl erased many of Finck's guitar parts. In March, drummer Josh Freese left to work on the variety of projects he's often involved with. Both Finck and Freese refuse to talk about their experiences.

They might be wise. Over the last few years most who have been part of the G N' R circus have found themselves in the midst of legal wrangling. Gilby Clarke was involved in an ongoing suit with G N' R for "misappropriation of his name, likeness, photograph, voice, and performance".

The Guns' management company sued Slash and Duff McKagan over the recently released live album. The Allstar music website reports Big F D Entertainment wants no less than $400,000 in money the pair received for *Live Era '87–'93* for representation the management company did on their behalf.

"When we were in airports and people are ignoring Duff and asking for my autograph, that didn't go over so well. The guys would say, you know, 'what am I? Wood?' " There was an effort to bring me down," 'It was a king of the mountain thing." So said Axl of his old friends. He had a surprise visitor one day when Izzy Stradlin turned up at his mansion. After being viewed on the hi–tech security system Izzy was refused entry. "It wouldn't be healthy for me," Axl said of his decision not to hook up with his long lost pal. "Izzy went back to Indiana, that pretty much explains the absurdity of the whole goddamn thing. The fucking idea of going back to Indiana – I am not even bagging on Indiana – I just know how much Izzy hated it. I went to high school with this guy. It's pitiful. I think it really has to do with what it takes to face that big audience. I wouldn't call it stage fright. It's something else, and to psyche yourself up for that, the old Guns doesn't seem to be able to do it without medication."

As for Slash the feelings are similar. "I am watching this guy and I don't understand it" Axl says. "Playing with everyone from Space

Ghost to Michael Jackson. I don't get it. I wanted the world to love and respect him. I just watched him throw it away."

"Along the time we were trying to put it together with the other fellas, I certainly had my doubts," Doug Goldstein remarks of the old line up attempting to release a new album. "But now Axl has a group of guys that he appears to be friends with, and it's a very cohesive unit, which wasn't necessarily the case in the past. Everything I've heard is spectacular. It's exciting and diverse and – I think – absolutely well worth the wait."

According to Axl the next record was always going to be much more emotional. He felt the new songs were purposely written from a simplistic perspective, meaning many should be able to relate to his experiences. However weird or twisted the record eventually turns out to be, one thing is certain, it should be akin to the *Use Your Illusion* set. Whether it is a double album, trilogy or single CD the album will certainly be brimming with music, 76 minutes seems to be Axl's desired length. The music unsurprisingly will also encompass a variety of themes and styles, much like *Use Your Illusion.*

There is a strong suggestion that people in the business end of things do not even know what is going on with Axl and G N' R. They are still unclear as to whether there will be one or two CDs and getting hold of the front man is nigh on impossible. From fax to e-mail it seems Axl is unlikely to give much away. The master tapes for *Chinese Democracy* are heavily guarded.

"I really believe in what we're doing. And I think the longer its gone on, the more I've had to invest in what I'm doing. I want to see it through. I still think I have a lot to prove with this band. I have a lot invested in it and I want to see it happen. It always seems like its just around the corner that its going to come, so why quit now? And then you get around the corner, and it's around the corner again. But still, at this point, it's the same thing: Why quit now? And I guess I haven't done anything stupid to get fired" Dizzy Reed

LYRICS

"This wasn't Guns N' Roses, but I feel it is Guns N' Roses now"
Axl Rose

Though the album itself is something of a mystery, there have been the aforementioned clues to its content. Songs such as 'Madagascar' and 'Chinese Democracy' have been played live and consequently their lyrics can be deciphered. Below are some lyrics from the songs so far played live, and notes on their possible meaning.

'Rhiad & The Bedouins' is perhaps one of the more confusing titles and subjects, returning to the Axl theme of mixing up several different meanings within the same song. Firstly the word bedouin relates to a desert dweller, an Arab tribesman. This would fit in with the capital of Saudi Arabia, but this is of course spelt Riyadh. So, whether this is a play on words by Axl or simply a misspelling on the part of the many G N' R enthusiasts worldwide remains to be seen. There is also the "Half the time they're bedouins, Nomads and/or Aryans" line, which again begs confusion. Overall it seems to be a plea from Axl to his many detractors to cease their poor treatment of him. ("Caught in the lies if you ignore this world. Somewhere in time people will like me there"). Is he also talking of himself as a desert dweller lost in the wilderness and his enemies, the liars he must escape from?

A song of particular beauty and maturity, 'Madagascar' will threaten charts the world over if released at the right time. The lyrics are somewhat saintly, appearing as if the singer views himself as something of a messiah, who must forgive those who trespass against him ("Forgive them that tear down my soul, bless them that they might grow old"). This seems to especially refer to anyone who doubts his convictions and intentions.

"I won't be told anymore that I've been brought down in this storm" Axl croons, perhaps pointing at the 'storm' he sang of in 'Estranged'? There is a veiled warning that he will not be told he "can't find (my) way back, (my) way anymore". Subliminal assurance perhaps that there will be a studio album eventually.

The title track is a song rather reminiscent of 'You Could Be Mine' in its attacking simplicity and varied lyrics. The song seems to be more about phrases that fit well together rather than any inherent meaning. The song title, taken from the album itself is clearly a politically motivated diatribe but its specific topic is unclear. Lines such as "Our baby got to rule the nation but all I got is precious time" seem particularly cryptic.

The self–explanatory title of 'The Blues' only hints at the pain contained within the lyrics. The music accompanies the words in succinct agony, as Axl refers to a relationship gone wrong throughout the song. "Now there's a hell I can't describe" can be interpreted in many ways but seems to centre on a depression he cannot shake, which as evidenced in other chapters is entirely real. There is a discreet mention of what life as Axl Rose might be like, "So now I wander through my day trying to find my way", is a fitting epitaph to innocence lost.

'Back Off Bitch' looks tame in comparison to 'Silk Worms' with tasteful lines like "Kneeling fucking virgin, you know that's what you are. Pussy for a maggot, isn't that a shock." Whoever wronged Axl clearly did not endear themselves to him. The title most probably suggests a woman (with a face of an angel and love of a witch)... A worm who crawled through Axl's soul, covered in silk so she slid right in ("Parasitic demons sucking acid through your heart").

ALBUM INFORMATION

Producer(s): Axl Rose, Sean Beavan, Caram Costanzo, Roy Thomas Baker
Engineering: Critter, Eric Caudieux
Current tracks:
Today, Tomorrow, Forever
Silk Worms
Hearts Always Get Killed
I.R.S
Rhiad & The Bedouins
Chinese Democracy

Cock–a–roach Soup
This Life
Closing In On You
Something Always
Catcher in the Rye
T.W.A.T. (There Was A Time)
No Love Remains
Strange Disease
Suckerpunched
Oklahoma
Friend or Foe
Never Had It
Oh My God
This I Love
The Blues
Prostitute
Zip It
Additional Musicians:
Paul Huge: Guitar
Richard Fortus: Guitar
Stevie Salas: Guitar
Zakk Wylde: Guitar
Brian May: Guitar
Dave Navarro: Guitar on 'Oh My God'
Gary Sunshine: Guitar on 'Oh My God'
Chris Pittman: Keyboards
Shaquille O'Neal: Additional Vocals
Dave Abbruzzese: Drums
Josh Freese: Drums

Film composer Marco Beltrami has also revealed he was asked in
2002 to supply orchestral arrangements for the tracks, 'Thyme',
'Seven', 'General' and 'Leave Me Alone'.

"How the fuck did I get so fucking important!?" Axl Rose

Circulating stories regarding Guns N' Roses have only served to fuel uncertainty and/or despair in those awaiting *Chinese Democracy*. Ex members have been in trouble. A report on the APB News website, July 25 1999, stated that Steven Adler had been sentenced to 150 days in jail for beating two women and violating his probation from an earlier domestic violence conviction. "Adler, 33, pleaded no contest to two counts of battery and a probation violation stemming from a 1997 domestic violence conviction", said city attorney's spokesman Mike Qualls. Municipal Court Commissioner Joseph S. Biderman also placed Adler on three years probation and ordered him to undergo one year of domestic violence counselling.

But despite his ongoing problems– of every kind possible, Adler was not the only former Guns' member to be in trouble with the police. It was reported during the same month, by Slash's girlfriend, that he had beaten her. The report ran as follows: 'West Hollywood, California (AP). Former Guns N' Roses lead guitarist Saul Hudson, better known by his stage name Slash, was arrested for allegedly beating his live–in girlfriend, authorities said Sunday. Hudson, 34, was arrested Saturday night at his Sunset Boulevard recording studio after his girlfriend told Los Angeles County sheriff deputies that he beat her on July 19 at the Le Parc Hotel in West Hollywood. Hudson was freed after posting $50,000 bail.' The girlfriend's name was not released.

Axl himself has been busy with the press. Bizarrely, *The New York Post* reported, on May 9th 2003, that Axl was spotted (in the company of "a sexy Asian woman") asking the deejay at Suite 16 in Manhattan to stop playing the group's hit 'Paradise City'". Punk band The Offspring thought they were having fun when they claimed to be calling their newest album *Chinese Democracy*, in parody of G N' R and its lengthy hiatus. Axl was not amused and the band was threatened with the worn phrase of "legal action" should they go ahead and steal Axl's title. The issue of copyright would seem to favour G N' R only because they had toured under the banner of *The Chinese Democracy* tour. The Offspring changed their album name to *Splinter*.

Meanwhile in a story unrelated to Axl (though strange enough to be so), G N' R fans in Hungary were victims of an outrageous hoax in which 3,000 fake tickets were sold at a cost of around £30 each ($50). The hoax culled around £64,000 ($110,000) for its perpetrators who promptly disappeared, with the band none the wiser. Posters had suggested and advertised a show to be played by G N'R on a disused airport site in Budapest, on September 26th 2003.

After unofficially leaving Guns N' Roses in 2003, in 2004 Buckethead's departure was confirmed. According to many close to the band, he essentially used Axl and G N' R to boost his own career, and had no intention of staying with the group. Despite this flagrant show of disloyalty, it is alleged that Buckethead is still on the Guns' pay roll. Whether this is a contractual obligation is unclear, but a close source suggests that Axl is paying Buckethead in the hope he might rejoin. After Roy Thomas Baker was, allegedly, accidentally sacked from his production duties, he was paid for months afterwards.

For those curious about Buckethead's G N' R perspective and personal history, the following might be of interest. He was born Brian Carroll in 1969 in Marietta, Georgia, USA. It is true that Buckethead considers himself to be from another planet. Take a look at his website at www.bucketheadland.com, and you will be inundated with a plethora of odd images, sights and sounds. Like all the best freaks, the guitarist prefers to remain unseen from the neck upwards, and persists in wearing an upturned bucket, whenever he appears in public. Must get uncomfortable!

But behind the veneer of a Sci–fi villain and Disneyland addict lays a relatively normal rock n' roll upbringing. As a youth his influences were like many of his generation. A huge interest in heavy metal, particularly with axe slingers such as AC/DC's Angus Young, widdler extraordinaire Yngwie Malmsteen and the late Ozzy Osbourne Band guitarist Randy Rhoads, was present at an early age.. Carroll's playing was equally influenced by classical elements and his increasingly unique style was compounded by a base knowledge of musical theory.

His childlike nature played a big part in his development as a guitarist with his own style. He was a very shy child and spent most of his time ensconced in his bedroom, which was brimming with video games, martial art movie memorabilia and comics. To add a truly weird streak was his obsession with Disneyland, which although a place for children, could equally be seen as sinister with its cartoon characters and their permanently etched smiles. Oddly, he also found a hero in a most unlikely form, that of Michael Jackson. The recent hullabaloo surrounding Jackson led Buckethead to state, "It is very tragic. He was the last innocent, a hero that children could believe and love."

But the real inspiration for Buckethead's choice of headwear was the *Halloween* movies. Immediately after seeing the 1988 sequel *Halloween 4: The Return of Michael Myers* Carroll went out and bought himself the essential white mask. And a revelation occurred as he was eating take out food that evening. While eating the fried chicken (from KFC of course) Carroll suddenly put the Myers mask on, followed by the empty KFC bucket. "I went to the mirror and said out loud, Buckethead. That's Buckethead right there. It was just one of those things. After that I wanted to be that thing all the time." There has apparently never been a problem using the KFC brand name, the outlet has never approached him or threatened him in any way, but if it were to happen, he says, "If they have a problem it's no problem for me, I have other buckets ready for me."

It has never been admitted or expounded on by Carroll, but perhaps his decision to remain in camouflage permanently was a product of the typical rock star syndrome, for which the archetypal outcast kid at school had no interest. He is an artist first and foremost and, to use a cliché, prefers his guitar playing to do the talking. Perhaps the irony is that in not wanting to let his image detract from the music, he has actually drawn more attention to it. And therein lies another facet of the Buckethead make up – that of the entertainer. Carroll takes pride in his solo output and the aforementioned website, both of which take you into another world whether you want to go or not.

And his solo music is not something requiring technical knowledge to appreciate. In contrast with his early idols such as Yngwie Malmsteen, Carroll's path has taken him into uncharted musical areas, those of huge riffs, sparkling dynamics, simple melody and occasionally pure noise. His own knowledge is perpetual and incessant, at one time he wrote a column for *Guitar Player* magazine called 'Psychobuddy', yet his ability to talk of arpeggios and 9th intervals is diminished by his sheer enthusiasm and ability to make a guitar talk to its listener. A rare quality that was no doubt the reason Axl Rose felt he had his man.

His CV reads as impressive. Like his ex band mate Brian Mantia, he has performed with Primus but also performed with Bill Laswell, Bootsy Collins, Iggy Pop and the late drummer Tony Williams (of the Miles Davis quintet). Buckethead has kudos.

Axl Rose worked hard to engage Carroll – Guns N' Roses was not really an ideal home for the versatile but hermit like musician. But Axl persevered and invited Buckethead over to his house one Christmas. The rare Leatherface doll (from *The Texas Chainsaw Massacre*) he had been seeking, hadn't arrived in his Christmas stocking, but when he got to Axl's pad, there was the very object of his desire. Upon making his feelings known, Axl graciously gave it to him. He took it as a sign that the Guns' front man "understood him, somehow".

What this prolific player really wants to do apparently is make an all–Disney album, incorporating the same dynamics as within his favourite tune, 'When You Wish Upon A Star'. Such a harmless, uncomplicated yet beautiful song is typical of Carroll's approach. At odds with the supposed loving world of Disney cartoons and pretty scenery, he practices guitar in front of a makeshift altar containing the Michael Myers mask, a plastic replica of KFC's Colonel Sanders and, of course, his prized Leatherface doll. Not to mention a rubber chicken!

Are things not quite right in the mind of Brian 'Buckethead' Carroll one wonders?

Buckethead says of the Colonel Sanders doll, "It's like your father; maybe he beats you, but he's still your father, and you love him… it's complicated." The Buckethead character was raised by chickens (what else?) and Carroll has taken it upon himself to tell the world about the ongoing chicken holocaust in fast food restaurants all over the world.

In an interview by MTV, Buckethead decided that 'Herbie' would answer all questions. Herbie was a full–headed rubber monster mask that was draped over his right hand. In an attempt to explain his own chicken obsession, Buckethead said that the evil man who owned the chicken farm where he was raised, came to the coop one day and placed fired chicken pieces inside.

Herbie said, "And for the first time he realised they were cooking chickens. And they were his family, so he tried to put them back together, and he just kind of went nuts. And he put the bucket on his head 'cause he thought he could help all those dead chickens come back to life. So when he plays, it's like the sound of all those dead chickens coming through his hands. This rubber chicken is kind of sad; it makes him play more pretty. When he sees this, he thinks of lullabies and that sort of stuff. But it's not real, and he knows it's not real."

There is also the revelation, spoken in third person of course, that the character "goes to the grave. Bury it, burn it, cut it. It goes to the grave. There is no mask."

THE GREATEST?

Come 2004 it was clear Geffen was becoming tired of waiting around for new Guns N' Roses material, and so a long mooted idea was cobbled together, the familiar death knell for an artist's career, *The Greatest Hits*. It's worth considering that bands who have managed to stave off the idea of a 'best of' compilation, are usually the most successful and integral; Metallica or AC/DC for example.

For many the idea of a greatest hits package so late after many of the songs' initial impact was a definite cash in. No one associated with the band seemed happy about it. Axl Rose worked in conjunction with Slash and Duff (albeit indirectly) to try to prevent Geffen from releasing the album, claiming that the alteration of the master songs without permission constituted a breach of contract.

A statement claimed, "We have not been given the opportunity to approve the choice of songs, the artwork, the release date or the re–mastering done on the tracks included on this compilation."

There was also a precise diatribe from Axl, stating he was concerned "that not only will their audience be misled into believing that the planned compilation is an unauthorised release, but that it will hinder the release of the band's long–awaited new studio album *Chinese Democracy*."

However a court in Los Angeles dismissed the lawsuit. Peter LoFrumento, a spokesman for Geffen, said: "Their lawsuit is merit less. Fortunately, since the court has denied their application for a temporary restraining order, the album will be released as scheduled on March 23." So it became. True fans of course would have already owned the tracks and with no extras, bonus material, or even some decent packaging, it was a dreadful dismissal of the true Guns N' Roses' legacy.

Duff later said, "It annoyed us. We had no say in the track listing. I actually agree with it not coming out sort of, but it was like, you two guys aren't even in the fucking band so fuck all y'all". Here he was referring to Axl, who supposedly chose the tracks against Duff and Slash's wishes. The songs themselves were in part unusual. The single only release 'Sympathy For The Devil' was included, as were two other cover versions in 'Since I Don't Have You' and 'Ain't It Fun'. Not exactly the ideal advert for original G N' R music.

Regardless, the album sold well, mainly to casual music buyers who only knew the most familiar singles, such as 'Sweet Child O' Mine' and 'Paradise City'.

It also seems somewhat penny pinching not to release a more 'value for money' double disc set at a similar price – even the one disc was not filled with music. A typically shoddy and disrespectful move from the record company left a sour taste with all Guns' members past and present.

Come early 2005, the rumours were even stronger that *Chinese Democracy* was soon to appear. At first, February was the suggested month of release, but with little in the way of confirmation and no advance advertising, this idea soon fizzled out. Instead it appeared that spring was a likely target.

From a good beginning, working with Sean Beavan in late 1998, came delay after delay and change after change, more of each than could ever be catalogued, until by 2004 the band were still recording at The Village Studios in Los Angeles with producer and engineer Caram Costanzo and ProTools engineer Eric Cadieux.

As of January 2005 the line up of Guns N' Roses is: Axl Rose (vocals and guitar), Dizzy Reed (keyboards), Richard Fortus (guitar), Tommy Stinson (bass), Brain (drums) and Robin Finck (guitar).

"I prefer the studio. Live is fun interesting and a blast but the live thing is like a one night stand – which is great, but the things that last are the songs" Axl Rose

Over their career Guns N' Roses have performed to literally millions of people all over the world. From humble beginnings in the alleys, bedrooms, parties and back yards of their L.A. brethren they progressed to the stadiums and outdoor arenas and venues from London to Japan. Axl once said "Usually when we're on the road. I'm very stressed about the shows, which are the most important thing to me. Nothing ever really works right for this band. Slash once said that God didn't want us to happen, and I somewhat believe that. When an interviewer comes in, and I'd rather be sleeping or they know I'm not in the mood, the impression left is 'He's losing it'. In a nutshell, that's why that happens."

The following is a full list of the official concerts the band has played in their troubled history. Despite having averaged a pitiful number of gigs in recent years, this was not always the case as is immediately clear looking at the touring schedule for both *Appetite For Destruction* and the *Use Your Illusion* double set. In fact it would be with some justification Axl Rose might claim to have been put off by the rigours of such a demanding itinerary and therefore decided to limit his appearances to those concerts, which he both knows about and feels fit and willing to play.

Of course, despite the shortage of live performances in recent times (though the band seems back on course in that regard), it is still the case the band has played shows without any new material to support and it is up to the individual to decide whether they would rather see *Chinese Democracy* released or the band play more gigs where they fulfil their obligations.

Duff was in agreement when he said of the current G N' R line–up: "Fans will be the real test. The group is likely to get away with it if they can go on a big tour, but I'm not even sure the public will come. When Led Zeppelin reformed without their bassist John Paul Jones, I didn't go see them. Page & Plant wasn't Led Zeppelin. In my opinion, John Paul Jones played as big a role as the others and the band without him was worth nothing. I didn't go see Aerosmith on tour with Jimmy Crespo and Rick Dufay it wasn't Aerosmith to me."

LIVE SHOWS

"Izzy agrees with writing stuff but he's not interested in touring... He doesn't want to deal with Axl y'know? The Rockstar thing... Like me, he just wanna play... We never thought G N' R would become so big" Slash

1983

April 1: *Rose* (pre– G N' R and pre Hollywood Rose) performed at the Troubadour in Hollywood, CA.
1984 *Hollywood Rose*
March 16: Madame Wong's East in Los Angeles, CA.
July 10: Troubadour in Hollywood, CA.
August 29: Troubadour in Hollywood, CA.
August 31: After hours party at Shamrock Studios in Santa Monica, CA.
December 31: San Pedro, CA.

1985 *Guns N' Roses*

April 11: Guns N' Roses (Axl, Izzy, Duff, Tracii Guns & Rob Gardener) performed at Radio City in Anaheim, CA.
June 6: The first Guns N' Roses show that included Axl, Izzy, Duff, Slash & Steven. They performed at the Troubadour in Hollywood, CA.
June 8: Guns N' Roses performed at the Rock Theater in Seattle, WA.
June: 'Hell Tour' starts in Portland, OR, the band also played in Eugene, OR, Sacramento, CA, San Francisco, CA
June 28: Stardust Ballroom in Hollywood, CA.
July 20: Troubadour in Hollywood, CA.

August 30: Stardust Ballroom in Hollywood, CA.
September 20: Troubadour in Hollywood, CA.
October 18: Chuck Landis' Country Club in Reseda, CA.
October 31: Radio City in Anaheim, CA.
November 22: Troubadour in Hollywood, CA.
December 20: Music Machine in Los Angeles, CA
That year Axl and Tracii Guns also joined Shark Island onstage in
Los Angeles to play a cover of Zeppelin's 'Rock and Roll'.

1986

1986: Axl, Duff, Izzy and Slash play a three song acoustical set at
the Central in Hollywood.
1986: Opened for Cheap Trick in Los Angeles.
January 1: Troubadour in Hollywood, CA.
January 18: Roxy in Hollywood, CA.
February 1: Roxy in Hollywood, CA.
February 28: Troubadour in Hollywood, CA.
March 11: Music Machine in Los Angeles, CA.
March 21: Opened for Johnny Thunders at Fenders Ballroom in
Long Beach, CA.
March 28: Performed two sets at the Roxy in Hollywood, CA.
March 29: Opened for The Lords of the New Church (with Stiv
Bators) at Fenders Ballroom in Long Beach, CA.
April 5 Whiskey A Go Go in Hollywood, CA.
May 3: Roxy in Hollywood, CA.
July 11: Troubadour in Hollywood, CA.
July 31: Opened for The Lords of the New Church at Timbers
Ballroom in Glendora, CA.
August 23: Whiskey A Go Go in Hollywood, CA.
August 30: Opened for Ted Nugent at the Santa Monica Civic Center
in Santa Monica, CA.
August 31: Roxy in Hollywood, CA.
September 13: Music Machine in Los Angeles, CA.
September 21: Performed a short set at the Street Scene in Hollywood,
CA. The show ends early after Axl is hit with a bottle.

October 31: Opened for the Red Hot Chili Peppers at Ackerman Hall, UCLA in Los Angeles, CA.
November 15: Opened for the Dead Boys at Fenders Ballroom in Long Beach, CA.

1987

March 16: Whiskey A Go Go in Hollywood, CA.
March 29: Roxy in Hollywood, CA.
May 10: The Drunk Fux (G N' R with West Arkeen & Del James) performed in Hollywood, CA.
June 19: Marquee in London, England
June 22: Marquee in London, England.
June 28: Marquee in London, England.
August 14: Cult in Halifax, Canada
August 15: Waterloo, Canada.
August 17: Verdun Auditorium in Montreal, Canada
August 18: Superskate in Kitchener, Canada
August 19: CNE Grandstand in Toronto, Canada
August 21: State Theater in Detroit, MI
August 24: Winnipeg Arena in Winnipeg, Canada
August 27: Max Bell Arena in Calgary, Alberta
August 29: Coliseum Theatre Stage in Vancouver, Canada
August 30: Paramount Theatre in Seattle, WA
September 2: Warfield Theatre in San Francisco, CA
September 3: Santa Cruz Civic Auditorium in Santa Cruz, CA
September 4: Open Air Theatre in San Diego, CA
September 5: Long Beach Arena in Long Beach, CA
September 11: Sunken Garden Amphitheatre in San Antonio, TX
September 12: Palmer Auditorium in Austin, TX
September 13: Bronco Bowl Auditorium in Dallas, TX.
September 16: Houston Music Hall in Houston, TX
September 17: Sanegar Theater in New Orleans, LA
September 29: Markethälle in Hamburg, Germany.
September 30: Tor 3 in Dusseldorf, Germany.
October 2: Paradiso in Amsterdam, Holland.

October 4: Newcastle City Hall in Newcastle, England.
October 5: Rock City in Nottingham, England.
October 6: Manchester Apollo in Manchester, England.
October 7: Bristol Colston Hall in Bristol, England.
October 8: Hammersmith Odeon in London, England.
October 16: The Sundance in Bay Shore, NY.
October 17: Airport Music Hall in Allentown, PA.
October 18: Baltimore, MD.
October 20: Philadelphia Experiment in Philadelphia, PA.
October 21: Albany, NY
October 22: Obsessions in Randolph, NJ.
October 23: The Ritz in New York, NY.
October 25: The Chance in Poughkeepsie, NY.
October 26: Providence, RI.
October 27: Paradise in Boston, MA.
October 29: L'Amour in Brooklyn, NY.
October 30: CBGB's in New York, NY.
October 31: The Horizon in Syracuse, NY.
November 1: Washington, DC.
November 3: Mobile Municipal Auditorium in Mobile, AL
November 4: Albany Civic Center in Albany, GA
November 6: Cajun Dome in Lafayette, LA
November 7: Lake Front Arena in New Orleans, LA
November 8: Mississippi Coliseum in Jackson, MS
November 10: Huntsville Civic Center in Huntsville, AL
November 11: Charlotte, NC
November 12: Savannah, GA
November 14: Colombia, SC
November 17: Knoxville Civic Coliseum in Knoxville, TN
November 20: The Omni in Atlanta, GA
November 21: UTC Arena in Chattanooga, TN
Novmeber 22: The Omni in Atlanta, GA
November 24: Lakeland Civic Center in Lakeland, FL
November 25: Lakeland Civic Center in Lakeland, FL
November 26: Jacksonville, FL
November 27: Lee Civic Center in Fort Myers, FL

November 29: Sportarium in Hollywood, FL

December 3: Houston, TX

December 4: Reunion Arena in Dallas, TX

December 17: Roy Wilkins Auditorium in St. Paul, MN

December 18: UIC Pavilion (University Of Illinois) in Chicago, IL

December 19: Dane County Coliseum in Madison, WI $

December 26: Perkins Palace in Pasadena, CA

December 27: Perkins Palace in Pasadena, CA

December 28: Perkins Palace in Pasadena, CA

December 30: Perkins Palace in Pasadena, CA

December 31: The Glamour in Los Angeles, CA

December 31: Axl sings 'Honkey Tonk Women' at The Central in Hollywood, CA after G N' R's performance at The Glamour.

1988

January 5: Opened for Great White at the Santa Monica Civic Center in Santa Monica, CA.

January 14: The Drunk Fux (GN'R plus Del James and West Arkeen) performed at the Coconut Teaszer in Hollywood, CA.

January 21: The Cathouse in Hollywood, CA.

January 31: The Limelight in New York, NY.

February 2: The Ritz in New York, NY (Also broadcast on MTV)

February 4: Crest Theatre in Sacramento, CA.

February 5: Warfield Theatre in San Francisco, CA.

February 6: Fresno, CA

February 8: Montezuma Hall, SDSU in San Diego, CA.

February 9: Celebrity Theatre in Anaheim, CA.

February 10: Celebrity Theatre in Anaheim, CA.

February 12: Celebrity Theatre in Phoenix, AZ.

February 13: Celebrity Theatre in Phoenix, AZ.

February 26: Axl, Izzy & Slash joined Alice Cooper onstage at the Long Beach Arena in Long Beach, CA to perform 'Under My Wheels'.

March 31: Appeared on the Fox Late Show performing 'You're Crazy' and 'Used To Love Her' acoustically.

April 26: Memorial Auditorium in Burlington, IA.

April 27: Oshkosh Centre in Oshkosh, WI.

April 29: Coronado Theatre in Rockford, IL.

April 30: Danville Civic Center in Danville, IL.

May 1: Toledo Sports Arena in Toledo, OH

May 3: Devos Hall in Grand Rapids, MI.

May 5: Music Hall in Cleveland, OH.

May 6: Saginaw Civic Center in Saginaw, MI.

May 7: State Theater in Detroit, MI.

May 9: Felt Forum in New York, NY.

May 10: Tower Theatre in Upper Darby, PA.

May 11: Orpheum Theatre in Boston, MA.

May 13: Moncton Coliseum in Moncton, Canada

May 14: Metro Centre in Halifax, Canada

May 16: Quebec Coliseum in Quebec City, Canada

May 17: Montreal Forum in Montreal, Canada

May 18: Ottawa Civic Center in Ottawa, Canada

May 20: CNE Grandstand in Toronto, Canada

May 23: Winnipeg Arena in Winnipeg, Canada

May 26: Northlands Arena in Edmonton, Canada

May 27: Saddledome in Calgary, Canada

May 30: PNE Coliseum in Vancouver, Canada

May 31: Spokane Coliseum in Spokane, WA

June 1: Seattle Center Coliseum in Seattle, WA

June 3: Salt Palace in Salt Lake City, UT

June 5: Shoreline Amphitheatre in Mountain View, CA

June 6: California Exhibition Center in Sacramento, CA

June 8: LA Guns opened for Iron Maiden after Axl blew his throat. Slash & Izzy joined them onstage for a jam.

June 9: G N' R (without Axl) perform two songs (with Duff on vocals) to please the crowd at Irvine Meadows in Irvine, CA. The band quit the Iron Maiden tour after this show due to Axl's recurrent throat problems.

Juy 9: Celebrity Theatre in Phoenix, AZ.

July 10: Celebrity Theatre in Phoenix, AZ.

July 17: Poplar Creek Music Theatre in Hoffman Estates, IL

July 19: Richfield Coliseum in Richfield, OH
July 20: Wheeling Civic Center in Wheeling, WV $
July 22: Show Me Center in Cape Girardeau, MO
July 24: Starplex Amphitheatre in Dallas, TX
July 26: Sandstone Amphitheatre in Bonner Springs, KS
July 27: Hilton Coliseum in Ames, IA
July 29: Alpine Valley Music Theatre in East Troy, WI
July 30: Val Du Lakes Amphitheatre in Mears, MI
August 1: Riverbend Music Center in Cincinnati, OH
August 2: Market Square Arena in Indianapolis, IN
August 4: Philadelphia Spectrum in Philadelphia, PA
August 5: Philadelphia Spectrum in Philadelphia, PA
August 6: Performing Arts Center in Saratoga Springs, NY
August 7: Orange County Fairgrounds in Middletown, NY
August 9: Cayuga County Fairgrounds in Weedsport, NY
August 11: Pine Knob Music Theatre in Clarkston, MI
August 12: Pine Knob Music Theatre in Clarkston, MI
August 13: Pine Knob Music Theatre in Clarkston, MI
August 16: Giants Stadium in East Rutherford, NJ
August 17: Merriweather Post Pavilion in Columbia, MI
August 20: Castle Donington Park in Donington, England (Monsters
of Rock Festival)
August 24: Great Woods in Mansfield, MA
August 25: Great Woods in Mansfield, MA
August 26: Great Woods in Mansfield, MA
August 28: Buckeye Lake in Hebron, OH
August 30: Pocono Downs in Wilkes–Barre, PA
August 31: Pittsburgh Civic Arena in Pittsburgh, PA
September 2: Starwood Amphitheatre in Antioch, TN
September 3: St. Louis Arena in St. Louis, MO
September 7: MTV Music Awards at the Universal Amphitheatre in
Los Angeles, CA
September 8: Concord Pavilion in Concord, CA
September 10: Shoreline Amphitheatre in Mountain View, CA
September 12: Compton Terrace in Chandler, AZ
September 14: Pacific Amphitheatre in Costa Mesa, CA

September 15: Pacific Amphitheatre in Costa Mesa, CA
September 17: Opened for Aerosmith & INXS at Texas Stadium in Irving, TX. (Texas Jam Festival)
December 4: NHK Hall in Tokyo, Japan
December 5: Festival Hall in Osaka, Japan.
December 7: Nakano Sunplaza in Tokyo, Japan.
December 9: NHK Hall in Tokyo, Japan.
December 10: Nippon Budokan in Tokyo, Japan.
December 14: Entertainment Centre in Melbourne, Australia.
December 15: Entertainment Centre in Melbourne, Australia.
December 17: Sydney Entertainment Centre in Sydney, Australia.
December 19: Big Top in Mount Smart in Auckland, New Zealand.

1989

January 30: American Music Awards at the Shrine Auditorium in Los Angeles, CA (The band played 'Patience' with Don Henley taking Steven's place on drums)
August 26: Axl performed 'Free Fallin' and 'Knockin' On Heaven's Door' with Tom Petty at the American Music Awards at the New York State Fairgrounds in Syracuse, NY.
September 6: Axl performed 'Free Fallin' and 'Heartbreak Hotel' with Tom Petty at the MTV Video Music Awards at the Universal Amphitheatre in Los Angeles, CA.
October 11: The Cathouse in Hollywood, CA.
October 13: Park Plaza Hotel in Los Angeles, CA.
October 18: Los Angeles Coliseum in Los Angeles, CA
October 19: Los Angeles Coliseum in Los Angeles, CA
October 21: Los Angeles Coliseum in Los Angeles, CA
October 22: Los Angeles Coliseum in Los Angeles, CA
December: Axl & Slash perform 'White Light White Heat' with Ian Hunter & Mick Ronson from Mott The Hoople at a club in Los Angeles, CA.
December 12: Axl performed 'Dead, Jail or Rock 'n' Roll' with Mike Monroe and Slash joined them for 'Looking At You' at the Whiskey A Go Go in Hollywood, CA.

December 17: Axl & Izzy performed 'Salt of the Earth' with the Rolling Stones at the Convention Center in Atlantic City, NJ.

December 19: Axl & Izzy performed 'Salt of the Earth' with the Rolling Stones at the Convention Center in Atlantic City, NJ.

December 20: Axl & Izzy performed 'Salt of the Earth' with the Rolling Stones at the Convention Center in Atlantic City, NJ. Axl also sang back up vocals on 'Mixed Emotions'.

1990

March 3: Axl & Slash performed 'Train Kept A Rollin' with Aerosmith at the Great Western Forum in Inglewood, CA.

April 7: Farm Aid VI at Hoosier Dome in Indianapolis, IN (Short 2 song set)

June 21: Slash performed 'It's A Sin' with the Black Crowes at the Marquee in New York, NY.

November 9: GAK, a band featuring Axl, Slash, Duff, Sebastian Bach (Skid Row), James Hetfield & Lars Ulrich (of Metallica) performed at RIP magazine's birthday party at the Hollywood Palladium in Hollywood, CA.

1991

January 20: Rock In Rio II Festivial at Maracana Stadium in Rio de Janeiro, Brazil.

January 23: Rock In Rio II Festivial at Maracana Stadium in Rio de Janeiro, Brazil.

May 9: Warfield Theater in San Francisco, CA

May 11: Pantages Theatre in Los Angeles, CA.

May 16: The Ritz in New York, NY

May 24: Alpine Valley Music Theatre in East Troy, WI.

May 25: Alpine Valley Music Theatre in East Troy, WI.

May 28: Deer Creek Music Center in Noblesville, IN.

May 29: Deer Creek Music Center in Noblesville, IN.

June 1: Capital Music Center in Grove City, OH.

June 2: Toledo Speedway in Toledo, OH.

June 4: Richfield Coliseum in Richfield, OH.
June 5: Richfield Coliseum in Richfield, OH.
June 7: CNE Grandstand in Toronto, Canada.
June 8: CNE Grandstand in Toronto, Canada.
June 10: Performing Arts Center in Saratoga Springs, NY.
June 11: Hershey Park Stadium in Hershey, PA.
June 13: Philadelphia Spectrum in Philadelphia, PA.
June 15: Lake Compounce Amphitheatre in Bristol, CT.
June 17: Nassau Coliseum in Uniondale, NY.
June 19: Capitol Centre in Landover, MD.
June 20: Capitol Centre in Landover, MD.
June 22: Hampton Coliseum in Hampton, VA.
June 23: Charlotte Coliseum in Charlotte, NC.
June 25: Greensboro Coliseum in Greensboro, NC.
June 26: Thompson–Boling Center in Knoxville, TN.
June 30: Birmingham Race Course in Birmingham, AL.
July 2: Riverport Amphitheatre in Maryland Heights, MI,
July 8: Starplex Amphitheatre in Dallas, TX.
July 9: Starplex Amphitheatre in Dallas, TX.
July 11: McNichols Sports Arena in Denver, CO.
July 12: Starplex Amphitheatre in Englewood, CO.
July 13: Salt Palace in Salt Lake City, UT.
July 16: Tacoma Dome in Tacoma, WA.
July 17: Tacoma Dome in Tacoma, WA.
July 19: Shoreline Amphitheatre in Mountain View, CA.
July 20: Shoreline Amphitheatre in Mountain View, CA.
July 23: ARCO Arena in Sacramento, CA.
July 25: Pacific Amphitheatre in Costa Mesa, CA.
July 26: Pacific Amphitheatre in Costa Mesa, CA.
July 29: Great Western Forum in Inglewood, CA.
July 30: Great Western Forum in Inglewood, CA.
August 2: Great Western Forum in Inglewood, CA.
August 3: Great Western Forum in Inglewood, CA.
August 13: Jäahalli in Helsinki, Finland.
August 14: Jäahalli in Helsinki, Finland.
August 16: Globen in Stockholm, Sweden.

August 17: Globen in Stockholm, Sweden.
August 19: Copenhagen Forum in Copenhagen, Denmark.
August 24: Mäimarktgelände in Mannheim, Germany.
August 31: Wembley Stadium in London, England
December 5: Worcester Centrum Centre in Worcester, MA.
December 6: Worcester Centrum Centre in Worcester, MA.
December 9: Madison Square Garden in New York, NY.
December 10: Madison Square Garden in New York, NY.
December 13: Madison Square Garden in New York, NY.
December 16: Philadelphia Spectrum in Philadelphia, PA.
Decmeber 17: Philadelphia Spectrum in Philadelphia, PA.
December 28: Suncoast Dome in St. Petersburg, FL.
December 31: Joe Robbie Stadium in Miami, FL.

1992

January 3: LSU Assembly Center in Baton Rouge, LA.
January 4: Mississippi Coast Coliseum in Biloxi, MS.
January 7: The Pyramid in Memphis, TN.
January 7: The Pyramid in Memphis, TN., (after the show the band
went to a local club called Rascals and played with the band on
stage, Son of Sam).
January 9: Summit in Houston, TX.
January 10: Summit in Houston, TX.
January 13: Erwin–Nutter Center in Dayton, OH.
January 14: Erwin–Nutter Center in Dayton, OH.
January 21: Target Center in Minneapolis, MN.
January 22: Target Center in Minneapolis, MN.
January 25: Thomas & Mack Center in Las Vegas, NV.
January 27: San Diego Sports Arena in San Diego, CA.
January 31: Compton Terrace in Chandler, AZ.
February 1: Compton Terrace in Chandler, AZ.
February 19: Tokyo Dome in Tokyo, Japan.
February 20: Tokyo Dome in Tokyo, Japan.
February 22: Tokyo Dome in Tokyo, Japan. (This show was released
as the 'Use Your Illusion' home video double set)

April 1: Palacio De Los Deportes in Mexico City, Mexico.

April 2: Palacio De Los Deportes in Mexico City, Mexico.

April 6: Myriad Arena in Oklahoma City, OK.

April 9: Rosemont Horizon in Rosemont, IL.

April 20: G N' R performed a two–song set at the Freddy Mercury Tribute Concert (A Concert For Life) at Wembley Stadium in London, England. Slash and Axl also performed with Queen and Axl alone played with Elton John.

May 16: Slane Castle in Slane, Ireland.

May 20: Strahov Stadium in Prague, Czechoslovakia.

May 22: Népstadion in Budapest, Hungary.

May 23: Donauinsel Stadium in Vienna, Austria.

May 24: Axl joined U2 for a duet with Bono on 'Knockin' On Heaven's Door' at Donauinsel Stadium in Vienna, Austria.

May 26: Olympic Stadium in Berlin, Germany.

May 28: Cannstatter Wasen in Stuttgart, Germany.

May 30: Müngersdorfer Stadion in Cologne, Germany.

June 3: Niedersachsenstadion in Hannover, Germany.

June 6: Hippodrome De Vincennes in Paris, France. (Pay Per View show with guest appearances by Lenny Kravitz and Steven Tyler and Joe Perry from Aerosmith)

June 13: Wembley Stadium in London, England.

June 14: Manchester City Football Ground, Maine Road in Manchester, England.

June 16: Gateshead International Stadium in Gateshead, England.

June 20: Talavera–Mainwiese in Würzburg, Germany.

June 21: Fussballstadion St. Jakob in Basel, Switzerland.

June 23: Feyenoord Stadion in Rotterdam, Holland.

June 27: Stadio Delle Alpi in Turin, Italy.

June 30: Estadio Benito Villamarin in Seville, Spain.

July 2: Alvalade Stadium in Lisbon, Portugal.

July 17: RFK Stadium in Washington, DC.

July 18: Giants Stadium in East Rutherford, NJ.

July 21: Pontiac Silverdome in Pontiac, MI.

July 22: Hoosier Dome in Indianapolis, IN.

July 25: Rich Stadium in Orchard Park, NY.

July 26: Three Rivers Stadium in Pittsburgh, PA.

July 29: Giants Stadium in East Rutherford, NJ.

August 8 Stade Du Parc Olympique in Montreal, Canada,

August 25: Phoenix International Raceway in Phoenix, AZ.

August 27: Aggie Memorial Stadium in Las Cruces, NM.

August 29: Louisiana Superdome in New Orleans, LA.

September 2: Citrus Bowl in Orlando, FL.

September 4: Astrodome in Houston, TX

September 5: Texas Stadium, Irving, TX.

September 7: Williams–Brice Stadium in Columbia, SC.

September 9: performed 'November Rain' at MTV's Music Video Awards with Elton John at the Pauley Pavilion, UCLA in Los Angeles, CA.

September 11: Foxboro Stadium in Foxboro, MA.

September 13: Exhibition Stadium in Toronto, Canada.

September 15: Metrodome in Minneapolis, MN.

September 17: Arrowhead Stadium in Kansas City, MO.

September 19: Mile High Stadium in Denver, CO.

September 24: Oakland Coliseum in Oakland, CA.

September 27: Los Angeles Coliseum in Los Angeles, CA.

September 30: Jack Murphy Stadium in San Diego, CA.

October 3: Rose Bowl in Pasadena, CA.

October 6: Kingdome in Seattle, WA.

November 25: Poliedro de Caracas in Caracas, Venezuela.

November 27: Estadio El Campín in Bogota, Colombia.

November 30: Estadio El Campín in Bogota, Colombia.

December 2: Estadio Nacional in Santiago, Chile.

December 5: Estadio River Plate in Buenos Aires, Argentina.

December 6: Estadio River Plate in Buenos Aires, Argentina.

December 10: Estacionamento Do Anhenbi in Sao Paulo, Brazil.

December 12: Estacionamento Do Anhenbi in Sao Paulo, Brazil.

December 13: Autodromo in Rio de Janeiro, Brazil.

1993

January 12: Tokyo Dome in Tokyo, Japan.
January 14: Tokyo Dome in Tokyo, Japan.
January 15: Tokyo Dome in Tokyo, Japan.
January 30: Eastern Creek Raceway in Sydney, Australia.
January 31: Slash & Duff performed songs with Rose Tattoo at the
Palace Club in Melbourne, Australia.
February 1: Calder Park Raceway in Melbourne, Australia
February 6: Mount Smart Stadium in Auckland, New Zealand.
February 23: Frank Erwin Center in Austin, TX.
February 25: Jefferson Center in Birmingham, AL.
March 6: New Haven Coliseum in New Haven, CT.
March 8: Cumberland Civic Center in Portland, ME.
March 9: Hartford Civic Center in Hartford, CT.
March 12: Copps Coliseum in Hamilton, Canada.
March 16: Augusta Civic Center in Augusta, ME.
March 17: Boston Garden in Boston, MA.
March 20: Carver–Hawkeye Arena in Iowa City, IA.
March 21: Fargo Dome in Fargo, ND.
March 24: Winnipeg Arena in Winnipeg, Canada.
March 26: Saskatchewan Place in Saskatoon, Canada.
March 28: Northlands Coliseum in Edmonton, Canada.
March 30: British Columbia Place in Vancouver, Canada.
April 1: Portland Coliseum in Portland, OR.
April 3: ARCO Arena in Sacramento, CA.
April 3: Lawler Events Center in Reno, NV.
April 7: Delta Center in Salt Lake City, UT.
April 9: Rushmore Plaza Civic Center in Rapid City, SD.
April 10: Omaha Civic Auditorium in Omaha, NE.
April 13: The Palace Of Auburn Hills in Auburn Hills, MI.
April 15: Roanoke Civic Center in Roanoke, VA
April 16: Dean Smith Center in Chapel Hill, NC.
April 21: Estadio Jalisco in Guadalajara, Mexico.
April 23: Palacio De Los Deportes in Mexico City, Mexico.
April 24: Palacio De Los Deportes in Mexico City, Mexico.

April 27: Estadio Universitario in Monterrey, Mexico.

April 28: Estadio Universitario in Monterrey, Mexico.

May 14: (As the Drunk Fux) Hollywood Palladium in Hollywood, CA. The line up: Slash, Duff, Matt, Gilby, Zakk Wylde and Lemmy of Motorhead

May 22: Hayarkon Park in Tel Aviv, Israel.

May 24: Olympic Stadium in Athens, Greece.

May 26: Inonu Stadium in Istanbul, Turkey.

May 29: National Bowl in Milton Keynes, England.

May 30: National Bowl in Milton Keynes, England.

June 2: Praterstadion in Vienna, Austria.

June 5: Stadspark De Goffert in Nijmegen, Holland.

June 6: Stadspark De Goffert in Nijmegen, Holland.

June 8: Gentofte Stadion in Copenhagen, Denmark.

June 10: Valle Hovin in Oslo, Norway.

June 11: Slash jammed with guitar legend John Mayall at a club in Oslo, Norway.

June 12: Stockholms Stadion in Stockholm, Sweden.

June 16: Fussballstadion St. Jakob in Basel, Switzerland.

June 18: Weserstadion in Bremen, Germany.

June 19: Müngersdorfer Stadion in Cologne, Germany.

June 22: Wildparkstadion in Karlsruhe, Germany.

June 25: Waldstadion in Frankfurt, Germany.

June 26: Olympiastadion in Munich, Germany.

June 29: Modena Stadio in Modena, Italy.

June 30: Modena Stadio in Modena, Italy.

July 5: Estadi Olimpic in Barcelona, Spain.

July 6: Vicente Calderon Stadium in Madrid, Spain.

July 8: Zenith de Nancy in Nancy, France.

July 9: Halle Tony Garnier in Lyon, France.

July 11: Werchter Festival Ground in Werchter, Belgium.

July 13: Palais Omnisports de Bercy in Paris, France.

July 16: Estadio River Plate in Buenos Aires, Argentina.

July 17: Estadio River Plate in Buenos Aires, Argentina.

"I was treated great. Look, I was paid well; I was in a rock band that I liked to be in. I never had any problems on the road. It's kind of hard to have problems or complain about the lifestyle in the band when you are selling out stadiums every show you play, and people are buying the records. There's a lot of controversy that comes with it, but as far as I'm concerned life could be a lot worse. The guys were always great, we hung out every day together" Gilby Clarke

1994

January 20: Axl performs 'Come Together' with Bruce Springsteen at the 1994 Rock N' Roll Hall Of Fame Induction Ceremony at the Waldorf Astoria Hotel in New York, NY.

It is fairly clear looking at the gigs the band has played throughout their career their lean spell creatively speaking coincided with their dwindling live performances. The upheaval of personnel led to only ex members remaining busy on the road. While Slash, Duff, Matt and Gilby were active individually; they also collaborated occasionally and performed at the odd concert collectively. One example was the Randy Castillo tribute show at the Key Club in Los Angeles along with other guests such as Steven Tyler, members of Buckcherry and Sen Dog of Cypress Hill. Slash, Duff and Matt also played at the likes of Club Vodka in Hollywood with Shooter Jennings from Stargun.

Unbelievably it was a full six years before Axl Rose returned to perform on a public stage of any kind. Clearly the years of media spotlight led to him feeling happier away from the public gaze and he spent most of that interim period away from virtually anybody. For those confused as to Axl's eternal lateness on stage, he had this to say (and this was back in 1992 so it's clear that some things never change) "I pretty much follow my own internal clock, and I perform better later at night. Nothing seems to work out for me until later at night. And it is our show. I don't want to make people sit around and wait it drives me nuts. That hour and a half or two hour time period that I'm late going onstage is living hell, because I'm wishing there was any way on earth I could get out of where I am and knowing

I'm not going to be able to make it. I'm late to everything. I've always wanted to have it written in my will that when I die, the coffin shows up a half hour late and says on the side, in gold, SORRY I'M LATE".

There has usually been a good reason, at least in Axl's own mind for either failing to show up on time, or at all. He has given an explanation in the past stating; "I'm usually an emotional wreck before a show because of something else that's going on in my life. I mean, as I say, somethin' weird just always happens to me two seconds before I'm supposed to go onstage, you know? Like I found William Rose. Turns out, he was murdered in '84 and buried somewhere in Illinois, and I found that out like two days before a show and I was fucking whacked! I mean I've been trying to uncover this mystery since I was a little kid. I didn't even know he existed until I was a teenager, you know?" Life in the period of 1993 until the new century was not easy for varying reasons but thankfully the band seems to now be finding its feet again.

The following is a focus on the return to more acceptable touring standards for Guns N' Roses and brings us up to date with their concert activity.

June 2000

Just 250 of the assembled throng see Axl Rose appear on stage completely unannounced at the Cat Club in West Hollywood with the club's house band The Starfuckers, of course led by former G N' R guitarist Gilby Clarke. Rose's first live appearance since 1994 is an impromptu rendition of two Rolling Stones songs, 'Wild Horses' and 'Dead Flowers'.

Axl also appeared in *Rolling Stone* magazine for a rare interview.

He updated fans on the current state of the *Chinese Democracy* recording, reputed at the time to have cost at least $6 million. He also reveals that the entire *Appetite For Destruction* album has been completely revamped, though oddly this has gone on record as being minus the songs 'Patience' and 'You Could Be Mine'. Whether this was Axl's memory serving him poorly or simply a misquote or

misprint remains to be seen but the explanation for the re–recording was given by Axl as thus. "Why did we do that? Well, we had
to rehearse them anyway to be able to perform them live again, and
there were a lot of recording techniques that subtly could use a little sprucing up".

December 2000

The first Guns N' Roses live show in seven years is confirmed, with
the announcement of a full–length tour to come. The new line up was
due to debut at the Rock In Rio III festival in Brazil on January 14th,
along side other rock and metal acts such as Iron Maiden, Halford,
Queens Of The Stone Age, Sepultura, Foo Fighters, Red Hot Chili
Peppers. Not to mention such bizarre guests as Sting, Oasis, Neil
Young, Britney Spears, and REM. It is leaked the band will certainly feature former Nine Inch Nails guitarist Robin Finck and the virtually unknown guitarist Buckethead who fans are intrigued to learn
plays wearing an upturned bucket of Kentucky Fried Chicken on
his head.

December 2000

Axl unveils the new look band – the aforementioned Buckethead
and Robin Finck plus guitarist Paul Tobias, former Replacements
bassist Tommy Stinson, keyboard players Dizzy Reed and Chris
Pittman and ex Primus drummer Brian Mantia – with a double act
of New Year shows in Las Vegas. A packed venue of 1,800 fans pays
$180 per head for the privilege of watching the band at the House
Of Blues.

*"We've done four or so new songs at the live shows but we are still
holding our big guns back" Axl Rose*

January 2001

January 1: House of Blues in Las Vegas, NV
  This show was most notable for being Axl's first G N' R concert in 7 and a half years. He seems in happy mood, introducing himself as 'Uncle Axl' and athletically bounding around the stage, flitting between front man and fan (watching the band from side–stage). The set was focused on material from *Appetite For Destruction* and even included 'Think About You' which hasn't been documented as being played since 1986.
  There were new tracks too, the first time these had been aired. 'Oh My God' was melodically reworked. Axl told the crowd he had written 'Chinese Democracy' after seeing the movie *Kundun*. Other new songs played were 'The Blues' and 'Silkworms'. After 'Chinese Democracy,' and a short drum solo, Buckethead took centre stage, playing numchukas before throwing them into the crowd. He then threw chocolate roses from a KFC bucket into the audience. 'Paradise City,' closed proceedings, Axl thanked the crowd wishing everyone a happy new year. The G N' R return has been a success, a 2 hour plus show without negative incident!

January 15: Rock In Rio III at Rock City, Barra da Tijuca in Rio de Janeiro, Brazil.
Attendance: 200,000
Opening acts: Pato Fú, Carlinhos Brown, IRA! e Ultraje a Rigor, Papa Roach, Oasis
Sound check: It's So Easy, November Rain, My Michelle, Oh My God, Knockin' On Heaven's Door
Set: Welcome To The Jungle, It's So Easy, Mr Brownstone, Live And Let Die, Oh My God, Think About You, You Could Be Mine, Sossego [Robin Finck solo], Sweet Child O' Mine, Knockin' On Heaven's Door, Madagascar, Guitar Solo [Buckethead], November Rain, Out Ta Get Me, Rocket Queen, Chinese Democracy, Chicken Binge [Buckethead], Instrumental Jam, The Blues, Patience, Nightrain
Encore: Instrumental Jam, My Michelle, Silkworms, Paradise City

Guns N' Roses appear at Rock In Rio after several rumours of rifts in the ranks and a rumour the band is not going to turn up at all. 200,000 fans witness a full two and a half hour set including four new songs.

At one point Axl states: "I know that many of you are disappointed that some of the people you know and love could not be with us here today. Regardless of what you have learned or read, my former friends have worked very hard to do everything they could so I wouldn't be here today. I say fuck that." He uses the set as an excuse to set the record straight on as number of issues and seems to be in fine ranting form. At one point the front man ejects a fan for taunting him.

For the second show Axl makes a speech about Paul Tobias, saying that without Paul, there would be no more Guns N' Roses. After 'Patience,' Axl tells the crowd he used to surf the Internet, but "it seems to be a big garbage can". So he doesn't read the garbage that is written anymore. After a blistering 'Paradise City,' Axl happily tells the audience about his Brazilian family. He says Beta has been a mother and manager to him. Beta was his translator. Axl leaves the stage promising fans the band will "Be back next summer with a whole bunch of new songs!"

March 2001

The band announces there will be the first UK shows in years with appearances scheduled for London, Glasgow, Manchester and Birmingham in June later in the year.

May 2001

A US report states that Axl Rose is refusing to perform live and that the European tour is very much in doubt. Their reasoning? That Axl has undergone a secret batch of hair transplants leaving him with "big, scarred patches on the back of his head". Another report also suggests he has had liposuction leaving him needing time to recover. (In 2004 Hollywood weekly magazine, National Enquirer featured Axl in 'before' and 'after' modes allegedly proving he'd had surgery to his cheekbones, forehead and mouth. The pictures certainly showed a marked difference from an older shot but equally the 2004 picture was heavily lighted and appeared airbrushed.)

There are also rumours of a mystery stomach illness being suffered by Buckethead as well as the need to finish off the *Chinese Democracy* album, with reports suggesting Roy Thomas Baker (Queen) has taken over production duties. Official sources only confirm that the four UK shows have been rescheduled for between December 13 and 19 of 2001.

November 2001

As rumours fly to the effect that Buckethead has left the band there are once again no concrete confirmations of the tour actually going ahead. In an interview with a Canadian magazine Slash suggests he is aware of the current G N' R plight by stating that "Now that I know a little bit more about that stuff I'm trying to look for a loophole," when talking of the remaining original ex members (himself, Steven, Izzy and Duff) seeking to take part control of the Guns N' Roses name back.

December 2001

The entire 14 dates of the band's European tour are cancelled at the last minute. In a later interview Axl will state that he was entirely unaware of the fact he was even meant to be doing a tour, leaving manager Doug Goldstein to embarrassingly admit he neglected to tell Axl of the scheduled shows. The official statement from Goldstein read: "Following the euphoria of 'Rock In Rio', I jumped the gun and arranged a European tour, as our plan was to have the new album out this year. I'm very sorry to disappoint our fans. I made a plan, and unfortunately it did not work out." Goldstein also points out that Axl has spent "every waking hour of every day during the last five years" working on *Chinese Democracy*.

December 29: The Joint Las Vegas, NV

Attendance: 1,400
Set: Welcome To The Jungle, It's So Easy, Mr. Brownstone, Live And Let Die, Guitar Solo [Buckethead], Oh My God, Think About You, You Could Be Mine, Sweet Child O' Mine, Knockin' On Heaven's Door, Out Ta Get Me, Madagascar, Rocket Queen, November Rain, Chinese Democracy, The Blues, Acoustic Guitar Solo [Buckethead], Patience, Silkworms, My Michelle, Paradise City

G N' R played from 10:52 p.m. until 1 a.m. Due to constant sound problems at the beginning of the show Axl left and returned several times. At one point Robin Finck, also angry at the sound hurled his guitar whilst playing 'Oh My God'. Surprisingly the band persevered, despite Axl getting angry with the sound engineer. It later emerged Axl had heard Slash was due to appear at the club. He insisted the security should turn Slash away and in thinking he was in the venue on a couple of occasions, stopped the band immediately. Slash later stated that "I was trying to be discreet, but apparently Guns N' Roses' management found out and it was major pandemonium, it was like they sent out an all points bulletin."

Axl explained about the current Guns' situation, saying the Vegas shows were the first he had wanted to play since the *Use Your Illusion* tour. He told the crowd how the European 2001 tour had been booked by Doug Goldstein without his knowledge, and it was only from the Internet he knew G N' R were meant to be doing it.

Axl played new songs once more with a promise the album would surface soon.

December 31: Hard Rock Hotel Las Vegas, NV.
Attendance: 1,400
Set: Welcome To The Jungle, It's So Easy, Mr. Brownstone, Live And Let Die, Oh My God, Think About You, You Could Be Mine, Sweet Child O' Mine, Knockin' On Heaven's Door, Madagascar, November Rain, Out Ta Get Me, Guitar Solo [Buckethead], Rocket Queen, Chinese Democracy, Acoustic Guitar Solo [Buckethead], Patience, The Blues, Silkworms, My Michelle, Nightrain
Encore: Paradise City

The show was a huge improvement on the previous one. The sound was immense and the band performed the songs flawlessly with Axl often running to the side of the stage to watch the band carry off G N' R standards. At 11:54 p.m. Axl's bodyguard Earl told him it was almost midnight – the band then played the emotive 'Madagascar', finishing at exactly 12 a.m. The stage screens featured live pictures of the Vegas strip.

After 'Paradise City,' Axl screamed, "TWO THOUSAND FUCKIN' TWO! LAS VEGAS, NEVADA, GOOD...FUCKIN'... NIGHT!!!"

February 2002

Roy Thomas Baker is sacked from his duties on the *Chinese Democracy* project, just as Axl's former band mates take legal action to halt the use of the new recording of 'Welcome To The Jungle' being used in the *Black Hawk Down* soundtrack.

May 2002

G N' R announce an appearance at the Leeds Festival on August 23, and they are also asked to appear as headliners at the Reading version of the Carling festival but cannot due to playing the Pukkelpop Festival in Belgium.

July 2002

The band is set to play London's Docklands Arena on August 26 and 27 but no official confirmation is actually given. There is also the likelihood that the Leeds festival might not go ahead after improvements due to be made to the venue don't appear and the company's licence is not renewed.

"I was in Guns N' Roses because it was my favourite band and watching this band now is just as exciting as the old players if not more for me" Axl Rose

August 2002

August 14: Summer Sonic Festival at the Hong Kong Convention
And Exhibition Centre Hong Kong, China.
Attendance: 2,000 +
Set: Welcome To The Jungle, It's So Easy, Mr. Browstone, Live
And Let Die, Think About You, You Could Be Mine, Sweet Child
O' Mine, Knockin' On Heaven's Door, Out Ta Get Me, Madagascar,
Guitar Solo [Buckethead], Piano Solo, November Rain, Rocket
Queen, Chinese Democracy, Patience, The Blues, My Michelle,
Nightrain
Encore: Paradise City

G N' R introduced their newly added rhythm guitarist Richard
Fortus for their first ever show in China. Before playing 'Chinese
Democracy,' Axl explained the title of the album and the artwork
for the new album was displayed on a giant stage screen. Before
'Paradise City' the screen displayed China's flag, plus several views
of Hong Kong from a car and a helicopter. During the song fire-
works were set off followed by red and yellow confetti falling from
the ceiling.

August 23: Carling Weekend Leeds Festival at Temple Newsam
Park Leeds, England
Attendance: 52,000+
Set: Welcome To The Jungle, It's So Easy, Mr. Brownstone, Live
And Let Die, Think About You, You Could Be Mine, Sweet Child
O' Mine, Knockin' On Heaven's Door, Out Ta Get Me, Madagascar,
Guitar Solo [Buckethead], Piano Solo, November Rain, The Blues,
Patience, Rocket Queen, Nightrain
Encore: Guitar Solo [Robin], Paradise City

After rumours claiming the show wouldn't go ahead, G N' R arrived onstage shortly past 11 p.m. due to delays with previous set
changes. After 'Live And Let Die,' Axl said, "So I don't know... it
looks like a bunch of you motherfuckers thought I might actually

make it here tonight! Look at all these fuckin' people! You like that Bucket? This is called 'Think About You.'"

Before 'November Rain,' Axl remarked, "Well, it appears that we're gonna have an interesting evening. You see the...the city council and the promoters' say we have to end the show. And they'll say that I'm... they could say maybe I'm inciting a riot. Now I'm not 'cause I don't want anyone to get arrested or anyone to get in trouble or anything like that. But I think we got a good 7 or 8 fucking songs left at least to play for you. And I didn't fucking come all the way to fucking England to be told to go back home by some fucking ass-hole! All I've got for the last 8 years is shit after shit after shit in the fucking press and Axl's this, Axl's that – I'm here to play a fucking show and we wanna play! So...if you wanna stay, I wanna stay and we'll see what happens. Everybody – nobody try to get in trouble or anything and try to have a good time."

In the mid section of 'November Rain,' Axl momentarily stops the song and says, "So I've been told that we've got more time... and whoever is responsible for that I'd like to say thank you." During 'Patience,' Axl sees someone in the crowd wearing a 'Where is Slash?' t–shirt, "He's in my ass! That's where Slash is! Fuckhead! Go home!" Axl laughs.

The show ends with Axl saying to the crowd, "I would like to seri-ously thank you for coming tonight. And by the looks of things, we will be seeing you again! I'd like to thank whoever was responsible for giving us the extra time and uh... this is Mr. Robin Finck." Axl throws his microphone into the crowd at the end of 'Paradise City.'

August 26: London Arena, London, England
Attendance: 12,500
Set: Welcome To The Jungle, It's So Easy, Mr. Brownstone, Live And Let Die, Think About You, You Could Be Mine, Guitar Solo [Robin], Sweet Child O' Mine, Knockin' On Heaven's Door, Out Ta Get Me, Chinese Democracy, Madagascar, Rhiad And The Bedouins, Guitar Solo [Buckethead], Piano Solo, November Rain, The Blues, Acoustic Guitar Solo [Buckethead], Rocket Queen, Patience, My Michelle, Nightrain
Encore: Guitar Solo [Robin], Paradise City

After 'Chinese Democracy,' Axl says, "Now, there's been some concern... that if we play 5 or 6 new songs, then there can't that many more on the album. Au contraire mon frère! We're just playin' the songs we're not considering putting out as singles or anything. So you'll get 18 songs and about 10 extra tracks. And when the record company feels that has run it's course, then you'll get it all over again. And by that time, I should be done with the 3rd album! So we'll see if all goes well boys and girls! And if Uncle Axl proves not to be an asshole – we'll have to see, the jury's still out." He then asks Tommy "Wait, was that a rant? Does that qualify as a rant or was that just nonsense? It was under 5? OK, it's... it doesn't qualify, wasn't long enough!"

During the encore of 'Paradise City,' Axl shouts, "God save the Queen!" finishing another triumphant show in England for G N' R.

August 29: G N' R performed a medley ('Welcome to the Jungle', 'Madagascar', 'Paradise City') at the MTV Video Music Awards.

This was not confirmed until the day before the show (the band worked a set out on the day itself) and was a complete shock to most viewers. As usual there were problems with the band making the show at all. Police stopped Axl walking down the street to the venue and as the public convened around the scene trying to catch a glimpse of the star surrounded by law enforcement officers, a member of the crowd shouted "Hey – there goes Kid Rock!" referring to the amused Axl Rose. The equally bemused singer had to essentially sneak into the MTV studios, flanked by both the G N' R and MTV security in order to perform the show, with police tracking him all the way. Axl referred to the melee as "pretty interesting".

Guns N' Roses promoters Clear Channel confirm the band's Docklands Arena appearance, a single show on August 26. An interview with Axl appearing on the official site of the band sees him state he feels the need to "wrap up the baby" with regards to recording of *Chinese Democracy*, now believed to have cost somewhere in the region of $8 million. As for those waiting with baited breath for the album itself Axl has scant consolation, "Don't. Live your life. That's your responsibility, not mine."

November 2002

Guns N' Roses' first North American tour in nine years starts on November 7th at the General Motors Place in Vancouver. A riot ensues after the promoter cancels the first show. Of the riot guitarist Buckethead said: "I felt Shocked and dismayed I mean, I didn't even know what the hell was going on. Tommy and Dizzy were doing an interview backstage with Kurt Loder from MTV, and they heard the announcement that the show was cancelled coming over the PA system in the arena. No one could believe it. And it was Robin's birthday too. It was such a drag. Axl had no idea, either, because he was on his way there. His plane was delayed, and we knew that he wasn't going to make it to the sound check, but there was never any question that he'd be there in time for the gig. Apparently, the venue just pulled the plug. It was pretty disappointing. And even worse, when you turn on the TV and see people getting their teeth knocked out, it's not something that you want to be a party to. So now the lawsuits will fly."

After subsequent shows, which go ahead minus problems, another riot is caused by the failure of G N' R to play their scheduled date in Philadelphia on December 6th. Axl later admits to watching a basketball game in his hotel room when due on stage. A full cancellation then places the entire tour under scrutiny from more frustrated fans and press after just one month.

"So now I wander through my day trying to find my way" 'The Blues'

Guns N' Roses are no strangers to controversy. Throughout their career, decadence and self–belief has been paramount to their longevity. They are still here. There is an album due. Despite, or perhaps because of Axl Rose's eccentricities there is still a band with the name now almost two decades old.

Like all the best artists Axl lives by his own agenda. He is now able to indulge in his passions and ambitious plans given his wealth. Although those plans are still not quite clear, it is hoped he returns soon with a studio album to silence the critics and please the fans.

Somehow along the way, G N' R turned into an unknown entity. Whoever was responsible for this transformation – there is no going back. It is very unlikely Guns' will become a cabaret act in the future, appearing to revisit old tunes and rake the millions in. Instead, Axl has spent his time ensuring his return will be a make or break for the band, once dubbed the most dangerous in the world.

He has a long way to go to restore such credibility, and perhaps in many ways does not seek to. For Axl it has always been about the music. As soon as this changed and the press homed in on his insecurities and temperament, he exploded in more ways than one. He virtually vanished to rediscover his roots. In shunning the spotlight, he has provided himself with the desired privacy to create as if he were unknown. Such anonymous status is attractive to Axl. Make no mistake; he is not a loveless, soulless brute, hell–bent on destruction and mayhem. Otherwise how could he live so reclusively and restfully, hidden away from the public eye?

Axl still seeks to please himself but he has obviously matured as a person. It seems clearer to him now the goals he must attain in life. It is not about money, status or even music. It's about inner peace. However life circumstances change, for better or worse, the demons remain from before the change. It was this that Axl had always struggled with. He had to come to terms with terrible revelations from his childhood, all in the centre of a media cyclone that took his quotable and likeable demeanour and distorted it to make him the hero or the villain – depending on the story and the writer.

Fans saw him as a demi–god, resplendent in body, mind and spirit, whilst the media knew he was reliable for a good quote. All the best one–liners emitted from Axl and his complex personality both welcomed the attention and denied the hostility. He could not, or would not put up with harassment in public. If he was challenged, he strained at the leash to attack. The best form of defence in his mind was to rip the opponents head off (verbally or otherwise) before he could be savaged.

Years of abuse, neglect and heartache drove Axl to his lowest point. It has taken a decade for him to reform himself. Although in Chapter 11 it seems that he has merely become stranger, this may only appear so to those with little understanding of traumatic life events. It is fact; everyone deals with inner fears, guilt or thoughts differently. For Axl, dealing with himself has been made more difficult by those who form opinions about him without knowing the truth.

The truth is still somewhat blurred through so many versions of events but there is a common theme throughout Axl's life. Self–preservation is his long–term defence mechanism. It is this immense strength of character and individual knowledge, which has kept him of interest to the public, and most importantly to himself.

As long as he believes in himself he will realise the world is interested in him. Occasionally he may lapse into insecurity regarding who he is and where he can go, but always he returns to the inner sanctuary of his own mind. Despite his demons, inside Axl there is a comfort blanket, which wraps around him every time a barbed sentiment is spewed or a punch thrown.

Axl is lucky. He no doubt has a spiritual force providing him shelter from the wrongdoers. This shield follows him in the form of new friends, uninterested in fame, fortune or excess. The path to enlightenment is the road, which Axl now walks. If we are respectfully curious and aware, the real W. Axl Rose may yet return.

"Well I jumped into the river too many times to make it home
I'm out here on my own an drifting all alone
If it doesn't show give it time
To read between the lines" *'Estranged'*

The Velvet Revolver Story

"This is the rock band I've always wanted to be in" Duff Mckagan

In 2002 at a benefit for Randy Castillo (the drummer for Ozzy Osbourne and Lita Ford, who had died of cancer aged 51), Slash, Duff and Matt Sorum came together. After playing with each other once again, the three decided they wanted to form another full time band.

Izzy Stradlin was invited to join them but he rejected the offer in favour of his solo career. Slash turned to old school friend Dave Kushner, who was no stranger to high profile rock bands having been in the Dave Navarro set up as well as Wasted Youth. He was also a friend of Duff's, having played with him in the bassist's Loaded project. Whilst trying to decide on a permanent name the group referred to themselves as 'The Project'. "Dave's our secret weapon," Duff later said. "He plays amazing textures and he can handle himself with Slash." It was important for Slash to be able to duet with an able guitarist who didn't have an overblown ego. In hindsight, the band were clearly better with Kushner in the ranks than they may have been with Stradlin, given Slash's reluctance to play alongside Izzy.

VH1 were invited to record the process of The Project searching for a lead singer. "We heard so many different singers, and every one lent towards a different vibe," Matt Sorum said after they had captured a vocalist. "Unfortunately, the vibes were usually not too good. As soon as we heard the vocals that people were sending in, we knew we were in trouble, and we knew we just couldn't put out some shabby rock tribute. It had to be something special."

A number of lead singers auditioned, including Josh Todd formerly of Buckcherry, Sebastian Bach ex of Skid Row, Kelly Shaefer of Atheist and Neurotica and Travis Meeks of Days of the New, but all were unsuccessful. Instead, a singer who offered his services a short while afterwards, was chosen. The former Stone Temple Pilots front man Scott Weiland had been friends with Duff for a while and had been socialising with him. He had also played alongside Kushner when he'd performed with the Electric Love Hogs.

Slash wanted to name the band Revolver, but Weiland suggested adding Velvet, and whether it was a deliberate irony at Guns N' Roses or not, the name was agreed on. As soon as the public knew a true super group had formed, the record labels' interest also peaked, and VR was approached to contribute a song to *The Hulk* soundtrack. In 2003 'Set Me Free' was recorded. They also did a cover of Pink Floyd's 'Money' for the remake movie, *The Italian Job*.

Come July the band played its first live show – at the El Rey Theatre in Los Angeles. "Doing the gig was worth more than any time in the studio or hanging out," said Weiland. "This was undeniable and the most sonically violent thing I've ever been a part of. Singing 'It's So Easy' with those guys at the El Rey was amazing. When I wrote 'Sex Type Thing' (from STP's debut album *Core*), it was sort of inspired by that low vocal of 'It's So Easy'."

For his new band mates, Scott Weiland was something of an unknown quantity, both up close and on stage. Slash, for one, had never seen him perform previously. He knew of course that Scott's voice would be just right for the material Velvet Revolver were creating, but playing onstage together, "the spontaneous chemistry sealed the deal on this whole collaboration" commented Slash.

The chemistry was helped by playing a relatively small venue, something that VR has continued since. This is in part a conscious choice by the band – they much prefer shows where the audience is not only visible but also audible. Duff alluded to this when he stated, "in the big stadium shows I played with Guns', the lights would be so bright, sometimes we couldn't even see the crowd. I mean we could hear them but that was it. We want to maintain a toe to toe relationship with our audience. We're gonna play the small venues too."

Despite Scott Weiland's court appearances for ongoing drug charges, and his rehabilitation commitments, the band managed to record a full length album at the end of the year, which they named *Contraband*. "This has been a pretty rough year for me," Weiland admitted. "The whole divorce thing really pulled me through a keyhole emotionally, so I fell backwards on a narcotic slide and had to pay the price. But these guys were there to catch my fall. This has been like a gang. And it helps that they've all been through it themselves a million times, so there's no judgment there. They've all kicked dope so it's not like I'm the lone junkie in the band or I'm the only one who knows what it's like to kick a three gram a day heroin habit. Through all the difficulties I've been through, they've all been there. That's more than I could ever ask for, more than I've ever experienced before." Duff said the band had been through a lot with Scott: "We got him to come up to the mountains, to Washington State, and he was learning martial arts and learning how to live a different way. Whatever happens, he has some tools that he didn't have before."

"Appetite For Destruction was one of those records that made me believe, that became my bible and taught me everything" Scott Weiland

Weiland also commented on the creativity of song writing and how that process had been such a godsend for Velvet Revolver. "We're looking to get back that same feeling we had when we all first started making music, the sense of doing it for the pure joy of making music. Along the way the whole idea that got us into this had been raped and sodomized. We were all in mourning of that and wondering if we could somehow get it back. As it turns out, the only way we could get it all back was to start it all new. Now we have that opportunity and it's amazing. This music is just vicious, very aggressive and it forces you to lace your boots up and sort of get ready for the fight."

It was no wonder Weiland felt the way he did – full of critical acclaim for Stone Temple Pilots' work yet plundering the depths of drug addiction had lead to an impossible reconciliation with the STP set up. It seemed Slash and Duff were made for Scott Weiland. With the problems the ex G N' R members had endured in just wanting to make rock n' roll the time was right to join up with a front man who had been and done everything before, yet wanted a more sober stab at the big time.

"There is no real concept to me," Slash stated. "We set out to make music we enjoy and can feel proud of playing, music that people we like will want to listen to. As soon as you start thinking beyond that, about wanting to keep up with the Joneses or about fitting in with somebody else's format that's when you lose the map. So we've just done what we do, and tried to have a cool time doing it." This was an almost lazy assurance in the ideals of Velvet Revolver, namely that there were very few ideals beyond playing rock music and enjoying doing so. For many fans this was a welcome theory. It showed how quickly a very strong record could be created when all musicians were working from the same page.

As for a producer, the band decided to co produce with Josh Abraham who had previously worked with the likes of Korn and Linkin Park. It seemed strange on paper but Abraham was more than able to produce classic rock music, and he managed to make the band feel relevant to the current music scene, without taking away their own experience and influences. For the rock veterans, they were aware they could not simply release an 'old' sounding record and get away with it. Hiring Abraham was all about being able to compete in the current music market.

The *Contraband* album was released in June 2004 debuting at #1 on the Billboard album charts, #2 in the Australian charts and #11 on the British album charts. Originally the album was to be titled *Uppers & Downers*, which came from a fan website. Though the band liked this title they decided *Contraband* was far snappier. In terms of the songs, the band had the arsenal they needed. As Duff would say, "it's an album. It's twelve songs. It's not a single with eleven fillers. It's a journey." And Slash confirmed, "Every song sounds different," he also said. "Everything has got a vibe to it. Each song is its own style."

And perhaps more importantly, the Velvet Revolver experience was not about trying to recapture a sound used by either Guns N' Roses or Stone Temple Pilots. Other so called super groups often had an obvious link, sonically, to their previous projects whereas with VR, though Weiland's voice was distinctive, the music itself was a separate experience to anything the band members had come up with before.

"This is the most effort I've ever put into anything. I put as much effort into the first STP album, but now I know so much more" Scott Weiland

Duff made a typical punk fuelled statement, "Our music is very aggressive. There's always that 'Fuck you' element to it. Really that's all we know how to do. We can't play nice or play radio. Slash, Matt and I were always that way in Guns, and Scott and Dave are very like–minded. To me, this is the first dangerous band that's come around in a while, truly dangerous. People are going to say, 'Oh a super group. These guys have everything.' And I can understand that, but we're not coming at this that way. We really hope to bring some chaos back into the whole world of rock."

INSPIRATION

"In a nutshell, this whole album for me is pretty much about the poisonous, toxic relationship that I had been in and the catastrophic effects my break–up and subsequent divorce has had on me. It's complete honesty so if people relate, great" Scott Weiland

Just like Guns N' Roses, Velvet Revolver has much to say, making their music even more meaningful and propelling it to greater heights than many of their current peers. Thanks to Scott Weiland's experiences and articulation in expressing them, there is a story worth hearing behind every song. Lyrics can be deciphered by the individual and are easily understood. One of Weiland's great capabilities is to connect with the listener in a clearly definable manner. He certainly did that with the Stone Temple Pilots and on his solo album *12 Bar Blues*.

What follows are some revelations on the way certain songs were recorded or created.

'Big Machine' is a modern glam rock anthem incorporating such icons as Sweet and T–Rex with a hint of upbeat grunge. The song was initially written by the VR musicians who then passed it to Weiland. According to Duff, "Scott chopped the shit out of it in Pro Tools and gave us this thing that was like – whoa! Then we played it like he'd rearranged it, and it totally made sense." One of the many songs to recall STP's finer melodies, this has an obvious Scott Weiland stamp.

'Fall To Pieces' was initially going to feature a cello playing the bass line. This was Duff's idea and he said, "We thought it would be great to have a cello with that line but everybody liked the bass just being the bass and so it's more of a sparse song." Recalling the more ballad style material from Stone Temple Pilot's *Purple* album, the song is a strong build up between a quiet verse and a huge chorus. Like many of *Contraband*'s tracks it merges the various band members trademark strengths – luscious guitar playing from Slash, Duff's plaintive bass work and Weiland's soulful croon.

'Slither' was the first track to be released from the album and was an assured indication that this was no side project. The lead riff is a full on groove–laden beast. The initial riffs were written by Slash, and Dave Kushner found this way of working easier for him as he merely added his own touch to the existing guitar lines. It's no wonder the riff sounds so thick, Duff, Slash and Dave are all playing the same notes together. Weiland says of 'Slither,' "it's a dark, prodding heavy one that definitely has an old STP vibe to it." The solo even sounds like a Dean Deleo (STP) lead.

'Sucker Train Blues' is the opening number; hurtling into the brimstone the quintet creates after a typically noxious Duff bass line. Though it appears first, it was actually the last song written for the album. The introductory guitar licks are played by Dave Kushner and all the rhythm guitars were played on a 1956 Telecaster. Best of all the solo was done in one take – whammy bar notwithstanding! The band considered this song as the first single.

'Superhuman' features two guitars played simultaneously, both by Slash. Duff also doubled his bass tracks for an extra thick sound. Unlike his usual clear bass lines, Duff used a fuzz pedal for a dirtier sound. As Duff quaintly put it, "It's almost inaudible but it'll rattle your nuts".

'You Got No Right' is a Beatles flavoured acoustic song, which Slash played on a Takamine guitar, recorded via microphone and pickup, which is very clear when you hear the song. Though it sounds marginally electric, the song itself was the only one from *Contraband* that was written on an acoustic. Slash acknowledged the chord changes were down to him, but the vocal lines Scott put on top of the music were amazing, and changed the whole outlook of the song. Slash admitted, "I wouldn't have come up with anything like that".

GUNS N' ROSES

ALBUMS

Live ?!*@ Like A Suicide: *Reckless Life/Nice Boys/Move To The City/Mama Kin*
LP –1986
Appetite For Destruction: *Welcome To The Jungle/It's So Easy/ Nightrain/Out Ta Get Me/Mr. Brownstone/Paradise City/My Michelle/Think About You/Sweet Child O Mine/You're Crazy/ Anything Goes/Rocket Queen*
LP, CD, Cassette, – Geffen 1991
Gn'R Lies: *Reckless Life/Nice Boys/Move To The City/Mama Kin/ Patience/Used To Love Her/You're Crazy/One In A Million*
LP, CD, Cassette – Geffen 1991
Use Your Illusion 1: *Right Next Door To Hell/Dust N Bones/Live And Let Die/Don't Cry (original)/Perfect Crime/You Ain't The First/ Bad Obsession/Back Off Bitch/Double Talkin Jive/November Rain/ The Garden/Garden Of Eden/Don't Damn Me/Bad Apples/Dead Horse/Coma*
2xLP, CD, Cassette – Geffen 1991
Use Your Illusion 2: *Civil War/14 Years/Yesterdays/Knockin On Heaven's Door/Get In The Ring/Shotgun Blues/Breakdown/Pretty Tied Up/Locomotive/So Fine/Estranged/You Could Be Mine/Don't Cry (alt. Lyrics)/My World*
2xLP, CD, Cassette – Geffen 1991
The Spaghetti Incident: *Since I Don't Have You/New Rose/Down On The Farm/Human Being/Raw Power/Ain't It Fun/Buick Makane/ Hair Of The Dog/Attitude/Black Leather/You Can't Put Your Arms Around A Memory/I Don't Care About You*
LP, CD, Cassette – Geffen 1993
Live Era '87–'93: Disc 1: *Nightrain/Mr. Brownstone/It's So Easy/ Welcome To The Jungle/Dust N Bones/My Michelle/You're Crazy/ Used To Love Her/Patience/It's Alright/November Rain*

Disc 2: *Out Ta Get Me/Pretty Tied Up/Yesterdays/Move To The City/*
You Could Be Mine/Rocket Queen/Sweet Child O Mine/Knockin On
Heaven's Door/Don't Cry/Estranged/Paradise City
2xLP, 2xCD – Geffen 1999

SINGLES

It's So Easy/Mr. Brownstone
7", 12" – Geffen 1987
Welcome To The Jungle
7", 12", CD – Geffen 1987
Sweet Child O Mine
7", 12", CD – Geffen 1988
Paradise City
7", 12", CD – Geffen 1989
Patience
7", 12", CD – Geffen 1989
Nightrain
7", 12", CD – Geffen 1989
You Could Be Mine
7", 12", CD – Geffen 1991
Don't Cry
7", 12", CD – Geffen 1991
Live And Let Die
7", 12", CD – Geffen 1991
November Rain
7", 12", CD – Geffen 1992
Knockin' On Heaven's Door
7", 12", CD – Geffen 1992
Yesterdays
7", 12", CD – Geffen 1992
The Civil War EP
7", 12", CD – Geffen 1993
Sympathy For The Devil
7", 12", CD – Geffen 1994
Since I Don't Have You
CD – Geffen 1994

SOUNDTRACKS

Lean On Me: *Welcome To The Jungle*
1989
Nobody's Child: The Romanian Angel Appeal: *Civil War*
1990
Days Of Thunder: *Knockin' On Heaven's Door*
1991
Interview With The Vampire: *Sympathy For The Devil*
1994
Grosse Point Blank: *Live And Let Die*
1997
Can't Hardly Wait: *Paradise City*
1998
End Of Days: *Oh My God*
1999

BOOTLEGS

Music Machine (Live In California) 11/03/86
Seattle '87 30/08/87
Marquee '87 06/06/87
Amsterdam '87
Madison, Wisconsin 1988
Ritz: 02/02/88
Jack Daniels Tour 09/05/88
Middletown, NY 07/08/88
Osaka '88 05/12/88
LA 1989 18/10/89
Farm Aid 07/04/90
Banzai 1991
2 x CDS
Live In Chile 1991
2 x CDS
Rock In Rio 2 1991
2 x CDS
For Motherfuckers Only Indiana 29/05/91

2 x CDS
Miami '91 31/12/91
3 x CDS
World Tour '92 Paris 1992
2 x CDS
World Tour '92 Japan 1992
Live In Germany 1992
2 x CDS
Berlin '92 26/05/92
2 x CDS
God Bless America 17/07/92
Live In Mexico 1993
2 x CDS
Frankfurt '93 25/06/93
2 x CDS
Back In The Jungle 01/01/01
2 x CDS
Rocking Rio 15/01/01
2 x CDS
Unplugged '87–'93

VARIOUS DATES

Rare Tracks 1
Rare Tracks 2

Rare Tracks 3
Unwanted Illusions
Live And Alive
Illusion On Tour
2 x CDS
November Rain
2 x CDS
Make My Day

SELECT PROMOS

Note: As with many collectible bands, the prices for promotional items can be fairly high, and in Guns N' Roses' case for some of the following items it might well be astronomical. Unusually for a high profile band they (or at least Geffen) has managed to keep very close tabs on the amount of promotional items that got sent to reviewers and radio stations.

Thus many of these are in very small circulation. The 1991 'Use Your Illusion I and II' US Promo Bible double CD was limited to 2000 copies, which when you think of the amount of Guns N' Roses fans around the world is rather paltry. This item is worth around £100 but really to a true collector you could go as high as £250– £300.

The most sought after item perhaps of the whole Guns' back catalogue would be the flexi disc, which came out in 1987. The square shaped item was basically an interview with Slash and Izzy talking over 3 tracks from 'Appetite For Destruction.' Today, CDs are often produced when a big band produces an album so that radio stations can play the pre–recorded interviews, sanctioned by the record companies. However this was scarcer in 1987 and given that this item was also a flexi disc (that now almost extinct format of vinyl) gives more credence to its scarcity. Expect not to get much change out of £200.

As collectors will often state the value of something is merely based upon how much a person is willing to pay, but the promo only items listed below rate as the crème da la crème of the Guns N' Roses collecting world and you should expect to pay rather a lot to complete your collection!

APPETITE FOR DESTRUCTION 7" SQUARE FLEXI DISC (USA) 1029221CS: *Welcome To The Jungle (sample)/Out Ta Get Me (sample)/Nighttrain (sample)/(Izzy and Slash interviews played over the samples)*
1987
GN'R (JAPAN) 12" PRS–10: *Paradise City/Welcome to The Jungle/ Patience/Sweet Child O Mine*

1989

SAMPLE YOUR ILLUSION (UK) 5" CD RADIO PROMO: *You Could Be Mine/Don't Cry/November Rain/Bad Obsession/Civil War/Double Talkin' Jive/Estranged*

1991

GUNS N RADIO (USE YOUR ILLUSION) 5" CD PRO–CD–4340: *Don't Cry (original)/Live And Let Die/Locomotive/Pretty Tied Up/ Dust N Bones/The Garden/Bad Obsession/Breakdown/Knockin On Heaven's Door/November Rain/14 Years/Estranged*

1991

GUNS N ROSES ON TOUR NOW 5" CD (USA) PRO–CD–4441: *Locomotive/Don't Cry (original)/Yesterdays/Live And Let Die/You Could Be Mine/The Garden/14 Years/November Rain/Civil War/ Knockin' On Heaven's Door/Estranged*

1991

USE YOUR ILLUSION 1 & 2 PROMO BIBLE 2XCDs (JAPAN) GEFFEN/MCA MVCG 43/44: *All Tracks from UYI 1 & 2*

1991

USE YOUR ILLUSION 1 & 2 PROMO BIBLE 2XCDs (USA) PRO–CD–4244: *All Tracks from UYI 1 & 2*

1991

GUNS N ROSES AUSTRALIA (AUSTRALIA) GNRD1: *Civil War/Don't Cry (alt.lyrics)/Live and Let Die (live at Wembley stadium 1991)/Shadow Of Your Love (demo)/Sweet Child O Mine/Patience/ Knockin' On Heaven's Door (live at Wembley stadium 1992)*

1992

GUNS N ROSES AUSTRALIA PROMO CASSETTE (AUSTRALIA) GNRC1: *Civil War/Don't Cry (alt.lyrics)/Live and Let Die (live at Wembley stadium 1991)/Shadow Of Your Love (demo)/Sweet Child O Mine/Patience/Knockin' On Heaven's Door (live at Wembley stadium 1992)*

1992

SANITIZED FOR YOUR PROTECTION CASSETTE (CANADA) GEFC91104: *Selections From UYI 1 & 2 – Censored For In–store play*

No date

BOX SETS

CD and T–SHIRT BOX SET (JAPAN) 37PZ2400
1988
APPETITE FOR COLLECTION (GERMANY) WE221: *Lies LP/
It's So Easy 12"/Paradise City 12"/Welcome to The Jungle 12"*
Bandana, Two Cloth Badges
1989
GUNS N ROSES BOX NR.1 (SWEDEN) NO CATALOGUE
NUMBER, ISSUED THROUGH WEA LABEL: *Paradise City
12"/Welcome to The Jungle 12"/Sweet Child O Mine 12"*
T–Shirt, Stickers, Badge, Patch
1989
USE YOUR ILLUSION 1 BOX SET (5,000) (AUSTRALIA)
GEFD–24415/GNRD1: *Use Your Illusion 1 CD/7 Track CD EP*
Bandana
1992
CELEBRATION PACK (AUSTRALIA) GEFD–24415: *Use Your
Illusion 1 Gold Picture CD*
'Coma' T–Shirt
1992
CELEBRATION PACK (AUSTRALIA) GEFC–24415: *Use Your
Illusion 1 Cassette*
'Coma' T–Shirt
1992
(The above CD and Cassette Boxes were also released for the UYI
II Album, with 'Coma' Shirt).
DESTRUCTION, LIES, THE ROAD TO ILLUSION (GERMANY)
GED 24434: *Appetite For Destruction CD/Lies CD/November Rain
Picture Disc*
Poster
1992
LIMITED EDITION BOX SET 1 (5,000) (JAPAN) MVZZ–2:
Appetite For Destruction CD/Lies CD/Holiday Greetings 3" CD
Poster
1993

LIMITED EDITION BOX SET II (5,000) (JAPAN) MVZZ–3: *Use Your Illusion I & II CDs/Holiday Greetings 3" CD*
Poster
1993
TOP HAT VOLUME 1 (500, 8" BOX) (GERMANY) NO CATALOGUE NUMBER: *Civil War/Don't Cry/Knockin' On Heaven's door/Live And Let die/November Rain/Yesterdays/You Could Be Mine CD Singles*
Certificate of Authenticity, Five Post Cards, Bandana, Six Removable Tattoos, "Kill Your Idols" T–Shirt, Poster Flag, Guns N Roses Pen, Watch and Key Ring
1993
TOP HAT VOLUME II (500, 8" BOX) (GERMANY) NO CATALOGUE NUMBER: *The Spaghetti Incident CD/The Tortellini Accident CD*
Certificate of Authenticity/Leather Wallet & Chain, 1993 Laminated Crew Pass, G n' R buckle–Leather Belt, G n' R Calendar
MAKING F@*KING BOXES (SWEDEN) GED 24450: *Use Your Illusion I & II CD/Slash Interview CD*
Poster, Badge
MAKING F@*KING VIDEOS BOX SET (USA) GEF–39542: *Making F@*king Videos Part 1 – Don't Cry/Part II – November Rain*
"Making A F@*king Fashion Statement" T–Shirt

BOOKS

Guns N' Roses: The World's Most Outrageous Hard Rock Band, Paul Elliot
Appetite For Destruction: The Days Of Guns N' Roses, Danny Sugerman
The Most Dangerous Band In The World, Mick Wall
Over The Top: The True Story of Guns N' Roses, Mark Putterford
In Their Own Words, Mark Putterford
The Pictures, George Chin
Lowlife In The Fast Lane, Eddy McSquare
Live! Mick St. Michael

AUDIO BOOKS

Maximum Guns N Roses, The Unauthorised Biography of Guns N Roses, Chrome Dreams 2000

VIDEOS

Use Your Illusion 1 – Live in Tokyo
Geffen 1992
Use Your Illusion I1 – Live in Tokyo
Geffen 1992
Making Fuckin' Videos Vol. 1
The Making Of Don't Cry
Geffen 1993
Making Fuckin' Videos Vol. 2
The Making Of November Rain
Geffen 1993
Making Fuckin' Videos Vol. 3
The Making Of Estranged
Geffen 1994
Welcome To The Videos
Geffen 1998
Sex N' Drugs N' Rock N' Roll (cat number cvis 326)
Chrome Dreams 2003

DVDS

Sex N' Drugs N' Rock N' Roll
Chrome Dreams 2003
Welcome to the Videos
Geffen 2003
Use Your Illusion I (World Tour 1992 in Tokyo)
Geffen 2003
Use Your Illusion II (World Tour 1992 in Tokyo)
Geffen 2003

WEBSITES

www.gnronline.com (official)
www.dopeshow.org/gnr
gnrunlimited.com
www.mygnr.com
www.lostrose.com
www.heretodaygonetohell.com
www.gnr.org.co.uk

CHART PLACINGS

ALBUMS

Appetite For Destruction – #1 on The Billboard 200 in 1988
GN'R Lies – #1 on The Billboard 200 in 1989
Use Your Illusion I – #2 on The Billboard 200 in 1991
Use Your Illusion II – #1 on The Billboard 200 in 1991
The Spaghetti Incident? – #4 on The Billboard 200 in 1993
Live Era '87–'93 – #45 on The Billboard 200 in 1999

SINGLES

1988: Sweet Child O' Mine – #1 on The Billboard Hot 100
1988: Welcome To The Jungle – #7 on The Billboard Hot 100
1989: Nightrain – #93 on The Billboard Hot 100
1989: Paradise City – #5 on The Billboard Hot 100
1989: Patience – #4 on The Billboard Hot 100
1991: Don't Cry – #10 on The Billboard Hot 100
1991: You Could Be Mine – #29 on The Billboard Hot 100
1992: Live And Let Die – #33 on The Billboard Hot 100
1992: November Rain – #3 on The Billboard Hot 100
1992: Yesterdays – #72 on The Billboard Hot 100
1992: November Rain – #19 on Top 40 Mainstream
1994: Since I Don't Have You – #69 on The Billboard Hot 100

1994: Sympathy For The Devil ("Interview With The Vampire") –
#62 on The Billboard Hot 100
1995: Sympathy For The Devil ("Interview With The Vampire") –
#55 on The Billboard Hot 100

G N' R BIRTHDAYS

1960
November 19 – Matt Sorum

1962
February 6 – William Bruce Bailey (W. Axl Rose)
April 8 – Jeffrey Isbell (Izzy Stradlin)
August 7 – Gilby Clarke

1963
June 18 – Darren Reed (Dizzy)

1964
February 5 – Michael McKagan (Duff)

1965
January 22 – Steven Adler
July 23 – Saul Hudson (Slash)

1966
October 6 – Tommy Stinson

1971
November 7 – Robin Finck

1976
February 25 – Chris C. Pitman

VELVET REVOLVER

ALBUMS

Contraband: *Sucker Train Blues/Do It For The Kids/Big Machine/ Illegal i Song/Spectacle/Fall To Pieces/Headspace/Superhuman/Set Me Free/You Got No Right/Slither/Dirty Little Thing/Loving The Alien*
CD, 2 x LP, Cassette – RCA 2004

SINGLES

Slither CD1: Slither/Negative Creep/Bodies (Live)
Slither CD2: Slither/Money/Set Me Free (Live)
CD, 12" – BMG 2004
Fall To Pieces: Fall To Pieces/Surrender
CD, DVD, 7", 12" – BMG 2004

SOUNDTRACKS

The Italian Job: *Money*
2003
The Hulk: *Set Me Free*
2003

AUDIO BOOKS

Maximum Velvet Revolver, The Unauthorised Biography of Velvet Revolver, Chrome Dreams 2005

Note: The author's knowledge comes from many years experience in both the new and second hand record collecting world. Up until recently he worked for a specialist retailer of collectibles and rarities, and prices given are from several years experience. For great prices on unusual items, visit the auction site www.ebay.com, or rarity paradise www.gemm.com.

INDEX

NOTE ABOUT THE AUTHOR

Paul Stenning is a writer and journalist (Terrorizer, Record Collector and Powerplay magazines) with many years experience in the nefarious world of hard rock and heavy metal. He lives in Manchester, England where he buys records by day and plays them by night, sometimes pausing to eat, sleep and rock some more.

This book is the result of a teenage obsession and adult continuation with Guns N Roses and the lifestyle/music they embody continuously - enjoy the ride!